# THE NEW HIGH PRIESTS

Contributions in Legal Studies
Series Editor: *Paul L. Murphy*

Crime and Punishment in Revolutionary Paris
*Antoinette Wills*

American Legal Culture, 1908–1940
*John W. Johnson*

Governmental Secrecy and the Founding Fathers: A Study in Constitutional Controls
*Daniel N. Hoffman*

Torture and English Law: An Administrative and Legal History from the Plantagenets to the Stuarts
*James Heath*

Essays on New York Colonial Legal History
*Herbert S. Johnson*

The Origins of the American Business Corporation, 1784–1855: Broadening the Concept of Public Service During Industrialization
*Ronald E. Seavoy*

Prologue to Nuremberg: The Politics and Diplomacy of Punishing War Criminals of the First World War
*James F. Willis*

The Network of Control: State Supreme Courts and State Security Statutes, 1920–1970
*Carol E. Jenson*

Drugs and Information Control: The Role of Men and Manipulation in the Control of Drug Trafficking
*Jerald W. Cloyd*

State Supreme Courts: Policymakers in the Federal System
*Mary Cornelia Porter and G. Alan Tarr, editors*

The Future of Our Liberties: Perspectives on the Bill of Rights
*Stephen C. Halpern, editor*

Tightening the Reins of Justice in America: A Comparative Analysis of the Criminal Jury Trial in England and the United States
*Michael H. Graham*

The Development of Law on the Rocky Mountain Frontier
*Gordon M. Bakken*

Clients and Lawyers: Securing the Rights of Disabled Persons
*Susan M. Olson*

# THE NEW HIGH PRIESTS

## *Lawyers in Post–Civil War America*

*Edited by*

**GERARD W. GAWALT**

Contributions in Legal Studies, Number 29

GREENWOOD PRESS
Westport, Connecticut • London, England

**Library of Congress Cataloging in Publication Data**

Main entry under title:

The New high priests.

(Contributions in legal studies, ISSN 0147-1074 ; no. 29)
Bibliography: p.
Includes index.
1. Lawyers—United States—History—Addresses, essays, lectures. 2. Practice of law—United States—History—Addresses, essays, lectures. I. Gawalt, Gerard W. II. Series.
KF297.A2N43 1984 344.73′0176134 83-18328
347.304176134
ISBN 0-313-24021-3 (lib. bdg.)



Library of Congress Catalog Card Number: 83-18328
ISBN: 0-313-24021-3
ISSN: 0147-1074

First published in 1984

Greenwood Press
A division of Congressional Information Service, Inc.
88 Post Road West
Westport, Connecticut 06881

Printed in the United States of America

10 9 8 7 6 5 4 3 2 1

# *Contents*

Introduction
*Gerard W. Gawalt* vii

Symbol of the New Profession: Emergence of the Large Law Firm, 1870–1915
*Wayne K. Hobson* 3

Constitutional Machinery and Judicial Professionalism: The Careers of Midwestern State Appellate Court Judges, 1861–1899
*Kermit L. Hall* 29

"The Ideal and the Actual in the Law": Fantasies and Practices of New York City Lawyers, 1870–1910
*Robert W. Gordon* 51

"The Best Men of the Bar": The Founding of the American Bar Association
*John A. Matzko* 75

The Impact of Industrialization on the Legal Profession in Massachusetts, 1870–1900
*Gerard W. Gawalt* 97

Industrialization and the Nineteenth-Century California Bar
*Gordon Morris Bakken* 125

From Deference to Confrontation: The Early Black Lawyers of Galveston, Texas, 1895–1920
*Maxwell Bloomfield* 151

The Virginia Bar, 1870–1900
*W. Hamilton Bryson and E. Lee Shepard* 171

Another False Start: Mississippi's Second State Bar Association, 1886–1892
*Michael de L. Landon* 187

Bibliographic Essay
*Gerard W. Gawalt* 201

Index 205

About the Editor and Contributors 213

*GERARD W. GAWALT*

# *Introduction*

Lawyers are now the dominant profession in American society. Where once they were often distrusted and occasionally outlawed, professional attorneys now hold sway from courtroom to boardroom. They affect our destinies from before our birth to long after our death. How and when did this profession move from a scattering of largely ill-trained practitioners on the periphery of society in the eighteenth century to the present, enormous, highly trained profession with extensive political, economic, social, and legal power? This book of historical essays examines the most critical period of this process of professionalization—the post–Civil War period of America—when law replaced religion as the controlling element in American society, and lawyers clearly established their role as formulators, advocates, and arbiters of the law. Brandishing their view of the ''scientific'' nature of the law as a justification for their power, lawyers became the new high priests of an increasingly legalistic, industrial society.

By 1900, American society had shifted from a largely rural, homogeneous population of British ancestry clustered on the eastern seaboard and centered in small towns and commercial centers to a heterogeneous, industrial society of increasingly variant ethnic stock spread across a continent and concentrated in urban areas and industrial-commercial centers. Statistical and documentary evidence indicates that the legal profession not only adjusted to this transformation, but pioneered or adopted many aspects of industrialization for use in the teaching and practice of law. Rather than opposing the rise of this new dominant force in society, the legal profession joined with the business community on many levels and consequently shared in both its socioeconomic advances and its increasingly national outlook at the expense of professional and individual autonomy.

An important element of the legal profession moved toward the formation of a national profession as it seized on the ethos of the emerging industrial society. Despite some regional variations in recruitment, training, office practice, and professional structure the most influential or elite part of the profession acquired a national perspective in training, practice, and professional institutions. Simultaneously, the exclusive, inbred, homogeneous composition of the profession was giving way under the pressure of an expanding, heterogeneous, inclusive-minded population. Much of this transition was due to the impact of industrialization on both American society and the legal profession.

The authors of these essays explore the extent of the legal profession's involvement in the growth of industrial America by focusing on the state of the profession in various geographic regions of the country and on the profession's institutions and plans for education, regulation, reform, and practice in the post–Civil War period. While wrestling with this general, theoretical question, some essays provide detailed views of particular aspects of professional development—the corporate law firm, judicial officeholding, and national professional institutions. Other essays explore professional development within states to examine in detail the applications of national trends on a regional level. All the essays address the central question: How was the nature and structure of the legal profession in post–Civil War America molded by the growth of urban-industrial society?

Such a question can be easily asked, but it cannot be easily answered. These essays utilize sophisticated statistical and prosopographic methods in addition to extensive research in personal, professional, and public papers to analyze this complex question. They measure changes in the profession's composition and orientation which indicate that the profession was more open to immigrant and minority participation than has traditionally been asserted. They examine the growing complexity and specialization of legal practice. They portray both the power and self-doubt of the "Wall Street" corporate lawyer. They study the changing demands on legal education and the adaptations of law schools. They assess the profession's interest in law reform, and the concurrent resurgence of the bar association as a vehicle for professional and legal reform. They describe the elite reformers' transformation from utopian idealogue seeking a society in which general laws were impartially and predictably applied by idealistic lawyer-advocates and lawyer-arbitrators to an apolitical technician without any ideology except a denial of any public role. They evaluate the impact of business and industrial organization on procedural law, substantive law, and the conduct of law-office business. They analyze the profession's control of the judiciary and the socioeconomic background of people attracted to arbitration rather than litigation and advocacy. They demonstrate the emerging bifurcation of the legal profession into a relatively small but growing number of increasingly influential lawyers whose legal interests and practices were national in scope and the larger but proportionately diminishing group of lawyers whose perspective remained provincial and whose practice remained basically unchanged despite the growth of the industrial-commercial society. These studies, in brief, examine the institutional as well as individual responses of the profession to societal shifts and occupational demands and also evaluate the roles lawyers have played in engineering these alterations in American society.

Because these essays cover such a wide variety of topics and spotlight several geographic regions, they clearly show that although the impact of these societal shifts was most immediate in the northeast and midwest—the lines of greatest industrial development—they also had a vital, though usually delayed, influence on the profession in the south and far west. The first two essays emphasize two developments which have proven to be among the most central to the legal profession: the emergence of the large corporate law firm and the importance of lawyers as arbiters. The reforming impulse of the profession is examined from both theoretical and institutional perspectives in the next two essays on the elite lawyer as a reformer and the formation of the American Bar Association. These are followed by studies of the legal profession in five states—Massachusetts, California, Texas, Virginia, and Mississippi—that provide not only a close-up view of the application of national developments on a local level, but a detailed view of the heterogeneous nature of the profession and the regional variations within the octopus-like occupation. The full range of subjects covered by these essays can best be appreciated by individually examining each one.

Wayne K. Hobson carefully scrutinizes the national growth of the corporate law firm and produces a fresh, insightful interpretation of professional growth in his heavily documented essay, "Symbol of the New Profession: Emergence of the Large Law Firm, 1870–1915." Hobson eschews the moral overtones that have burdened many previous examinations of the "commercialization" and "deprofessionalization" of the bar that occurred as the leadership in the American legal profession shifted from the solo practitioner to the large firm partner.

In his study, Hobson provides readers with a substantial accumulation of statistical data that will alter scholars' views on the development of the large law firm, which Hobson euphemistically refers to as a law factory. The trend toward large firms was a response to the needs of corporations for many specialized services, Hobson argues. "Only when industrial corporations requiring continuous legal supervision became the main clients did corporation law practice require large law firms." But there were mitigating circumstances. The formation of large firms was not depersonalized, according to Hobson: "The pace at which leading lawyers bureaucratized their firms was influenced by cultural factors as well as by the requirements of their corporate clients. The choices that were made reveal some of the temperamental, cultural, and generational fault lines within the legal elite."

Although New York City was the center of the corporate bar, large and major law firms proliferated in the industrial cities of the northeast and midwest during the early twentieth century. In the process, the image and the reality of the lawyer as learned professional was replaced by the image of skilled negotiator and facilitator, the practical man of business. These corporate law attorneys became the recognized elite of the profession and the molding force in the profession even though membership in the large law firm was and remains reserved for a very small percentage of American lawyers.

In "Constitutional Machinery and Judicial Professionalism: The Careers of

Midwestern State Appellate Court Judges, 1861–1899,'' Kermit L. Hall continues to examine the expanding role of the lawyer as it improved its power and position from advocate to arbiter within the legal system of America's industrial heartland. Hall begins with the revisionary thesis that popular election of the judiciary was ''a lawyer's reform'' to ''enhance the quality of the bench by curbing the influence party leaders had enjoyed under the appointive system.'' But in the late nineteenth century, as ''state judicial activities broadened in response to industrialization,'' a split grew between bar organization leaders and scientifically oriented lawyers, who wanted to reform the selection process by returning to an appointive method, and politically minded lawyers, who wanted to retain the popular sovereignty.

Hall expands this theme by analyzing the composition of the popularly elected appellate judges of the midwest and comparing them to the appointed judges of the lower federal courts. His important findings contradict contemporary studies and assertions used to oppose the popular election of judges; moreover, they revise recent historical studies on the topic. The popular election of judges still put on the bench state appellate judges who resembled lower federal judges in their high quality and limited social diversity. ''What state judges lacked in formal and prestigious academic training, they compensated for with prior judicial service, prosperous middle-class origins, and extensive kinship connections,'' Hall concludes.

Robert W. Gordon's essay, '' 'The Ideal and the Actual in the Law': Fantasies and Practices of New York City Lawyers, 1870–1910,'' nominally discusses only New York City lawyers, but in actuality his essay has a national sweep. Gordon focuses on how the reformist ideals of New York City's elite lawyers were mutated and manipulated in actual practice. In this essay, he argues that although ''reform in the name of scientific professionalism was, among other things, an idealogy of middle-class, native-born whites,'' its aim was not entirely cynical self-interest. Rather, Gordon examines these elitist reformers from their own perspective—as ''having 'ideal interests' as well as material ones, and as struggling to work out a relationship between their beliefs and their practices—between the ideal and the actual—with which they could live in comfort.'' These lawyers, Gordon argues, were ''classical liberals'' who sought to both restore society to an earlier, purer stage and eliminate the evils of ''lack of generality in framing laws, and lack of predictability and impartiality in applying them.''

When this ''fantasy'' failed to achieve its goals, lawyers saw this as a problem of ''scientific reform of the case law of common law and the Constitution'' rather than ''a problem in political economy.'' Thus, they sought to improve legal science as a means of creating the ideal, ''liberal social order'' and making these legal principles ''nationally effective.'' But the lawyers found mostly failure when theory was confronted with reality.

As members of the legal elite, the reformers' occupation severed them from legal science and forced them increasingly into the business world. They were, in fact, justified when they complained that law had changed "from a profession to a business"; and here Gordon is careful to argue that this change can not be described as a decline. Gordon argues that in its efforts to merge the ideal and the actual, the elite divided into three parts: a small number of reactionary idealogues; an equally small number of schizophrenics who split their time between public service and private practice; and most commonly, apolitical technicians with no ideology save that of craftsmanlike client service.

John A. Matzko, in his essay, " 'The Best Men of the Bar': The Founding of the American Bar Association," continues the national overview with his study of the American Bar Association—the first serious effort to erect a national bar institution across state lines that focused on national problems rather than provincial concerns. Matzko posits the thesis that the founders of the American Bar Association did not oppose the reform spirit of the age. On the contrary, he asserts, the organization of the American Bar Association "was itself a manifestation of that spirit to which its founders were highly sympathetic." Matzko attributes this desire to the status anxiety of elite lawyers who feared threats both from within the "scrambling bar" and non-English immigrant lawyers and from outside the profession through domination by corporate clients and the threat of "scientific" professions. It was these elite but insecure lawyers who sought to reform and revitalize their profession through a national bar association. The founders of the American Bar Association, according to Matzko, were well educated, highly trained elitists, moderates in politics, and representatives of the interests of national economic development. Matzko, like Hobson and Hall, found that the elite lawyers' ties to industrial America made them anxious about their professional status as well as powerful and prosperous.

Studying a state in the forefront of industrial development, Gerard W. Gawalt, in "The Impact of Industrialization on the Legal Profession in Massachusetts, 1870–1900," takes a detailed look at the profession in a single state, but his findings establish a paradigm for a national study. Gawalt uses extensive prosopographic, census, and documentary evidence to demonstrate "how the learned professions adjusted from a homogeneous, rural-small community society with pockets of commercial urbanization to a heterogeneous, urban-industrial society with pockets of rural-small community life." He finds that industrialization significantly altered the profession's patterns of recruitment, marriage, geographic mobility, wealth, and education. He found distinct differences between urban and rural regions and between law school graduates and the profession as a whole.

Gawalt's essay examines the effects of the growing emphasis of corporate and business law and the adaptation of industrial techniques of mass production in both law school education and legal practice. The statistical and documentary evidence shows that "rather than opposing the rise of this new dominant group in society, the legal profession joined the business community in many forms and, as a result, shared in its socioeconomic advances at the expense of professional and individual autonomy.'' Gawalt concludes that the legal and other learned professions ''were not conservative strongholds wedded to a less complicated and more idealistic, individualistic, or humanistic past. Rather the learned professions were full participants and often leaders in the headlong drive toward a modern, heterogeneous, industrial, institutional society.''

Demonstrating the broad reach of professional changes due to the growth of industrial society, Gordon M. Bakken, in ''Industrialization and the Nineteenth-Century California Bar,'' combines the use of computer and traditional research to analyze the impact of industrialization on the structure and practice of the profession in the far west. Bakken, like Gawalt, found that the growth of modern industrial society fundamentally altered the composition of both the profession and the nature of legal practice. His evidence shows the incredible growth of the urban bar and the increasing diversity within the profession. Bakken documents the extent of the migrant status of the California bar throughout the nineteenth century. His findings strengthen the concept that the frontier bar was highly educated, both collegially and in law.

As in other developing regions of the country, first land, then laws and administrative regulations, and then commerce and industry provided lawyers with opportunities for profitable practices and speculative profits. Bakken traces the shift from land law to tort and regulatory law as the initial rush of settlement gave way to commercial and industrial growth. Railroad law, corporate law, and commercial law attracted the largest number of lawyer specialists, who concentrated in Los Angeles and San Francisco. But most lawyers remained in general practice. As Bakken so succinctly puts it: ''The lawyer followed the practice of the dollar and some specialized to meet the needs of a rapidly urbanizing and industrializing population.''

Exploring the racial rather than the ethnic side of the ''scrambling bar,'' Maxwell Bloomfield, in ''From Deference to Confrontation: The Early Black Lawyers of Galveston, Texas, 1895–1920,'' presents the first detailed study of black lawyers in a southern state. He challenges the traditional view that ''black attorneys were the passive victims of Jim Crow legislation in the South. They either would not, or could not, resist an unjust legal system.'' Bloomfield's study of a representative southern city during the peak of anti-black activities argues that black lawyers, although quantitatively limited and undoubtedly restricted by Jim Crow legislation and tradition, ''served their community and the law far more effectively than conventional mythology suggests. As spokesmen for racial justice, they sometimes used their legal skills in creative ways to attack the institutionalized racism of the New South.'' Bloomfield examines several civil rights cases pursued by black lawyers from Galveston involving public accommodations on railroads and streetcars. Black lawyers also helped to organize the Anti-Lynching and Protective Association of Texas in Galveston. Bloomfield concludes that the black lawyers of this period ''did much to keep the promise of equal justice alive during a period of often brutal repression.''

Using court records, personal papers, and census-type data, Bloomfield has been able to examine the backgrounds and careers of nearly all the black lawyers who practiced in Galveston during a twenty-five year period. Bloomfield details the differences as well as some surprising similarities between black and white lawyers in family background, age on entering the profession, education, geographic mobility, etc. As professionals, they pursued a broad range of legal practice, but the restrictive nature of their clients' concerns limited their involvement in the legal aspects of industrial society. In practice, they handled both civil and criminal cases, and though most cases were in the lower courts, they did pursue cases through the appellate courts even to the United States Supreme Court. None of the black lawyers handled large industrial, banking, transportation, commercial, or trust cases—the core of power in the legal system of modern industrial America.

In their joint essay, "The Virginia Bar, 1870–1900," W. Hamilton Bryson and E. Lee Shepard portray the lawyers of Virginia as men who remained provincially oriented and steeped in the rural-planter tradition. Hesitant to embark on new courses in post–Civil War America and inhibited by an agriculture-based economy, Virginia lawyers only belatedly entered modern industrial society. Nevertheless, the urban-industrial areas of the state claimed the dominant share of the profession, and thirty-eight black lawyers were practicing law in the state in 1890. The demand for corporations, particularly railroad, banking, and mining firms, allowed many urban lawyers to specialize their practice rather than rely on a miscellaneous practice. On the other hand, the solo practitioner and dual partnership firm remained dominant in the Virginia bar until well into the twentieth century. Not until 1901, for example, was there a multimember (four) corporate law firm in Virginia. Despite the business connections of leading lawyers, Bryson and Shepard found that lawyers individually and as representatives of the state bar association were in the forefront of the fight to regulate corporations through a state Corporation Commission and by limitations on the fellow-servant rule. Lawyers were also deeply concerned with proposed codification reform and alterations in the system of land registry. Bryson and Shepard conclude that the state bar association "was a leader in the area of legal reform—the primary forum for public debate on these issues."

In contrast to other state studies in this book, Michael de L. Landon's essay, "Another False Start: Mississippi's Second State Bar Association, 1886–1892," concludes that the impact of industrial society on the legal profession was minimal. Landon discusses the difficulties of attempting to establish a formal institutional organization for the legal profession in a rural-small town oriented state. This widespread distribution of lawyers fostered a profession steeped in individual practice and local organization, but one generally opposed to central authority. Despite the reformist instincts of a few "elite" lawyers, the majority of lawyers were conservative populists. Consequently, bar reformers had little impact on either the new state constitution or the new code of race relations, according to Landon. He concludes that "although a few of the brightest and best of its lawyers might have wanted it to, Mississippi was not yet ready to join modern industrial America."

These essays, however, leave no doubt that the American legal profession adapted readily to industrial society in both functional and Weberian theoretical ways, and that the profession and the modern business community became interdependent and mutually supportive in post–Civil War America.

# THE
# NEW HIGH
# PRIESTS

*WAYNE K. HOBSON*

# *Symbol of the New Profession: Emergence of the Large Law Firm, 1870–1915*

The legal profession, like much of the rest of American society, was transformed between the 1870s and the 1920s. During this time, the counselor replaced the advocate at the head of the profession, as the skills of rhetoric and courtroom advocacy came to seem less important than technical competence and the skills of the negotiator and facilitator.[1] In a closely related change, the law school replaced reading in a law office as the most common route into the profession. Within the law school, the case method supplanted the lecture/textbook method. Organization and bureaucratization began to characterize professional life. Title and trust companies took over a significant portion of the bread-and-butter business of nineteenth-century lawyers. Bar admission standards became increasingly uniform and bureaucratized. Bar associations grew in size, representativeness, and influence as the legal profession shifted from being a largely unorganized profession to being at least a loosely organized profession. Although most lawyers in 1930 still practiced alone or with one partner, the leaders of the profession were no longer men in such firms; they were now all in large firms.

Searching for a symbol to capsulize and give meaning to this profound transformation of the American legal profession, commentators and historians, then and now, have often pointed to the corporation lawyer in the large law firm. Located in his modern, well-appointed, efficiently run, businesslike office high above Wall Street, or above the financial district of some other large American city, the corporation lawyer in the large law firm seems to symbolize what has become of the legal profession in modern America, at least until recently. The meaning of the symbol can be positive or negative, depending very much on how one feels about the lure of great wealth, the concentration of wealth and power, and the proper use of the country's best legal minds. Because Americans habitually respect wealth and power, the corporate lawyer, as an individual, can expect deference and even awe. But ever since the large firms became a visible presence and appropriate symbol of modern trends, thoughtful observers inside and outside the profession have been troubled by the implications of the rise to professional prominence of lawyers connected with such firms. To such observers, the rise of the large law firm and the corporation lawyer has symbolized commercialization, deprofessionalization, and bureaucratization. In this view, because of their thralldom to large corporations and/or because of the organizational requirements of large firms, the modern legal elite lost their personal and professional independence and adopted a blind conservatism during the transformation of their firms and their legal practices in the late nineteenth and early twentieth centuries.

James D. Andrews told the American Bar Association in 1906: "Instead of client and lawyer the relation of employer and employee has been substituted. . . . A great many of our lawyers, those who are now exercizing great weight and influence in the country, are employees."[2] As a result of this change, another leading lawyer lamented, "to become counsel for great railway corporations or large banking interests is to destroy every opportunity for securing popular confidence." Moreover, he concluded, "it has a basis in truth and reason."[3] Herbert Croly concluded that "the retainer which the American legal profession has accepted from the corporations inevitably increases its natural tendency to a blind conservatism."[4] Woodrow Wilson made similar points in several speeches delivered to bar associations. He called on the bar elite to resist the logic of specialization and to consider the public as well as their client's interest when conceptualizing their professional obligations. It was his purpose, he said, "to recall lawyers to the service of the nation as a whole, from which they have been drifting away."[5]

In many of these criticisms, the corporation lawyer was spoken of as if he were an independent practitioner who simply had to make a moral choice between blindly serving his client or serving the public interest. But some observers, especially those inside the profession, understood that bar leaders' commercialization and drift away from older conceptions of professionalism was not merely a personal characteristic. It could not be altered simply by a change of heart or a firm resolve to serve the public interest; instead, the new trends had become institutionalized in the atmosphere and operating assumptions of large law offices. John F. Dillon, who knew whereof he spoke, noticed in 1894 "in great law firms with their separate departments and head and subordinate bureaus and clerks with their staff of assistants, there is much resemblance to the business methods of the great mercantile and business establishments situated close by."[6]

On the other hand, unlike engineering, where the independent engineer gave way to the salaried corporate employee during these years, leading lawyers did retain at least a formal independence from their clients.[7] Bar leaders such as Elihu Root and Philander Knox insisted that this formal independence was crucial. Both claimed that they were not corporation lawyers, but lawyers who happened to have corporations among their clients. Root declared that "about half the practice of a decent lawyer consists in telling would-be clients that they are damned fools and should stop."[8]

Despite the actual and symbolic importance of the rise of the large law firm, we have surprisingly little concrete and detailed information about its development as a distinctive form within the profession. When did large firms begin to appear in significant numbers? How large were they? Did they appear at different times in different cities? Was their emergence a national phenomenon, or were there significant regional or local variations? Can the emergence of such firms be causally linked with such events as the turn-of-the-century merger movement? Did they reduce the independence of lawyers and channel in organizational directions the ambitions of young lawyers?

While numbers alone cannot answer all these questions, no inquiry can proceed without an understanding of the numbers of firms and lawyers involved. In order to develop a sense of chronology, *Hubbell's Legal Directory* was examined at five-year intervals between 1872 and 1915 to see how many large firms and how many law factories existed throughout the country.[9] In addition, the 1924 *Directory* was consulted for the five cities with the greatest number of such firms in 1915: New York, Chicago, Boston, Cleveland, and Kansas City. The result of this research has been the accumulation of objective data on the external features of large-firm development to supplement evidence on internal development gleaned from biographies, memoirs, and the few available firm histories.

The years between 1870 and 1915 were transition years in the development of the large law firm. The number of large firms increased yearly and at a rate far in excess of the growth of the legal profession as a whole. Some large firms grew steadily in size and a few became law factories. Large law firms and law factories, however, were only in the process of becoming institutionalized during this period. Many firms failed to sustain themselves as large firms over even a five-year period, appearing with five or six members in one year and then dropping back to two, three, or four members five years later. Some early large firms even failed to sustain themselves at all, their individual members appearing as independent practitioners or disappearing entirely from *Hubbell's*. Only 47 percent of large firms in 1893 remained as large firms in 1904. Between 1904 and 1915, the persistence rate was up to 54 percent. By the 1920s, large firms had become much more institutionalized. In the five cities with the greatest number of large firms in 1915, the 1904–1915 persistence rate increased from 55 percent to 71 percent between 1915 and 1924.

Even more significant, by the 1920s, legal factories had become common features of the professional landscape in all major cities. There were twenty-seven major firms, or law factories, in the five leading cities in 1915. By 1924, these five cities had 101 law factories. Not only had the number of firms dramatically increased, but the average size of these firms had also grown. In 1915, the average size of the twenty-seven major firms in the five leading cities was 8.8 lawyers; by 1924, the average size was 12.9 lawyers. The number of lawyers in law factories in these five cities increased 450 percent between 1915 and 1924, from 237 to 1303.

Because the 1870–1915 years were transitional, it is important to examine in these years the emergence not only of the law factories, but also of the more modest category I have called "large firms" (five or more partners and associates). The growth of these firms changed the overall shape of the legal elite more than did the growth of law factories in the years before 1915.

There were 368 firms in 78 cities that at some time during the 1872–1915 period reached large-firm size. (See Table 1.) After an initial spurt in the mid–1870s, the fastest growth rate occurred during the 1890s, just before the turn-of-the-century merger movement in the corporate world. Between 1893 and 1898, the number of large firms increased at an average rate of 17.2 percent per year, compared to an average annual increase of 8.2 percent between 1898 and 1904, 13.4 percent between 1904 and 1909, and 7.3 percent between 1909 and 1915.[10]

Although the lawyers in these large firms were an infinitesimal percentage of all the lawyers in the country (less than half of one percent in 1898 and only 1.28 percent in 1915), the growth rate of large firms far outpaced that of the profession as a whole. The number of lawyers in the country grew at an annual rate of 5.3 percent in the 1870s, 4.0 percent in the 1880s, 2.8 percent in the 1890s, .02 percent in the 1900s, and .7 percent in the 1910s. Even if we concentrate only on the larger cities, the large firms were growing much faster than the rest of the profession. The annual growth rate of all lawyers in New York, Chicago, and Boston between 1900 and 1915 was 1.7 percent, whereas lawyers in large firms in these three cities increased at an annual rate of 6.7 percent between 1898 and 1915. It is no wonder that the large firm began to be noticed in general circulation periodicals in the first years of the twentieth century.[11]

The trend toward large firms was a response to increasing industrialization and urbanization, particularly a response to the needs of corporations, which were increasing in both number and size. This generalization, which no one would dispute, summarizes a relationship that is more complex than is often supposed. It would be a mistake, for example, to assume that all large firms were engaged in corporation law practice. They all had corporations among their most important clients, to be sure, but that did not necessarily mean corporation law was the firm's specialization. Many firms did not specialize, but instead listed themselves as engaged in the general practice of law. They then listed a number of banks, railroads, and industrial corporations as references or clients.[12] The larger firms generally did specialize, but usually listed several specialties including insurance, probate, commercial, real estate, patent, bankruptcy, and corporation law. In fact, if a firm had several large corporations as clients, it had to be able to perform a wide range of legal services for the companies and their owners, including collections, personal injury, and probate, in addition to strictly corporation law business. Or, if a firm was unprepared to perform these services, it had to find other lawyers or firms who were. As the law grew in complexity, and elite lawyers increasingly specialized, law firms found it advantageous to grow in size in order to attract and keep corporate clients.

Advantageous, but not absolutely essential. Many of the leading corporation lawyers of the 1890s and early 1900s, the architects of major railroad reorga-

**TABLE 1**
**Large Firms (five or more partners and associates)**

| | 1872 | 1878 | 1882 | 1887 | 1893 | 1898 | 1904 | 1909 | 1915 |
|---|---|---|---|---|---|---|---|---|---|
| 5-member firms | 3 | 9 | 9 | 15 | 19 | 35 | 48 | 79 | 104 |
| 6-member firms | 1 | 2 | 2 | 3 | 10 | 14 | 28 | 41 | 53 |
| 7-member firms | 0 | 1 | 1 | 3 | 4 | 9 | 11 | 25 | 32 |
| 8-member firms | 0 | 2 | 2 | 1 | 2 | 7 | 7 | 10 | 19 |
| 9-11 member firms | 0 | 0 | 0 | 0 | 1 | 2 | 4 | 11 | 26 |
| 12-16 member firms | 0 | 0 | 0 | 0 | 0 | 0 | 2 | 1 | 6 |
| Total firms | 4 | 14 | 14 | 22 | 36 | 67 | 100 | 167 | 240 |
| Total cities | 1 | 4 | 4 | 6 | 14 | 21 | 29 | 44 | 70 |
| Total lawyers | 21 | 80 | 80 | 122 | 208 | 398 | 608 | 1021 | 1540 |

Source: <u>Hubbell's Legal Directory</u>

nizations and early industrial combinations, practiced in modest-sized law firms. When their accomplishments were described, they were always identified as individuals, rather than as members of particular firms.[13] During the 1890s, when Elihu Root was in the heyday of his practice, earning between $50,000 and $110,000 per year, supervising several important railroad reorganizations, serving as chief counsel for the Whitney-Ryan traction syndicate during its formative period, and assisting in the organization or dissolution of many large corporations in a wide range of industries, his firm, Root & Clarke, grew from three partners and no associates in 1893 to five partners and no associates in 1898. This qualified it as a large firm, but not as a law factory. Despite this modest size, the firm did not confine itself to corporation law. As a junior partner in the firm, Henry L. Stimson drew up and proved wills, conducted title searches, bill collections, mortgage foreclosures, and bankruptcies in addition to handling incorporations and dissolutions.[14]

Francis Lyne Stetson, well known as J. P. Morgan's lawyer, whose firm also handled the legal affairs of the Erie Railroad, the Guaranty Trust Company, and the International Paper Company, resisted the trend toward large law firms. The firm of Stetson, Tracy, Jennings & Russell did have seven partners in 1898, but it did not retain that size. Stetson preferred the informality of a small office; he was reluctant to assign his clients to other partners or associates.[15] Hence, the firm did not join the ranks of the truly large firms until 1919, when Stetson had become senile, and Jennings and Russell had gone into partial retirement. By 1924, under the name of Stetson, Jennings, Russell & Davis, the firm had fourteen partners. But until the 1920s, as long-time partner Lansing P. Reed reflected years later, "the firm was a firm only in name."[16]

James B. Dill, the father of the New Jersey incorporation act, was the senior partner in a three-partner, two-associate firm in 1898. By 1904, he had formed a new firm, Dill & Baldwin, which listed five partners. William D. Guthrie, Victor Morawetz, and Charles Steele, all eminent New York City corporation lawyers in the 1890s, were partners in the five-partner firm of Seward, Guthrie, Morawetz & Steele in 1898. The firm had grown from three partners in 1893, but it did not survive, the firm members going their separate ways. Of course, some corporation lawyers were in very large and enduring firms. William Nelson Cromwell, described by some as the leading corporation lawyer of his day, was listed in *Hubbell's* as the senior partner in Sullivan & Cromwell from 1893 through 1915. During that time, the firm never had fewer than seven members; in 1909 it had eleven partners.

During the early years of corporation law practice, when railroads, individual entrepreneurs, and investment bankers were the major clients, a large law firm was not essential. Only when industrial corporations requiring continuous legal supervision became the main clients did corporation law practice require large law firms. As Willard Hurst has argued, corporation law reflects the spirit of corporate thought and practice. Before the 1920s, corporation law was shaped by the investment banker and his lawyer. From the 1920s on, corporation law reflected the belief that "the promise of lasting growth. . . [lay] not in materials or money, but in large-scale organization; organization was the new factor of production. As the country moved into an expanding economy through the 1920s, prevailing opinion shared this faith. . . . The new corporation acts. . . were consistent in structure with this faith in the productivity of such organization."[17] Large law firms, indeed, law factories, were an essential facet of such industrial organization, in a way they had not had to be in earlier years.[18] From then on, Judge Learned Hand's statement that "sometimes I feel sorry for lawyers; they seem to me to be so earnest and to work so hard, and when all is said and done to get very little out of life, except, perhaps, money," would seem increasingly on the mark when applied to lawyers in large firms.[19]

Before about 1915, however, it was possible for an elite lawyer to exercise some discretion whether to remain in a medium- to large-sized firm or to join the trend toward the law factory. Therefore, the pace at which leading lawyers bureaucratized their firms was influenced by cultural factors as well as by the requirements of their corporate clients. The choices that were made reveal some of the temperamental, cultural, and generational fault lines within the legal elite.

Some of Elihu Root's career choices exemplify one of the options. He developed a reputation as a leading old-style advocate and court lawyer in the New York City bar during the final decades of the nineteenth century. In 1900, when he considered returning from government service to private practice, he was approached by several leading firms as a potential partner. He turned down a "generous offer" from the Cravath firm, one of the originators of the modern law factory. In a letter to William D. Guthrie of that firm, Root explained that he preferred to avoid the pace and pressures found in such a firm. "It would be more satisfactory to make less money and get more satisfaction out of doing things considerately and thoroughly."[20]

As Root suggested, Guthrie very likely sympathized with him. The Cravath firm's historian tells us that Guthrie, "the most driving and keenly analytical of any of the firm's many partners," resisted the innovations in staff organization made by Paul D. Cravath in the late 1890s. Rather than using the young law school graduates whom Cravath brought into the firm as associates, for example, Guthrie relied on his own older assistants.[21]

It seems clear that for Root and Guthrie, as well as others who resisted, the law factory was not only personally distasteful, but implied a new and not wholly welcome conception of bar professionalism. The nineteenth-century image of the law as a learned profession, with all that it implied in personal deference and respect, social prestige, and cultural power, was a major casualty of the new regime.[22] In its place came the image of the leading lawyer as a skilled negotiator and facilitator, the practical man of business. The new image, and the reality behind it, was not without its great compensations, of course. These came in the form of wealth and in new types of economic and political power. Men like Root and Guthrie did not oppose these compensations.

In retrospect, the large law firm of five or six members was a way station on the road to the law factory. Although the large firm may have seemed more desirable to some than a true law factory, it was itself inherently incompatible with the nineteenth-century image of the legal profession. A large firm was not simply five or six attorneys practicing together in place of the two-man partnership of former years. It was constructed with the assumption that its members would specialize, and that some would be exclusively office lawyers and not appear in court. In addition, the large firm utilized modern means of communication and modern forms of office organization. Indeed, it may be said that the telephone, the typewriter, and probably the female stenographer-typist made the proliferation of large law firms possible. Such firms required a nonlegal staff and the coordination of work.[23] All of these innovations spelled the end of the old-style law office. In fact, by 1914, when Theron G. Strong reflected back on the transformation of the New York City legal elite, he could think of only one firm which still practiced in what he considered an old-style law office.[24]

Still, a form of passive resistance appears to have been practiced by the older generation. This can be seen at Sullivan & Cromwell, a leading Wall Street firm. John Foster Dulles, who joined the firm as a clerk in 1911, reports that although the office had a telephone switchboard and operator, neither telephones nor stenographers were fully accepted. ''Some of the older partners felt that the only dignified way of communication between members of the legal profession was for them to write each other in Spencerian script, and to have the message thus expressed delivered by hand.'' Dulles thought these lawyers considered both telephone messages and dictation an affront to their sense of privacy and decorum.[25] However, Sullivan & Cromwell grew steadily in size and in wealth through all these years. The affront to privacy and decorum was real, but it did not get in the way of business.

So far, I have drawn entirely on New York City for illustrative examples. Most of the existing published information on the history of large law offices is about New York City firms. This emphasis does have justification. One-fourth of all large firms and 40 percent of all major firms (law factories) listed in *Hubbell's* between 1872 and 1915 were New York City firms. New York City accounted for more than half of all large firms until 1898 and more than half of all major firms until 1909. However, this exclusive focus on New York City has obscured the story of the large firm's emergence in other major metropolitan centers. Fourteen cities had six or more large firms during the 1872–1915 period. As late as 1909, three-fourths of all large-firm lawyers were in these cities. (See Table 2.)

Besides showing clearly the leadership of New York City, Table 2 reveals interesting patterns for particular cities. Philadelphia is especially conspicuous for its relative slowness to develop large law firms, considering its size, location, and commercial importance. On the other hand, several cities stand out because large firms developed relatively early in them, for example, Chicago, Detroit, and St. Louis. Cincinnati also had two large firms in 1887, although it never produced enough such firms to be among the fourteen leading cities. In addition,

**TABLE 2**
**Large Firms in Leading Cities**

| | 1872 | 1878 | 1882 | 1887 | 1893 | 1898 | 1904 | 1909 | 1915 |
|---|---|---|---|---|---|---|---|---|---|
| New York | 4 | 11 | 11 | 16 | 20 | 29 | 29 | 47 | 51 |
| Chicago | 0 | 1 | 0 | 1 | 3 | 8 | 11 | 17 | 27 |
| Boston | 0 | 0 | 0 | 1 | 1 | 5 | 12 | 11 | 10 |
| Cleveland | 0 | 0 | 0 | 0 | 2 | 2 | 4 | 9 | 10 |
| Kansas City | 0 | 0 | 0 | 0 | 0 | 1 | 4 | 6 | 9 |
| Philadelphia | 0 | 0 | 0 | 1 | 1 | 2 | 4 | 1 | 8 |
| Baltimore | 0 | 0 | 0 | 0 | 1 | 2 | 4 | 7 | 7 |
| Detroit | 0 | 0 | 1 | 0 | 0 | 2 | 3 | 2 | 8 |
| St. Louis | 0 | 1 | 1 | 0 | 0 | 0 | 1 | 7 | 2 |
| Atlanta | 0 | 0 | 0 | 0 | 0 | 1 | 0 | 3 | 3 |
| Milwaukee | 0 | 0 | 0 | 0 | 1 | 1 | 4 | 3 | 4 |
| Buffalo | 0 | 0 | 0 | 0 | 1 | 1 | 3 | 1 | 5 |
| Pittsburgh | 0 | 0 | 0 | 0 | 0 | 0 | 2 | 4 | 5 |
| San Francisco | 0 | 0 | 0 | 0 | 1 | 3 | 0 | 5 | 3 |
| Total firms | 4 | 13 | 13 | 19 | 31 | 57 | 81 | 123 | 152 |
| Total lawyers | 21 | 74 | 75 | 107 | 182 | 343 | 502 | 771 | 994 |
| Percent of all large firms | 100 | 92.9 | 92.9 | 86.4 | 86.1 | 85.1 | 81.0 | 73.7 | 63.3 |
| Percent of all lawyers in large firms | 100 | 92.5 | 93.8 | 87.7 | 87.5 | 86.2 | 82.6 | 75.5 | 64.6 |

Source: <u>Hubbell's Legal Directory</u>

Cleveland and Kansas City, although not particularly early in developing large firms, were conspicuous because the firms that did appear were extremely large for their time.[26]

The five-member St. Louis firm listed in 1878 and 1882 was Broadhead, Slayback & Haeussler. James O. Broadhead, the first president of the American Bar Association (1878–1879), was the senior partner. The firm also appeared in 1887 and 1893 with four partners, but was not listed from 1898 on.

Chicago consistently recorded nearly one-third of all midwest large firms and about 10 percent of all U.S. large firms. Four Chicago firms had five or more members before 1898, when six more firms joined the list. One of the early four (Douglas, Crawford & Blair) was short-lived, appearing in *Hubbell's* only in 1893. The other three were enduring firms, although none of them achieved major-firm size until the 1920s. The Tenney firm, which did not retain the same precise firm designation over any five-year interval, appeared in *Hubbell's* throughout the entire period; the firm alternated between four and five partners throughout the period. Until the late 1890s, the firm listed itself as devoted exclusively to commercial law and mercantile collections. From 1898 on, it listed its specialties as commercial and corporation law, indicating a typical evolution for large firms. Although a Tenney was always the senior partner, the list of junior partners constantly changed, as these men moved into other firms, judgeships, or government positions. Despite this revolving door, the firm obviously prospered; by 1924 it was a modest law factory with seven partners. One of the 1878 and 1882 partners, J. M. Flower, went on to become the senior partner in Flower, Smith & Musgrave, which appeared on the large-firm list with five members every year from 1893 on. The other early Chicago large firm (Aldrich, Payne & Defrees) had five partners in 1893, but dropped back to three or four between 1898 and 1915, until it mushroomed to a nine-partner, seventeen-associate firm in 1924. John Barton Payne, the second-listed partner in 1893, left the firm and became, by 1915, the senior partner in one of Chicago's most eminent firms, the law factory of Winston, Payne, Strawn & Shaw. He left private practice in 1917 to become General Counsel and then Chairman of the U.S. Shipping Board, as well as Counsel to the Director General of Railroads, and, in 1920, Secretary of the Interior in Wilson's cabinet. Payne's early career was typical of many leading Chicago lawyers. Born in Pruntytown, Virginia, he did not attend law school. He practiced for five years in Kingwood, West Virginia, serving as a circuit court judge at the age of twenty-five and mayor at twenty-seven, before relocating in Chicago at age twenty-eight.[27]

Two Cincinnati firms were on the large-firm list in 1887. King, Thompson, Richard & Thompson had five partners in 1887, but slipped to three in 1893, and then disappeared from *Hubbell's*. The two senior partners in 1887, Rufus King and Samuel J. Thompson, were in their forty-third and thirty-ninth years of law practice, respectively. Their firm failed to survive their retirement, although one of the junior partners, Lawrence Maxwell, went on to become the senior partner in the next Cincinnati firm to appear on the large-firm list, Maxwell

& Ramsey in 1909.[28] The other large firm in Cincinnati in 1887 had a more distinguished history. The firm appeared in 1872 as a two-man partnership, with former Ohio governor George Hoadly as the senior partner. Hoadly was at the head of the firm in 1887, but shortly thereafter he and the firm's second partner, Edgar M. Johnson, took their practice to New York City. They formed the large firm of Hoadly, Lauterbach & Johnson, which appeared on the New York City large-firm list in 1893 (six members), 1898 (eight members), 1904 (eight members), and 1909 (five members). This career move was very unusual for a well-established elite lawyer. After Hoadly left, the Cincinnati firm continued with the three junior partners, including Hoadly's son. They recruited Superior Court Judge Judson Harmon, who had read law in George Hoadly's office, as their new senior partner. The successor firm, Harmon, Colston, Goldsmith & Hoadly, listed four partners between 1893 and 1909, growing to six in 1915 and seven in 1924. Harmon was absent from the firm in 1895–1897 as Grover Cleveland's Attorney General, and in 1909–1913 he was Ohio's progressive governor.[29]

Two other midwestern cities, Milwaukee and Detroit, consistently had firms just below the large-firm threshold in the late nineteenth century. One of the five four-member firms outside New York City in 1872 and three of the fifteen firms in 1882 were in Milwaukee. The first Milwaukee large firm (Winkler, Flanders, Smith, Bottum & Vilas), which had five partners in 1898, specialized in corporation, commercial, and patent law. The firm retained that size through 1904, dropped to four partners in 1909 and 1915, and then grew to law-factory size, with nine partners in 1924. It continued to list the same specialties.

Kansas City did not have a four-member firm until 1893, but that firm (Lathrop, Morrow & Fox), is noteworthy because it early became one of the largest firms in the nation. By 1904, it had grown to fourteen members (seven partners and seven associates under the firm name Lathrop, Morrow, Fox & Moore), making it, along with the New York City firm of Carter, Hughes & Dwight, the largest firm in *Hubbell's* that year. The Lathrop firm grew to ten partners (eleven listed members) in 1915, and it continued growing in the 1920s. The firm's senior partner, Gardiner Lathrop, served as General Solicitor for the Atchison, Topeka, and Santa Fe Railway, and other partners served as local representatives for that railroad or as general counsel for other local railroads. Hence, at least in Kansas City, a law factory could emerge with railroads as its major clients.

In 1915, Kansas City had three law factories, as many as Chicago and Cleveland, and only one less than Boston. Two of the three Cleveland law factories had also been major firms in 1909. These firms are especially notable because of the size they obtained by the 1920s. Two grew from nine and ten members in 1915 to fifteen in 1924. One Cleveland firm (Squire, Sanders & Dempsey) skyrocketed from thirteen members (nine partners and four associates) in 1915 to twenty-nine partners in 1924, the largest in the nation. In addition, one other large firm in Cleveland in 1915 grew from five partners to nineteen partners by 1924.

Cities with a precocious record of large-firm development seem to have been predominantly midwestern cities. Several midwestern cities besides Chicago, St. Louis, Cincinnati, Milwaukee, Detroit, Kansas City, and Cleveland were congenial to large firms earlier than cities of similar size in other regions. Columbus, Toledo, Minneapolis, and St. Paul all present similar patterns. If the two largest cities in each region, New York and Chicago, are not included, the midwest consistently records more large firms than the east throughout the 1880s and 1890s; the two regions are nearly equal thereafter.

A particularly open and inventive brand of professionalism among lawyers seems to have developed in the midwest. This is shown by other evidence besides the record of large firms. Chicago, for example, was noteworthy in the early support its organized bar gave to reform efforts in the administration of justice and in the delivery of legal services.[30] A combination of economic, social, and cultural factors explains midwestern professionalism. Economic activity in the region had increased to the point that large firms were feasible. Urbanization, with its attendant problems, had also increased to the point that an innovative approach to law reform seemed called for. Compared to the eastern bar elite, the midwestern bar elite was newer and less aristocratic because most leading lawyers in the various midwestern cities came not from the upper class of those cities, but rather from elsewhere in the midwestern region.

Another factor explaining the newer, less aristocratic character of the midwestern legal elite was a greater variety in educational backgrounds than was found in the eastern bar elite. A college education and law school training were less "mandatory," at least prior to 1900. In addition, the number of lawyers in truly large firms or with an exclusively corporate clientele before the 1920s was never large enough in itself to constitute a visible bar elite. Hence, the elite was relatively inclusive and heterogeneous, maintaining, at the same time, its "standards."[31]

The contrast between the midwestern cities and eastern cities is strongest in the cases of Philadelphia and Boston, and weakest in the case of New York City. New York's elite was recruited from a wide region and was not notably home-grown. A college education and law school training was also not so "mandatory" a requirement before 1900. On the other hand, the absolute number of lawyers in large firms and with an exclusive corporate practice was always much greater in New York City, a factor which contributed to a greater homogeneity among leading lawyers and a greater social exclusiveness. In addition, the cultural traditions of the general urban elite in New York City had a long heritage, creating a predilection to aristocratic demeanor among the leaders of New York's bar.[32]

The contrasts among New York City, Philadelphia, and Boston are instructive. Throughout the period of this study, Philadelphia produced only two major firms, whereas New York City produced twenty-two, and Boston, a smaller city, produced four. New York City had ninety-six large firms, Boston had twenty, and Philadelphia had twelve. The first Philadelphia firm to appear on the large-firm list was Biddle & Ward. Significantly, the firm maintained a New York City office in addition to its main Philadelphia office.

The bar elite in Philadelphia, in contrast to New York City, had longer historic ties to the city's first families, those families that made their fortunes during the eighteenth and early nineteenth centuries. The strength of the family-firm tradition as well as certain other traditions peculiar to the Philadelphia upper-class milieu seem to have militated against the early creation of large firms. E. Digby Baltzell, the social historian of Philadelphia's upper class, has noted that no proper Philadelphia lawyer has ever been named to the U.S. Supreme Court. To explain this fact, he notes the apparent absence among upper-class Philadelphia lawyers of any strong "itch" for public office. He also cites a disinclination for the sustained abstract reasoning so characteristic of the Boston-Harvard tradition, where the family-firm tradition among the legal elite also was long-standing, but where the involvement in national politics came earlier. Baltzell believes the avoidance of abstractions is a clue to the values and attitudes of the Philadelphia upper class as a whole and not just of Philadelphia lawyers.[33]

One eminent Philadelphia lawyer who fits this pattern very well is John G. Johnson, one of the most highly regarded appellate court attorneys, especially in antitrust cases, during the late nineteenth and early twentieth centuries. He served as counsel in the E. C. Knight, Northern Securities, Standard Oil, American Tobacco, and U.S. Steel antitrust cases. Johnson displayed signs of what can be called an anti-organizational personal style that may have been characteristic of the nineteenth-century Philadelphia upper class. He never established a partnership, although he did employ young lawyers to assist him as his business grew. One lawyer, Frank P. Prichard, was associated with him for thirty-seven years, between 1883 and 1917, but always as an employee, not as a partner.[34]

As a sign of the winds of economic change which were eventually to blow over Philadelphia, several of the younger men in Johnson's office did leave the law for high business positions.[35] By the 1920s, Philadelphia had joined the national trend toward large law firms. Economic pressures were making the parochial attitudes of the Philadelphia legal elite increasingly anachronistic. The Biddle firm (now Biddle, Paul, Dawson & Yocum) had eleven members in 1924. One other firm (Roberts & Montgomery) was the same size, and three firms were larger. Dickson, Beitler & McCouch, with sixteen partners, was a very large firm by the national standards of the 1920s.

A bachelor's degree from an Ivy League college, attendance at Harvard Law School, and frequently an LL.B. were very common among the Boston bar elite during the Gilded Age. The elite was also conspicuously Boston-bred. All of these factors seem to have encouraged the Boston elite to be national-minded. Very likely, also, Boston's ties to the New York City bar, facilitated by the close connection that developed during the Gilded Age between the Harvard Law School and New York, encouraged the early emergence of large firms. Significantly, the three earliest major firms in Boston had important connections outside the city: two had senior partners with national reputations, Moorfield Storey and Louis D. Brandeis; the third (Fish, Richardson, Herrick & Neave) maintained a New York City office in 1904 and 1909, as did Storey's firm in 1915.

Brandeis was the true pioneer of modern forms of law firm organization in Boston. He was the first Boston lawyer to organize his office on the basis of taking bright young men quickly into partnership.[36] Beginning in 1881, he made it a practice to hire as salaried assistants those Harvard Law School graduates who stood high in their class.[37] That this was very rare in Boston in the 1880s is witnessed by Samuel Williston's report that no one in his Harvard class of 1888 was able to obtain a salaried position for his first year's work in an office.[38]

When Brandeis answered the complaints of several of the younger men in his firm in 1896 that their labors were contributing only to the firm's reputation, not to their own, he had to look to New York City for examples to prove his point that a lawyer could earn a reputation even though his name did not appear in the firm designation.[39]

Despite its leadership in the development of large firms, the New York City legal scene in the Gilded Age was still presided over by the great advocates who fought prominent cases through the courts. These advocates were generally remembered for their personal characteristics rather than for their legal erudition.[40] For example, in commenting upon Joseph H. Choate, probably foremost among New York City lawyers during the Gilded Age, the *New York Tribune* emphasized his courtroom manner rather than his legal arguments: "His method goes right home to the human heart. . . . He puts on no lofty airs, but often speaks with his hands in his pockets. He does not strive to stir up dark passions. While he is always a little keener, a little firmer, and more witty than the man in the box or on the bench, yet he is always a brother man to him."[41]

Yet, Choate was a partner in Evarts, Southmayd & Choate, one of the earliest major firms (eight partners in 1878). As if to underline Choate's and the firm's transitional status, it failed to grow beyond the eight partners it listed in 1882, falling back to seven in 1887 as Evarts, Choate & Beaman, and to four in 1904 as Evarts, Tracy & Sherman, after the death of the two senior partners and the departure of Choate to London as the American ambassador. The firm survived, with four partners in 1915 and six in 1924. The transition generation in New York City may have institutionalized the *large* firm in order to service the needs of its corporate clients, but it did not institutionalize the *major* firm. That development required lawyers with a temperament, professional outlook, and set of ambitions somewhat different from Choate, Root, and others of their generation.

This new breed came to the fore in the 1890s, creating the first enduring law factories. (See Table 3.) New York City lawyers pioneered the law factory, but did not necessarily create the largest firms in the pre–1920s period. Only one of the nine largest firms in this period was in New York City (Carter, Hughes & Dwight, with fourteen members in 1904). The other eight, ranging from twelve to sixteen members, were located in Boston, Kansas City, Philadelphia,

Providence, Pittsburgh, Chicago, Birmingham, and Houston. The largest of these was the Boston firm of Fish, Richardson, Herrick & Neave. It had sixteen members, nine partners, and seven associates, in 1909.

If only partners are considered, New York City had no more than two of the seven largest firms (eleven or more partners). Davies, Stone & Auerbach had eleven partners in 1904; Sullivan & Cromwell had eleven partners in 1909. The largest was the Pittsburgh firm of Reed, Smith, Shaw & Beal, which had eleven partners in 1909 and thirteen partners in 1915. The very fact that New York City had more law factories than any other city seems to be the reason that the very largest firms did not emerge there. The opportunities were so great in New York City that ambitious associates and even junior partners broke away from the budding law factories and formed their own firms, many of which soon became new law factories. In other cities, the opportunities were not so great. Fewer law factories developed, but they were able to grow to the largest size more quickly.[42]

Charles Evans Hughes was a representative figure among the generation of New York City lawyers who helped create the new type of law firm which would come to dominate the upper reaches of the profession. In 1883, the young Hughes entered the firm of Chamberlain, Carter & Hornblower, which had listed four partners in the 1882 *Hubbell's Directory*. The firm was small and unhurried enough that Hughes was able to do some essentially *pro bono* work, as counsel, in a long court fight, for a poor client who was trying to regain custody of his children.[43] But the firm was destined not only to become one of the largest firms in New York City, but also to serve as a ''seed'' firm for a number of other developing major firms.

The growth of Chamberlain, Carter & Hornblower during the 1880s was primarily due to Walter S. Carter, who not only brought most of the business into the firm and managed the office, but also established the practice of hiring a few outstanding graduates of leading law schools immediately after their graduation, with an eye to retaining a few of them as partners. The firm became a spawning ground for future eminent New York City law firms. In addition to Carter and Daniel H. Chamberlain, the Reconstruction governor of South Carolina, the other senior partner was William B. Hornblower, who left in 1887 with James Bryne to form his own firm, Hornblower, Bryne & Taylor, taking with him the business he had been handling. The Hornblower firm joined the list of major firms in the 1910s as Hornblower, Miller & Potter, with nine partners. By 1915, Bryne had gone on to form his own firm, Bryne & Cutcheon, with six partners.

At the same time that Hughes entered the Chamberlain, Carter & Hornblower firm, two future prominent Wall Street lawyers, Henry W. Taft (William Howard Taft's brother) and George W. Wickersham (Taft's Attorney General), were leaving. Wickersham went to Strong & Cadwalader, where he specialized in corporate reorganizations and served as a legal counsel for several major railroad and subway construction projects. Taft teamed up with William D. Page in Page

**TABLE 3**
**Major Firms (seven or more partners, or ten or more members)**

| | 1872 | 1878 | 1882 | 1887 | 1893 | 1898 | 1904 | 1909 | 1915 |
|---|---|---|---|---|---|---|---|---|---|
| Total firms | 0 | 3 | 3 | 4 | 3 | 10 | 9 | 22 | 39 |
| Total cities | 0 | 1 | 1 | 1 | 1 | 3 | 4 | 10 | 15 |
| Total lawyers | 0 | 23 | 23 | 29 | 21 | 80 | 84 | 193 | 369 |
| New York City's share of major firms (in percent) | -- | 100 | 100 | 100 | 100 | 70 | 56 | 32 | 36 |

Source: Hubbell's Legal Directory

& Taft and later joined Wickersham's firm, which in 1914 became Cadwalader, Wickersham & Taft, with eight members in the firm. As an indication of the true size of such a firm, it had a legal staff of fifteen who were not firm members and a nonlegal staff of twenty-nine.[44] Cadwalader, Wickersham & Taft became one of the handful of leading firms in the "financial bar" in New York City, handling legal business, including corporate reorganizations, for a wide range of financial institutions.[45] The rosters of many other leading Wall Street firms in subsequent years also contained the names of Carter's former associates and partners.[46]

Probably the most well known ex-partner in the Chamberlain, Carter & Hornblower firm, at least in the lore of the profession, was Paul D. Cravath. He joined Chamberlain, Carter & Hornblower after establishing a reputation as a brilliant student at Columbia Law School.[47] In 1888, his name was added to the firm's designation, when it became Carter, Hughes & Cravath. An important client of the firm was George Westinghouse. In 1899, Cravath moved to Seward, Guthrie & Steele as a partner, taking with him the business of the Westinghouse interests and the law office system Carter had pioneered.[48]

Prior to Cravath's arrival, the Seward firm had been staffed by friends of partners, colleagues, and clients, but most of them stayed only a few months. These men had not been much help in the important corporate matters which were increasingly dominating the firm's work. These men had not been paid and had been allowed to seek clients of their own. The lack of system and organization in the firm is revealed by the fact that in 1884 it employed no filing clerk and did not even have the semblance of a filing system. Though it did employ stenographers and copyists, it did not yet use typewriters.[49]

Cravath changed all that. He hired only young lawyers who had graduated from both college and law school, preferably with high scholastic marks from elite universities. Cravath also preferred men with forceful personalities and rugged physiques, recognizing that the new type of corporate law practice required hard work from high-strung, tense, and driving personalities. The young lawyers were paid and were not allowed to work for anyone but the firm. In return, they gained the experience of working on the major reorganizations and securities issues which were, by the late 1890s, almost the exclusive work of the firm.

Thus, by the late 1890s and early 1900s, Cravath was creating a system of law office organization which would, when it became the general rule in the 1920s, make nearly impossible the kind of career he and his young colleagues on the Carter firm had known. They had established major reputations as young men. Hughes, for example, was only twenty-six and Cravath twenty-five when they were made partners in Carter's firm in 1888.[50] These men had been able to move easily from firm to firm, often creating new firms themselves and carrying their clients with them. But the Cravath system, once institutionalized, churned out anonymous organization men, steadfastly loyal to the firm that had hired them fresh out of law school, moving only if the firm informed them it could not advance them to partnership.

A young lawyer in his third year with the Cravath firm, Mason Bigelow, was moved to complain in 1915 about his position in a revealing letter to his law school dean, Harlan Fiske Stone. He had worked on a wide variety of matters, including corporate organizations and reorganizations, construction contracts, and real estate transactions. In some of these matters, he had been given considerable personal responsibility. He had no complaints about the character of the work. But he wanted to leave the firm because "the number of older men in the office is so large that the outlook for advancement is not favorable, and. . . another office might, therefore, offer greater advantages."[51] Bigelow was not even listed as an associate of the Cravath firm in *Hubbell's*, its practice being to list only the partners. Stone advised Bigelow to look into Bowers & Sands, a five-partner firm.

By the 1920s the system Cravath had initiated was well established and regularized. The managing clerks of the leading law firms had even entered into a gentleman's agreement after World War I to eliminate the practice that had grown up of competitive bidding for the services of the most promising law school graduates. They established uniform beginning salaries and agreed not to pirate employees away from each other.[52]

It took some time, however, for the Cravath system to spread. Allen Wardwell, who went into Francis Lynde Stetson's firm right after graduating from Harvard Law School in the late 1890s, reported that at first he was not paid. For several years, he did routine work only a cut above that of a clerk, not moving into corporation work until around 1904.[53] But by 1905, William Draper Lewis was reporting that there was a heavy demand from large law offices for the best graduates of elite law schools, "and oftentimes at very fair salaries."[54] Lewis does not explain, however, what he considered a "fair salary" to be. Other evidence suggests that $40 to $50 per month was the best pay in the first years of the century, and many firms still expected beginning lawyers to work gratis, even those with law school degrees. By 1910–1915, a beginning salary in the $40 to $50 per month range was common. For those who were retained, moving from the clerk to the associate category, regular increases were the rule, up to about $5000 per year after five or so years, when a decision on admission to partnership was made.[55] The eagerness of elite law school graduates to become associated with a large and growing firm was a contributing factor to the increasing proliferation and the ever-growing size of these firms.

The emergence of large firms significantly transformed the character and outlook of the bar elite. What this development meant can be seen in the comments of several sensitive observers during the 1920s, when the implications of the large firm for the interests of justice and true professionalism became fully apparent. Roscoe Pound complained in 1926 that "I have seen more than one student who seems to me particularly suited for [legal aid work] get into the treadmill of a big office and have most of the milk of human kindness squeezed out of him therein.''[56] Felix Frankfurter believed the bar elite's commercialization poisoned the very atmosphere of the law schools. His students were dominated by a ''crass materialism,'' a desire to become ''big money-making lawyers in New York and Chicago.'' ''They hear from time to time noble talks. . . . But when all is said and done, these 'idealistic' influences, except in a negligibly few cases, are as nothing compared to the forces of example by 'leaders of the bar,' the career, the pursuits, the aims of those who are deemed the 'leaders.' ''[57]

Although young lawyers in large firms certainly went along with the system that promised them substantial material rewards, they did, at least occasionally, feel dissatisfied. One lawyer reported in 1932 to his former law school professor that in ten years of working for a large New York firm, he had noticed that ''there are a great number of young men who are dissatisfied spiritually, who have no respect for the older men for whom they work, who become more cynical, caring less and less each year to make more out of themselves than machines.'' It was the grinding hard work, long hours, and the lack of any aim higher than money and prestige that produced this cynicism and alienation.[58] This same young man lamented publicly (but anonymously) in *Scribners*: ''If there had been one real effort to strangle an injustice, one trial to overcome wrong at some personal sacrifice, a trying attention to banish some error—but I recall none.''[59]

A few leading lawyers were troubled by the implications of the circumstances surrounding their own professional success. George R. Nutter, long a partner in Louis D. Brandeis's firm, noted that for the ''men higher up at the bar,'' the practice of law had changed since 1880 ''from the determination of rights in court to advising and taking part in business enterprises. . . . The result is that while the business standards may have improved a good deal, I think that the legal standards, by contact with them, have deteriorated somewhat.'' Because of this, Nutter concluded, ''lawyers to a considerable extent become not persons whose advice is followed, but persons who are hired to carry through what their employers want to have done. One purchases legal brains now in the same way as he purchases industrial labor or anything else.''[60] Samuel Untermyer, a liberal New York City corporation lawyer, published a similar critique in 1933: ''Fifty years ago skill and eloquence in advocacy were the prime requisites of the leaders of our bar. Their reputations were made and had to be maintained in the courts.'' But then, large corporations began ''to draw away from advocacy the best minds of the bar and by money temptations convert them into highly paid clerks to teach financiers to keep 'prayerfully within the law.' '' When that happened, leading lawyers found that in addition to knowing the law, they had to develop business sense and expertise. As a consequence, Untermyer complained, the corporation lawyer's ''legal knowledge must not be thrust forward if he is to be of aid to his clients.''[61] The point is that not only did some lawyers become counselors to large corporations, but also these men were recognized both inside and outside the profession as the leaders of the bar. They were the best legal minds of their generation and they set the standards of professional conduct.

Harlan Fiske Stone was dismayed by that standard. He complained that the higher strata of the bar had become so commercialized that "they have little interest in raising [the bar's] standards, in improving its membership, or in improving the administration of the law in any substantial way." In addition, "you rarely find their services enlisted in any case which does not involve substantial remuneration, and almost never on the unpopular side of a case involving human rights and personal liberty."[62] Given these attitudes at the top, Stone thought it was not surprising that the bar as a whole "has so little professional and public spirit throughout that it is lagging behind the other professions."[63] If the law factory symbolized the transformation of the profession, thoughtful observers were profoundly uneasy about the meaning of that transformation.

## NOTES

1. James Willard Hurst, *The Growth of American Law: The Law Makers* (Boston, 1950), 297–308.

2. American Bar Association, *Reports* 29 (1906): 7–8 (hereafter cited as *ABA Rep*).

3. Julius H. Cohen, *The Law: Business or Profession?* (New York, 1916), 30. For similar views by lawyers with established reputations, see Theron G. Strong, *Landmarks of a Lawyer's Lifetime* (New York, 1914), 354; and Edward M. Shepard, "Lawyers and Corporate Capitalization," *Green Bag* 18 (July 1906): 603.

4. Herbert Croly, *The Promise of American Life* (New York, 1964; orig. pub. 1909), 136.

5. Woodrow Wilson, "The Lawyer and the Community," *North American Review* 192 (November 1910): 614. This was Wilson's 1910 address to the American Bar Association. See also, Wilson, "The Lawyer in Politics," *Kentucky State Bar Association Proceedings* 10 (1911): 19–22. A good discussion of the progressive era criticisms of corporate lawyers can be found in Jerold S. Auerbach, *Unequal Justice: Lawyers and Social Change in Modern America* (New York, 1976), 31–35.

6. John F. Dillon, "The True Professional Ideal," *ABA Rep* 17 (1894): 410. For similar statements, see John R. Dos Passos, *The American Lawyer* (New York, 1907), 47; Strong, *Landmarks*, 385; Harry D. Nims, "The Present Status of the Professions—The Law," *The World's Work* 5 (1903): 3085.

7. As late as 1930, 94 percent of the lawyers, judges, and justices were listed by the Census as either in the "Professional Service" (87 percent) or "Public Service" (7 percent) categories. Of the 6 percent employed directly by businesses, more than half were in either railroad companies, insurance companies, or banking, brokerage, and real estate firms, indicating the immaturity of the corporation law department in manufacturing industries. In comparison, only 42 percent of engineers were listed in "Professional Service," a figure inflated by the fact that engineers in management were not counted as engineers. Bureau of the Census, *Fifteenth Census*, vol. 5, *Population*, General Report on Occupations.

8. Philip C. Jessup, *Elihu Root*, 2 vols. (New York, 1938), 1:133; notes on a conversation with Elihu Root, May 4, 1930, Philip C. Jessup Papers, Box 243, Library of

Congress; note unsigned and undated, but attributed to Knox, Philander C. Knox Papers, Box 2, Library of Congress. Such statements can be read as self-serving rationalizations, of course. At the least, they need to be considered in the context of lists of leading lawyers who left legal practice to become high corporate executives in these years. For two such lists, see Cohen, *Law: Business or Profession?*, 210–211; Joseph Katz, "The American Legal Profession, 1890–1915," (M.A. thesis, Columbia University, 1953), 19–20.

9. The following editions of *Hubbell's* were examined: 1872, 1878, 1882, 1887, 1893, 1898, 1904, 1909, 1915. Although it began publication in 1870, 1872 was the first year it contained an adequate listing of attorneys. The other dates were selected on the basis of their availability in Southern California libraries. *Hubbell's* was the most satisfactory national directory for this research. *Martindale's American Law Directory* contained an alphabetical listing of lawyers and firms, but did not list the names of partners or associates. Local legal directories would be valuable in filling out the story of the development of the large firm in particular cities, but they would not have permitted the systematic collection of comparative data that the use of a single national directory allowed. A large firm was defined as one containing at least five members (partners and associates). A standard based only on the number of partners would be somewhat more reliable, since every firm gave a full list of partners, but occasionally associates were not listed. On the other hand, a list of firms which considered only partners could be a misleading indicator of the growth of the large firm. A firm with six members, even if only two of them have been admitted to partnership, is qualitatively different from a two-man partnership with no associates. For the early part of our period, a four-member firm was definitely a large firm. There were only fourteen of them in five cities in 1872. However, by 1915, there were 439 firms in 116 cities with at least four members. By then, a somewhat higher standard seemed desirable. By raising the standard to five members, we reduce the 1915 total of firms by nearly one-half, but only cut back the number of lawyers involved by 34 percent. We also cut back the number of cities from 106 to 70, omitting such places as Hastings, Nebraska; Atchison, Kansas; and Logansport, Indiana. The law factory, or major firm, was defined as one containing seven partners or a combination of ten partners and associates. The problem of the occasional nonlisting of associates was assumed to be a more serious one for the very largest firms. The major-firm threshold was determined by examining the size of the fifty largest firms listed in *Hubbell's* in 1915.

10. If we consider the number of lawyers in large firms, rather than the number of firms, the annual growth rates are even higher: 1893–1898: 18.3 percent; 1898–1904: 8.8 percent; 1904–1909: 13.6 percent; 1909–1915: 8.4 percent.

11. Bureau of the Census, *Sixteenth Census*, *Population*, Comparative Occupational Statistics for the United States, 1870 to 1940, by Alba M. Edwards (Washington, 1943), 111; Henry E. Howland, "Practice of Law in New York," *Century Magazine* 62 (October 1901): 802–25; Nims, "The Law," 3082–86; Ivy Lee, "The Modern Lawyer," *The World's Work* 8 (1904): 4873–80; H. M. Stevens, "New York's Famous Lawyers," *Harper's Weekly*, July 29, 1911, 17.

12. This information is drawn from *Hubbell's*, especially from the Appendix, in which firms could insert advertisements describing themselves.

13. Henry J. Fehrman, "The Duty of the Lawyer in the Conflict between the People and Leaders of Organized Wealth," *Case and Comment* 19 (July 1912): 93; Strong, *Landmarks*, 463.

14. Jessup, *Elihu Root*, 1:183–84; Richard W. Leopold, *Elihu Root and the Conservative Tradition* (Boston, 1954), 15–17; Elting E. Morison, *Turmoil and Tradition; A Study in the Life and Times of Henry L. Stimson* (Boston, 1960), 65–67, 71–75.

15. William Harbaugh, *Lawyer's Lawyer: The Life of John W. Davis* (New York, 1973), 186, drawing on the firm's privately printed history; Beryl H. Levy, *Corporation Lawyer—Saint or Sinner? The New Role of the Lawyer in Modern Society* (New York, 1961), 32, 70–73; Allen Wardwell, Oral Memoir, 1952, Columbia University, 38–41.

16. Harbaugh, *Lawyer's Lawyer*, 187.

17. James Willard Hurst, *The Legitimacy of the Business Corporation in the Law of the United States, 1780–1970* (Charlottesville, 1970), 72–75.

18. The contrast between Henry L. Stimson's firm's size and practice in the 1910s and in the 1920s is instructive. In the earlier period, the firm, Winthrop & Stimson, deliberately kept itself below law factory size (seven members in 1909, nine in 1915). In the 1920s, the firm did not practice, and probably could not have practiced, such a policy. Morison, *Turmoil and Tradition*, 204–5, 253–69.

19. Learned Hand to Felix Frankfurter, July 27, 1921, Frankfurter Papers, Box 63, Library of Congress. But see Charles Evans Hughes, *The Autobiographical Notes of Charles Evans Hughes*, ed. David J. Danelski and Joseph S. Tulchin (Cambridge, Mass., 1973), 114–15 for a statement about the pace and drudgery of an 1890s law factory.

20. Elihu Root to William D. Guthrie, May 22, 1900, copy in Jessup Papers, Box 252, Library of Congress. See also Root to Langdon Parker Marvin, November 19, 1903, copy in Jessup Papers, Box 252. Marvin was in the firm of Carter & Ledyard, another leading turn-of-the-century Wall Street firm. As it turned out, Root decided to remain in McKinley's Cabinet in 1900. It should be pointed out that Root was already quite wealthy and could look forward to a lucrative practice no matter what the circumstances.

21. Robert T. Swaine, *The Cravath Firm*, 3 vols. (New York, 1946–1948), 1:359, 776–78. When Guthrie withdrew from the firm in 1906, it was no surprise.

22. Strong, *Landmarks*, 377–78; Dos Passos, *American Lawyer*, 23–27; George F. Shelton, "Law as a Business," *Yale Law Journal* 10 (May 1901): 275–82.

23. In recognition of this fact, firm histories always dutifully report when the first telephone was installed, when typewriters began to be used for business letters, and when female clerical help was first hired. See Walter K. Earle, *Mr. Shearman and Mr. Sterling and How They Grew* (New Haven, 1963), 125; Otto E. Koegel, *Walter S. Carter: Collector of Young Masters; or, The Progenitor of Many Law Firms* (New York, 1953), 171; William W. Clary, *History of the Law Firm of O'Melveny & Myers, 1885–1965*, 2 vols. (Los Angeles, 1966), 1:1–2, 141–42; Morison, *Turmoil and Tradition*, 48–52; Hughes, *Autobiographical Notes*, 63, 75. Theron G. Strong estimated that these innovations tripled a lawyer's productivity, *Landmarks*, 393.

24. Strong, *Landmarks*, 385. The firm was DeWitt, Lockman & DeWitt. It was a two-family firm specializing in the handling of estates. The firm was listed continuously in *Hubbell's* from 1878. At its largest during this period, in 1904, six DeWitts and Lockmans were listed as partners. The firm did not appear in the 1924 [illegible].

25. John Foster Dulles, Foreword, in Arthur H. Dean, *William Nelson Cromwell, 1854–1948: An American Pioneer in Corporation, Comparative, and International Law* (New York, 1957), iii. The firm obtained a wall phone in 1881, desk phones about 1900, and female stenographers in the late 1890s. Ibid., 23–29.

26. These figures confirm the information Lord Bryce received from his informants: "The custom of forming legal partnerships is one which prevails much more extensively

in some parts of the Union than in others. In Boston and New York, for instance, it is common, and I think in the Western cities. . . in Philadelphia one is told that it is rather the exception.'' James Bryce, *American Commonwealth*, 2 vols. (New York, 1910, rev. ed.), 2:667.

27. Biographical data on Payne is from John W. Leonard, *Who's Who in Jurisprudence* (Brooklyn, 1925).

28. Two other of the King, Thompson junior partners were listed after 1893 as independent practitioners, clearly indicating that the firm did not survive its founders' retirement.

29. H. D. Peck, ''Judson Harmon,'' *Green Bag* 20 (May 1908): 239–43.

30. For example, Roscoe Pound, who was a close observer of the organized bar and of efforts to reform the administration of justice, reported: ''I think the liveliest local bar association in the country is the Chicago Bar Association.'' Pound to William B. Cockley, March 2, 1917, Roscoe Pound Papers, Box 8, Harvard Law School Library. See also Hurst, *Growth of American Law*, 154–63; and ''Report of the Committee on the Defense of Poor Persons Accused of Crime,'' *Chicago Bar Association Reports* 42 (1915): 65, which compares local bar association activities in New York City and Chicago.

31. Careers of leading lawyers reported in obituaries in the *ABA Rep*, 1900–1911, confirm these impressions. Only 4 percent of Chicago lawyers had been born in that city and only another 24 percent elsewhere in Illinois. In comparison, 84 percent of Philadelphia lawyers had been born in that city or elsewhere in Pennsylvania, and 63 percent of Boston lawyers had been born in that city or elsewhere in Massachusetts. New York City had a mixed pattern, with 42 percent born in that city or elsewhere in New York state. Interestingly, several major midwestern cities outside Chicago (Cincinnati, Cleveland, Kansas City, and Milwaukee) had a pattern very similar to Boston's, with 61 percent born either in the home city or state. However, the nonexclusiveness of the midwestern bar elite is reflected in the fact that only 35 percent had ever even attended law school, whereas 89 percent of the Boston lawyers appearing in the ABA obituaries had attended law school. In Chicago, success depended much more on law school attendance than it did elsewhere in the midwest. Of Chicago lawyers in the ABA obituaries, 40 percent had graduated from law school, and 56 percent had attended. The 40 percent figure compares favorably with the 42 percent of Boston elite lawyers who had graduated from law school. However, only 60 percent of the Chicago lawyers had ever attended an undergraduate college, compared to 85 percent of the Boston lawyers.

32. As mentioned above, only 42 percent of New York City lawyers whose careers were summarized in ABA obituaries between 1900 and 1911 were born in either New York City or New York State, compared to 63 percent of the Boston lawyers born in that city or Massachusetts and 84 percent of the Philadelphia lawyers born in that city or Pennsylvania. Only 63 percent of the New York City lawyers had a college degree, compared to 74 percent in Philadelphia and Boston. Twenty-eight percent of the New York City lawyers had never attended college, compared to 21 percent of the Philadelphia lawyers and 15 percent of the Boston lawyers. Only about half as many of the New York City lawyers (46 percent) had ever attended law school compared to the Boston lawyers (89 percent). Interestingly, only 42 percent of the Philadelphia lawyers had ever attended law school—reflecting, no doubt, the stronger hold that the clerkship system had in that city than elsewhere.

33. E. Digby Baltzell, *Philadelphia Gentlemen: The Making of a National Upper Class* (Glencoe, Ill., 1958), 146.

34. Barnie F. Winkelman, *John G. Johnson* (Philadelphia, 1942), 113, 117, 187, 189, 197.

35. Ibid., 189.

36. Samuel Williston, *Life and Law* (Boston, 1941), 112.

37. Louis D. Brandeis to Christopher Columbus Langdell, December 30, 1889, in Brandeis, *Letters of Louis D. Brandeis, Urban Reformer*, ed. Melvin I. Urofsky and David W. Levy (Albany, 1971), 86. For additional details on Brandeis's practice, see the impressively researched and very insightful Allon Gal, *Brandeis of Boston* (Cambridge, Mass., 1980), 1–95. See also, Urofsky, *A Mind of One Piece: Louis D. Brandeis and American Reform* (New York, 1971), 26–29; or the standard biography, Alpheus T. Mason, *Brandeis: A Free Man's Life* (New York, 1946), 56–95.

38. Williston, *Life and Law*, 104.

39. Brandeis to William Harrison Dunbar, August 19, 1896, in Brandeis, *Letters*, 124–25.

40. Morison, *Turmoil and Tradition*, 64; Edwin C. Austin, "Some Comments on Large Law Firms," *The Practical Lawyer* 3 (April 1957): 9; Robert T. Swaine, "Impact of Big Business on the Profession: An Answer to Critics of the Modern Bar," *American Bar Association Journal* 35 (February 1949): 91–92.

41. Edward Sandford Martin, *Life of Joseph Hodges Choate*, 2 vols. (New York, 1921), 1:445; see also 2:80–83.

42. Compare Walter S. Carter's statement about his ambitious, hard-driving junior partner, George M. Pinney, to Brandeis's letter to William Dunbar, quoted above. "Pinney ought to get out. He has got a good solid business of $12,000 to $15,000 a year, and it will be more before it will be less. He. . .hasn't got one jot of the raw material that goes to the make up of a lieutenant." Carter to Charles Evans Hughes, December 21, 1892, quoted in Koegel, *Carter*, 71–72. Brandeis, in Boston, urged his dissatisfied juniors to stick with the firm, where they could make more money than if they struck out on their own.

43. Hughes, *Autobiographical Notes*, 64–65.

44. In addition to *Hubbell's*, see Henry W. Taft, *A Century and a Half at the New York Bar* (New York, 1938), 176n; James C. German, Jr., "Taft's Attorney General: George W. Wickersham" (Ph.D. diss., New York University, 1969), 3–5.

45. Taft, *Century and a Half*, 191–200.

46. Koegel, *Carter*, Appendix VIII provides a "genealogical chart" of the major firms Carter's former associates or partners joined.

47. Beerits Memorandum, "Ancestry and Early Life," 18–19, Charles Evans Hughes Papers, Box 165, Library of Congress.

48. Hughes, *Autobiographical Notes*, 72–87.

49. Ibid., 64–65, 75; Swaine, *Cravath Firm*, 1:370–73, 657–58, 364–65.

50. Koegel, *Carter*, 462–63; George W. Wickersham, "Informal Talk," in Association of the Bar of the City of New York, *Lectures on Legal Topics* 6 (1924–25): 213–19.

51. Mason Bigelow to Harlan Fiske Stone, January 6, 1915, Harlan Fiske Stone Papers, Miscellaneous Correspondence, Columbia University Library. It is clear from Stone's correspondence while he was Columbia dean that his wide acquaintance with leading New York firms was most useful in placing graduates.

52. Swaine, *Cravath Firm*, 2:2–10; Erwin O. Smigel, "The Impact of Recruitment on the Organization of the Large Law Firm," *American Sociological Review* 25 (February

1960): 61. Apparently, the agreement among managing clerks to eliminate competitive bidding was confined to New York City, judging by a letter in 1925 to Felix Frankfurter from a partner in Hale & Dorr, a leading Boston firm: Joseph N. Welch to Frankfurter, November 27, 1925, Frankfurter Papers, Box 111.

53. Wardwell, Oral Memoir, 42.

54. *ABA Rep* 28 (1905): 553. Lewis's comments seem more applicable to New York City and cities such as Cleveland in which large firms were well established rather than to cities like Minneapolis–St. Paul, where as late as 1914 the supply of young law school graduates seeking places was greater than the number of firms able to take them on, despite the fact that in the Twin Cities, law school graduates were not paid during their first few months in a firm. For Cleveland, see Harold H. Burton to A. A. Stambaugh, May 17, 1913, Ezra R. Thayer Papers, Box 2, Harvard Law School Library; for the Twin Cities, see Rome G. Brown to Thayer, February 14, 1914, ibid., Box 1.

55. Howland, "Practice of Law," 808–10; Koegel, *Carter*, 468; Lee, "Modern Lawyer," 4876; Clary, *O'Melveny and Myers*, 186; Dulles, Foreword, in Dean, *William N. Cromwell*, i–ii; Harry Barnard, *The Forging of an American Jew: The Life and Times of Judge Julian W. Mack* (New York, 1974), 36.

56. Pound to John S. Bradbury, October 8, 1926, Pound Papers, Box 11.

57. Frankfurter to Learned Hand, October 3, 1924, Frankfurter Papers, Box 63.

58. Harrison S. Dimmitt to Zechariah C. Chaffee, Jr., February 12, 1932, copy in Frankfurter Papers, Box 152.

59. Harrison S. Dimmitt [William Maybree Downing], "Life in the United States: New York Lawyer," *Scribners*, January 1932, 23. Despite this numbing philistine atmosphere, the large law firms have never become fully bureaucratized or commercialized. The tension between professionalism and commercialism-bureaucratism that slowed their emergence has remained, although the balance has tipped in the direction of commercialism. Erwin Smigel's study of Wall Street law firms, conducted in the 1950s, concluded that, contrary to the popular image, the firms were "underbureaucratized." Smigel, *The Wall Street Lawyer* (New York, 1964), passim. See also William Delany and Alan H. Finegold, "Wall Street Lawyer in the Provinces," *Administrative Science Quarterly* 15 (June 1970): 197–98, which confirms Smigel's findings and concludes that loose supervision and lack of written rules and procedures are necessary to mitigate the alienation and conflict produced among junior partners and associates by the clash of professional and organizational goals, needs, and attitudes.

60. Nutter to Felix Frankfurter, March 19, 1929, Frankfurter Papers, Box 140.

61. Samuel Untermyer, "What Every Present-Day Lawyer Should Know," American Academy of Political and Social Science, *Annals* 167 (May 1933), 173–74.

62. Stone to Frederick Lewis Allen, n.d., copy enclosed in Allen to Zechariah Chafee, Jr., December 11, 1928, Zechariah Chafee, Jr., Papers, Box 1, Harvard Law School Library. The Stone letter is also printed in full in Alpheus T. Mason, *Harlan Fiske Stone: Pillar of the Law* (New York, 1957), 376–77n. Mason dates the letter as October 5, 1926.

63. Stone to Nicholas Murray Butler, December 3, 1926, reprinted in Mason, *Harlan Fiske Stone*, 210. Stone expressed these views privately in the 1920s and publicly in the 1930s. See ibid., 376–78; Stone, "The Public Influence of the Bar," *Harvard Law Review* 47 (November 1934): 1–14.

*KERMIT L. HALL*

# *Constitutional Machinery and Judicial Professionalism: The Careers of Midwestern State Appellate Court Judges, 1861–1899*

Finley Peter Dunne's Mr. Dooley once mused: "I wisht I was a German and believed in machinery."[1] Mr. Dooley did not. He understood that informal and personal pressures necessarily infringed upon the prescriptive power of constitutionally mandated processes. Yet historians have treated the constitutional machinery of state appellate court selection, when they have treated it at all, with little appreciation for its richness or its interconnectedness with the broader political and legal cultures. As James Willard Hurst observed three decades ago, and as is still the case today: "We have no broad studies concerning [the selection] of judges outside the great cities. . . nor have we studies which single out the elective courts."[2] Students of political science and judicial administration have treated the selection of state appellate court judges in the twentieth century, but less is known about the historical functioning of this process and its impact on judicial character and decision making.[3]

Between 1846 and 1912, the method of selecting state appellate judges rapidly and dramatically changed. Constitutional conventions in every new state entering the Union adopted the popular election of judges, and so, too, did most of the settled states. Lawyer-delegates controlled the committees on the judiciary of these conventions and led the debate in its favor. Popular election was a lawyer's reform. They believed that an infusion of popular sovereignty would enhance the quality of the bench by curbing the influence party leaders had enjoyed under the appointive scheme, that it would make judicial review more credible, and that it would stimulate public confidence in the state appellate judiciary.[4]

By the end of the nineteenth century, popular election was under attack. Lawyers led the assault. This time, however, the impetus for reform came from the newly organized American bar, with its national professional voice in the American Bar Association. A host of local and state bar associations joined with the national organization in urging restoration of the appointive method.[5] In 1904, Simon Fleischmann, a Buffalo lawyer and member of the ABA's committee on judicial selection, along with Frederick E. Wadhams, the secretary of the New York State Bar Association and the treasurer of the ABA, published the findings of a nationwide survey of lawyer's attitudes toward different methods of judicial selection. "The most favorable reports as to the character and ability of the judges and freedom from political considerations in their selection," they reported, "came from States having the appointive system. . . ." Elected judges were "only fairly competent."[6] Fleischmann and Wadhams, as did many critics of popular election, advanced the appointed lower federal judiciary as the model of ability and standing; its judges "averaged higher than that of the states" operating under the elective method.[7]

Lawyers had come to disagree among themselves about the machinery of judicial selection at the same time that the appellate courts became more important. Lawyers close to the political processes of the state constitutional conventions thought popular election a successful reform worth retaining; leaders of the bar thought it undermined the important task of making the bar and the judiciary apolitical instruments of the new science of law.[8] As the range and scale of state judicial activities broadened in response to industrialization during the last half of the nineteenth century, the gap widened.

State appellate courts emerged as important policy-makers. Their judges were the major interpreters of the common law, of state constitutional law, and of a rapidly expanding body of statutory law.[9] Whomsoever controlled their selection might hope to shape public policy.

The midwest was the first region to adopt uniformly popular election. By 1857, all the states from Ohio west to Iowa had begun to elect their appellate judges.[10] Lawyer-delegates in the constitutional conventions that engineered this development expected partisan election to infuse quality, independence, and accountability into the judiciary without degrading the social composition of the bench.[11] The judicial articles of the new constitutions did differ in the number of judges, the timing of judicial elections, the use of at-large and district voting divisions, the filling of vacancies, the length of tenure in office, and the levels of salaries. These differences were the result of compromises struck between competing groups in the conventions over how to either limit or accentuate the effects of popular election. In the aggregate, the constitutional rules affecting judicial selection in the midwest mirrored schemes adopted throughout the rest of the nation.[12]

Between 1861 and 1899, 153 judges sat on the appellate courts of the midwest. Of these, one-third (33.3 percent) were first appointed to fill vacancies caused by death or resignation, but only three of these judges never stood for election. At the same time, 218 judges were appointed to the federal district and circuit courts. It was these judges, Fleischmann and other critics of popular election believed, that ranked above the state appellate judiciary.

## QUALITY

Critics indicted popularly elected appellate judges as mediocrities at best and incompetents at worst. They charged, first, that popular election brought persons of questionable moral character and unfit judicial temperament to the bench; second, that elected judges lacked sufficient technical sophistication to understand fine points of law and to write able opinions; third, that these shortcomings stemmed from inadequate formal academic preparation, shoddy legal training, insufficient preelection judicial experience, and excessive political activism.[13]

Judicial quality is an elusive concept. Personal character and judicial temperament, although critical to the maintenance of the judicial process, are subjective qualities difficult to measure today, let alone a century ago. There were examples of corruption among late nineteenth-century judges, but these incidents, such as that involving Albert Cardozo and the Tweed Ring in New York City, were restricted to the lower state courts. At least in the midwest, corruption and charges of corruption against appellate judges were noticeably absent.[14] A cursory reading of the judges' opinions confirms Lawrence Friedman's view that they were "bombastic, diffuse, labored, drearily logical," and "crammed with unnecessary citations."[15] The implications are unclear; the same charge would fit the opinions of Thomas M. Cooley of the Michigan Supreme Court, who was uniformly praised as the greatest midwestern appellate judge during the post–Civil War era, as it would other appellate judges in the region.[16] The judges' patterns of formal academic education, legal training, prior legal and judicial experience, and political activism, however, offer relatively objective measures of the variable impact of elective and appointive methods of selection.

Lawrence Friedman has observed that state "high-court judges were . . ." often not "liberally educated," and those that were, usually attended "conservative schools. . . ."[17] The case was slightly more complex.

The appointive method most frequently brought to the bench judges with college degrees from prestigious institutions. At a time when the general population had little access to higher education, judges on both the lower federal and state appellate courts attained significant educational levels; two-thirds (66.9 percent) had either graduated from (53.5 percent) or attended (13.4 percent) a college or university (See Table 1). Yet 20 percent more lower federal judges had college degrees than did popularly elected state appellate judges. Almost as many state judges had not attended (40.2 percent) as had graduated (41.7 percent) from college. More frequently, the lower federal judiciary attended the most prestigious of the great "conservative institutions"; although slightly more than one-tenth (14.7 percent) of the state judges had attended Ivy League schools, more than two-fifths (44.3 percent) of the lower federal judiciary had passed some time at these institutions. College-educated state judges usually attended private (66.6 percent) or Big Ten institutions (20.7 percent) in the midwest.

Law school education was an important aspect of the movement to profes-

**TABLE 1**
**Judges' Levels of Academic Education, 1861–1899**
**(Adjusted Percentages)**

| Judges | Level of Education | | | | |
|---|---|---|---|---|---|
| | N | Grad. College | Attnd. College | Secondary | Little/None |
| State | 139 | 41.7 | 17.3 | 40.2 | .7 |
| Federal | 203 | 61.6 | 10.8 | 27.6 | — |
| Total | (342) | (183) | (46) | (112) | (1) |
| Percent | | 53.5 | 13.4 | 32.7 | .4 |
| Missing Cases | (36) | | | | |

sionalize the bar.[18] Most judges in the last half of the nineteenth century did not have such training; they had begun their careers before the rise of the law school. The majority (74.6 percent) of judges on both benches gained admission to the bar by reading law with either an attorney or a judge (See Table 2). As with academic education, federal judges more often had studied in a formal setting; approximately one-third (31.5 percent) of federal judges, in contrast to approximately one-fourth (23.9 percent) of state appellate judges, had either graduated from or attended a law school. In both the level and nature of legal education, the machinery of selection discriminated lightly. Yet, of those judges who did attend law school, federal judges were far more likely to have attended an Ivy League institution.[19] In their formal legal and academic educations, state judges were most often locals rather than cosmopolitans.

State judges built their careers at the local level. Election to a state appellate court in the midwest capped careers that included significant local and lower state court and public legal service. Two-thirds (66.9 percent) of the state judges had prior judicial service compared with about two-fifths (43.1 percent) of lower federal judges.[20] (See Table 3.) Popular election and partisan nomination promoted rather than restricted judicial experience. Within the legal community of every midwestern state, a small group of lawyers developed judicial apprenticeships in the local and lower state courts. Since service in these lower courts invariably required election, appellate judges usually had experience in the practical politics of winning judicial office. They were far more likely to feel comfortable with both judicial service and politics than were lawyers of equal or better credentials who lacked experience in one or the other.

Most appellate judges carved a place for themselves in their state political and

**TABLE 2**
**Judges' Levels of Legal Education, 1861–1899**
**(Adjusted Percentages)**

| Judges | Character of Legal Education | | |
|---|---|---|---|
| | | Grad. or Attnd. | |
| | N | Law School | Read Law |
| State | 138 | 23.9 | 76.1 |
| Federal | 200 | 31.5 | 68.5 |
| Total | (338) | (86) | (252) |
| Percent | | 25.4 | 74.6 |
| Missing Cases | (40) | | |

party systems. Both state and federal judges had pursued significant careers in elective politics; more than nine-tenths (91.9 percent) of the former, and eight-tenths (79.6 percent) of the latter had held elected public office (See Table 4). State judges, however, had overwhelmingly concentrated their careers on filling judicial and public legal posts; about eight-tenths (80.9 percent) of these judges, contrasted with about two-fifths (45.3 percent) of federal judges, had held either

**TABLE 3**
**Judges' Previous Highest Level of Judicial Experience, 1861–1899**
**(Adjusted Percentages)**

| Judges | Level of Highest Judicial Experience | | | | |
|---|---|---|---|---|---|
| | N | Local | State | Federal* | None |
| State | 136 | 65.4 | 1.5 | .7 | 32.4 |
| Federal | 197 | 17.3 | 15.7 | 10.1 | 56.9 |
| Total | (333) | (123) | (33) | (21) | (156) |
| Percent | | 36.9 | 9.9 | 6.3 | 46.9 |
| Missing Cases | (45) | | | | |

*Includes service on the territorial bench.

or both of these kinds of offices. These were truly political judges. Their political and legal careers converged on a relatively narrow path of public legal and judicial officeholding.

Differing schemes of selection had an impact on objective measures of quality. State judges had less extensive and less impressive levels of academic and formal legal education. They tended to be locals, not cosmopolitans. They were also political activists who, more frequently than federal judges, channeled their activism into judicial and public legal service. In this sense, the political and legal cultures of the era reinforced one another; the former emphasized popular sovereignty and partisan discipline, the latter stressed experience and preparation for high judicial office. Partisan ballots and popular elections fostered a distinctive career path for would-be state appellate judges that encouraged prior judicial and public legal service. The judges most likely to win nomination were those who had judicial experience, and those who had experience were also more likely to appreciate and understand the rigors of partisan nomination and campaigning. This may have denied the best legal talent access to the bench, but the process of popular election succeeded far more than the appointive method in placing experienced judges on the bench.

## INDEPENDENCE AND ACCOUNTABILITY

Critics viewed this political and partisan activism as a threat to the independence and accountability of the state appellate judiciary. Beneath this fear lay an essentially cynical attitude toward parties and, more especially, toward the ability of the public to make the judiciary accountable. Somewhat paradoxically, while critics of popular election complained about the threat of too much popular sovereignty, they also claimed that the electorate was apathetic toward judicial elections and that governors frequently subverted the entire process by filling vacancies with appointees that the public blindly accepted at the next election.[21]

Notions of independence and accountability contain powerful assumptions about the proper relationship among politics, law, and the judicial role. If the function of appellate judging is considered essentially technical, then popular election and limited tenure in office thrust unwanted and undesirable political considerations into the selection process and, ultimately, into the performance of the judicial role. In this sense, politics and judging work at cross-purposes. On the other hand, if the judicial role is more art than science, and an art that ought to be sensitive to political necessity as well as formal legal rules, then popular election offers a legitimate means of ensuring judicial accountability through the political process. This, however, presumes a sensitive, active, and informed electorate, a condition most studies of voting behavior suggest is seldom realized.[22]

Philip Dubois has recently argued that even when voter awareness of judicial candidates is low, party affiliation may actually enhance both the accountability

**TABLE 4**
**Judges' Previous Elected Political Experience, 1861–1899**
**(Adjusted Percentages)**

| Judges | Nature of Experience | | | | | | | | |
|---|---|---|---|---|---|---|---|---|---|
| | N | Legis. | Jud. & Legal | Exec. | 1 & 2 | 1 & 3 | 2 & 3 | 1, 2, & 3 | None |
| State | 136 | 7.4 | 39.0 | 1.5 | 29.4 | 2.2 | 6.6 | 5.9 | 8.1 |
| Federal | 216 | 26.8 | 19.4 | 2.8 | 23.6 | 4.6 | .5 | 1.8 | 20.4 |
| Total | (352) | (68) | (95) | (8) | (91) | (13) | (10) | (12) | (55) |
| Percent | | 19.3 | 26.9 | 2.3 | 25.9 | 3.7 | 2.8 | 3.4 | 15.6 |
| Missing Cases | (26) | | | | | | | | |

**TABLE 5**
**Judges' Length of Tenure, 1861–1899**
**(Adjusted Percentages)**

| Judges | Years of Service | | | | |
|---|---|---|---|---|---|
| | N | 4 or less | 5-10 | 11-20 | 21 and above |
| State | 153 | 20.3 | 36.6 | 30.7 | 12.4 |
| Federal | 218 | 11.5 | 17.6 | 41.2 | 29.6 |
| Total | (371) | (57) | (94) | (136) | (83) |
| Percent | | 15.4 | 25.4 | 36.8 | 22.4 |

and the independence of the appellate judiciary.[23] Presently, there are not sufficient data available on late nineteenth-century judicial elections to test this notion.[24] Nor have data been gathered on voting divisions in state courts of appeals, although such data might suggest a relationship between background characteristics such as party affiliation, and the development of voting blocs.[25] In crude ways, however, the judges' career paths do suggest that popular election imposed accountability on the judges without significantly undermining their judicial independence.

State judges had significantly briefer careers on the bench than did federal judges. The average term in office for a state judge was 8.9 years; the average term for a federal judge was 18.2 years (See Table 5). Rejection by party leaders and the electorate ended few state judicial careers; less than one-fifth (18.2 percent) were either defeated (15.9 percent) or failed to be renominated (2.3 percent)(See Table 6). State judges most frequently terminated their service because they refused to run for reelection; slightly more than one-third (35.8 percent) declined to seek another term. Some judges undoubtedly concluded that they could not win. Even if self-selection was decisive in their career choices, most (81.8 percent) judges who sought reelection won. Although turnover from death was almost twice as likely on the lower federal than the state courts (58.7 percent versus 25.7 percent), most state judges must have felt sufficiently secure to have sought reelection if they wished to remain on the bench. The courts were neither revolving doors nor judicial sinecures, a pattern that suggests a balancing of independence and accountability.

Elected incumbents enjoyed a healthy degree of security. Attempts by governors to use their power to fill interim vacancies was only marginally successful. One-third (33.3 percent) of all state judges served appointed interim terms. The constitutions of all of the midwestern states allowed governors to fill vacancies through appointment, but they also required that these appointees stand for office

**TABLE 6**
**Judges' Reasons for Termination of Service, 1861–1899**
**(Adjusted Percentages)**

| Judges | Reason for Termination | | | | | |
|---|---|---|---|---|---|---|
| | N | Death | Resigned | Refused to Run | Lost Election | Not Nominated |
| State | 132 | 21.2 | 25.7 | 35.8 | 15.9 | 2.3 |
| Federal | 217 | 41.3 | 58.7 | — | — | — |
| Total | (349) | (118) | (161) | (46) | (21) | (3) |
| Percent | | 33.8 | 46.1 | 13.2 | 6.1 | .8 |
| Missing Cases | (21) | | | | | |

either within a year or at the next judicial election.[26] These appointees bore the brunt of defeat at the polls; almost three-fifths (14 of 24, or 58.3 percent) of defeated judicial candidates were interim appointees. The electorate willingly returned judges for whom it had previously voted, but it exercised more discretion in approving interim appointees.[27]

In both the state and the federal courts, the term of office rather than the method of selection imposed the most significant restraint on the tenure of judges. Most critics of popular election understood this; even advocates believed that longer terms rather than shorter terms encouraged sound judicial behavior.[28] In the midwest, appellate judges' terms varied from five to ten years.[29] The end of a term brought opportunity as well as anxiety about reelection; sitting judges must have found it a significant temptation to parlay the prestige and experience gained in high judicial office into a potentially rewarding law practice. Of those judges who declined to seek reelection or resigned during their terms, fully four-fifths (80.2 percent) went immediately into private law practice. Unlike the lower federal courts, where death or retirement culminated judicial careers, most state appellate judges went on to private legal practice.[30]

Along with specified terms of office, the age structure of both federal and state judges determined the status of their postjudicial careers. The former were both older at appointment and older at leaving the bench than the latter (See Table 7). Federal judges averaged 58.9 years of age at appointment; state judges averaged 50.9 years at first election. State judges left the bench at an average age of 60 years (59.8 years); federal judges left at an average age of 77 years (77.1). Most appellate judges ended state service at ages that permitted private legal careers.

Popular election was important, but not determinative in establishing the independence and accountability of the state appellate judiciary. Limited terms of service rather than popular election created a turnover that was higher on the state bench than on the federal bench. State judges more frequently terminated service for reasons other than death; they reached the bench at younger ages (although with greater judicial experience); they served significantly briefer terms; and they left the bench at younger ages than did federal judges. Elected incumbents prospered; interim appointees, although usually winning election, composed the largest block of defeated sitting judges. Whatever their motivations—fear of election defeat, unhappiness with the job or salary, or the appeal of private practice—incumbent elected state appellate judges tended to shape their futures. They were, at once, more accountable, more dependent, and more free in their career decisions than federal judges.

## ACCESS

The accessibility of different social groups to judicial office is closely related to the concept of accountability. Judgeships are significant public offices. The extent to which the formal machinery of judicial selection promotes social diversity on the bench reveals the social biases and the relative openness of the political process during the last forty years of the nineteenth century. Accessibility also means the extent to which kinship and friendship penetrated the selection process. The issue is not so much whether, during these years, kinsmen acted as patrons to secure posts for one another, but whether, in a system predicated on popular election, successful candidates for judicial office benefitted from an environment of informal ties and indirect incentives that encouraged and sustained political activism and judicial service.[31]

Critics of popular election, perhaps revealing their conservative predispositions, claimed that it eroded the social standing of the appellate judiciary. The judges' lower social status meant a decline in the judiciary's "dignity; its just weight; its hold upon the general confidence."[32]

Historians have split over the issue. Mark Tushnet has argued that state judges were drawn from the ranks of "big capital" and were "affiliated by marriage and association with leading members of the capitalist class."[33] Hurst and Friedman have offered different opinions. The former has emphasized the increasing social openness of the bench and the responsiveness of the election process to professional considerations; the latter has insisted that judges were most frequently drawn from "good, solid middle-class backgrounds"—they were "elected—not elite."[34]

The social composition of the judiciary had little relationship to the method of selection. State and federal judges were, as Friedman has suggested, drawn from families of the prosperous and ambitious middle class. Paradoxically, popular election slightly more frequently tapped judges of elite social-class origins

**TABLE 7**
**Judges' Ages at Accession and Termination, 1861–1899**
**(Adjusted Percentages)**

| Judges | Ages at Accession | | | | | Ages at Termination | | | | |
|---|---|---|---|---|---|---|---|---|---|---|
| | | Below | | | Above | | Below | | | Above |
| | N | 30 | 30-40 | 41-50 | 50 | N | 30 | 30-40 | 41-50 | 50 |
| State | 138 | — | 21.8 | 34.8 | 43.5 | 139 | — | 2.9 | 30.3 | 66.9 |
| Federal | 216 | .9 | 11.9 | 36.2 | 50.0 | 218 | — | 2.7 | 5.9 | 91.4 |
| Total | (354) | (2) | (56) | (127) | (169) | (357) | (—) | (10) | (34) | (313) |
| Percent | | .6 | 15.8 | 35.9 | 47.7 | | | 2.8 | 9.5 | 87.7 |
| Missing Cases | (17) | | | | | | | | | |

**TABLE 8**
**Judges' Social-Class Origins, 1861–1899**
**(Adjusted Percentages)**

| Judges | Social Origins | | | |
|---|---|---|---|---|
| | N | Elite | Prominent | Modest |
| State | 127 | 18.0 | 68.6 | 13.4 |
| Federal | 180 | 19.0 | 62.7 | 18.3 |
| Total | (307) | (57) | (200) | (50) |
| Percent | | 18.6 | 65.1 | 16.3 |
| Missing Cases | (64) | | | |

(21.3 percent versus 20.6 percent) than did the appointive method.[35] (See Table 8.) The political culture, through the judicial selection process, did promote limited diversity on both benches. Contrary to critics' complaints, a slightly larger percentage (18.3 percent versus 13.4 percent) of these judges were appointed to the lower federal courts rather than elected to the state appellate judiciary.

Both methods of judicial selection favored persons with kinship connections to other political activists. Most judges had kinsmen active in the political and legal cultures. Approximately three-fourths (76.2 percent) of the state judges had kinship connections through blood or marriage to at least one other person who had held public office (See Table 9). Indeed, popularly elected judges were slightly more likely (75.2 percent versus 69.7 percent) to have these connections than were lower federal judges.

Although the United States has never developed an established class devoted to judging, there were significant kinship connections among judges. Political activism among the populace was unusual; judicial officeholding was restricted to a handful of persons. Nonetheless, one-half (50 percent) of the state appellate judiciary had such connections, a figure slightly larger than for the lower federal judiciary (44.2 percent)(See Table 10). Popular election did nothing to promote a socially random selection process; rather, it frequently tapped persons whose careers began in an environment in which the role models of kinsmen provided both encouragement and incentive. At the same time, Tushnet's belief in the sweep of the "hegemonic class" over the judiciary seems strained.

Popular election promoted limited social diversity. Not only were all judges white males, they were almost entirely Protestant (92.7 percent) and invariably native-born (91.7 percent). The same was true for the lower federal bench.[36] For groups outside the era's established social and political consensus—blacks,

**TABLE 9**
**Judges with Kinsmen in Public Office, 1861–1899**
**(Adjusted Percentages)**

| Judges | Kinship Connection | | | | | |
|---|---|---|---|---|---|---|
| | | (1) | (2) | (3) | | |
| | N | Blood | Mrg. | D.R.* | 1, 2, & 3 | None |
| State | 137 | 33.0 | 10.9 | 4 | 27.7 | 24.8 |
| Federal | 201 | 31.8 | 10.9 | 2.0 | 24.9 | 30.3 |
| Total | (338) | (109) | (37) | (9) | (88) | (95) |
| Percent | | 32.2 | 10.9 | 2.7 | 26.1 | 28.1 |
| Missing Cases | (31) | | | | | |

*Distant relative.

**TABLE 10**
**Judges with Kinsmen in Judgeships, 1861–1899**
**(Adjusted Percentages)**

| Judges | Kinship Connection | | | | | |
|---|---|---|---|---|---|---|
| | | (1) | (2) | (3) | | |
| | N | Blood | Mrg. | D.R.* | 1, 2, & 3 | None |
| State | 136 | 21.3 | 6.6 | 5.1 | 16.9 | 50.9 |
| Federal | 199 | 20.6 | 7.5 | 6.0 | 10.1 | 55.8 |
| Total | (335) | (70) | (24) | (19) | (43) | (179) |
| Percent | | 20.9 | 7.2 | 5.7 | 12.8 | 53.4 |
| Missing Cases | (36) | | | | | |

*Distant relative.

women, and, to a lesser extent, non-Protestants and immigrants—the method of judicial selection was irrelevant. Both methods narrowed and limited the judiciary to the upper end of the social spectrum, with emphasis on the prosperous middle class. Even within these limits, however, a disproportionate percentage of persons with kinship ties to political activists and judges gained the bench. Such judges were perhaps likely, as Lawrence Friedman has argued, to exalt the businessman's values that formed such a crucial part of the era's middle-class ethic and to expect that the law and the judicial role would restrain the vulgar rich and check the excesses of the masses.[37] Whatever troubled the critics of popular election, the social-class origins and kinship connections of most judges need not have.

## CONCLUSION

Tinkering with the machinery of judicial selection had only modest consequences. In their quality and social diversity, elected state appellate judges resembled lower federal judges. What state judges lacked in formal and prestigious academic training, they compensated for with prior judicial service, prosperous middle-class origins, and extensive kinship connections. State judges enjoyed less independence and suffered greater accountability than federal judges, but these limitations on the judicial role stemmed more from the former's fixed terms in office than from their method of selection.

From the perspective of Fleischmann and other critics, these results seem paradoxical and ironic. The method of selection they thought most threatening to the judiciary actually produced judges similar to those brought to the bench through appointment. In one respect, the critics were correct, however; politics penetrated the selection of state judges and permeated their preelection careers. Moreover, the critics were not so naive to believe that they could eliminate political influence; instead, they hoped that the appointive method would mitigate undesirable political effects and strengthen the judicial role. Most significantly, the newly organized bar, with its faith in legal science and legal formalism, seemed to believe it more likely to achieve this goal by intervening with elected officials who controlled the appointive process than with the "party wirepullers" who supposedly dominated the elective method.[38]

They were men of little faith. The electorate and state political parties proved more sensitive to the needs of the legal culture than critics supposed. While substantial numbers of judges were first appointed to fill vacant posts, the electorate was disposed to place its confidence in elected incumbents. Moreover, through the nominating process, political parties most frequently rewarded those aspirants for appellate duties who had extensive prior judicial and public legal service. As the Englishman James Bryce observed at the end of the nineteenth century, "party leaders. . .are. . .mostly lawyers themselves" and "have not only a professional dislike to the entrusting of law to incapable hands. . .but they have a personal interest in getting fairly competent men before whom to plead.''[39]

This, in turn, suggests a fundamental division among lawyers of the post–Civil War era over the proper balance to be struck among the judicial role, the bar, and the political culture. Historians only dimly understand these divisions, their relationship to the broader social and economic developments that flowed from industrialization and urbanization, and their implications for the shape of public policy. The newly organized bar groups that took exception to popular election labored to eliminate political and partisan influence from the law and the legal profession. They pressed to modernize the bar by making judging more impersonal, the law more formal, and politics less intrusive. For them, the infusion of popular will into the judicial selection process promised social disorder, legal instability, and diminished legitimacy for the rule of law. Other lawyers, perhaps best represented by those attorneys who both controlled most of the decision making relating to the judiciary articles of the constitutions of the midwestern states and guided the nominating processes of their parties, viewed the political and legal cultures of the era as complementary and reinforcing. Popular will in the selection process promised competent justice and a popularly based, and therefore more legitimate, rule of law. Like Mr. Dooley, they may have wished they were Germans and could find certainty in machinery, but they were politically astute enough to know better.

## APPENDIX

### *Social Class Origins*

Few historical phenomena are more illusive than social status. The ambiguity of the concept stems from scholarly disagreement over what socioeconomic and other attributes contribute to status, how best to measure status, and how most effectively to relate specific findings to society as a whole. While the customary separation of men into the ''better, middling, and inferior'' sorts undoubtedly holds for the late colonial and ante-bellum eras, delineating class levels is difficult.[40] The historical investigation of status has relied heavily upon occupation. Social origin has been viewed as the consequence of a father's occupational pursuits, and social-class position has been deemed the product of a son's particular calling. Occupational differences, if any, between father and son have been used to detect social mobility. Ralph Dahrendorf and Edward Pessen, among others, have argued persuasively that occupation, although useful, is an uncertain guide to status. Both social origins and social-class positions are multidimensional, involving other individual attributes such as wealth, level of education, public service, and religion.[41] This study attempts, within the bounds of collectable data, to take account of the multifaceted character of social status. Table 11 presents the indicators relied upon to reconstruct the social-class origins of the state and federal judiciaries.

### *Social Origins*

Seven separate indicators were combined to estimate social origins. These were drawn from the works of Sidney Aronson; Edward Pessen; Joseph Schneider; and Charles

**TABLE 11**
**Indicators of Judges' Social Origins**

| Indicator | Rank | Value |
|---|---|---|
| Father's Occupation | High Ranking | 10 |
| | Middle Ranking | 5 |
| | Low Ranking | 1 |
| Father's Wealth | Great--$25,000 plus | 10 |
| | Impressive--$5,000-$25,000 | 8 |
| | Modest--$1,000-$5,000 | 6 |
| Father's Political Activity | National Office | 8 |
| | State Office | 6 |
| | Local Office | 4 |
| Father's Highest Level of Education | College Graduate | 8 |
| | Attended College | 6 |
| | Secondary | 4 |
| Prominence of Father in Occupation | National | 6 |
| | State | 3 |
| | Local | 1 |
| Family's Generational Level in North America | 5 or More Generations | 3 |
| | 3-4 | 2 |
| | 1-2 | 1 |
| Father's Religion | Protestant (Non-Evangelical) | 6 |
| | Protestant (Evangelical) | 3 |
| | non-Protestant | 1 |

Westoff, Marvin Bressler, and Philip C. Sagi.[42] The specific weights assigned each indicator are attempts to give numerical relationship to the rank order developed by Schneider and Westoff et al. These are crude estimates intended to make specific impressionistic assertions about the relative importance and interrelationships of the different indicators. There is some logic behind such a stratified arrangement, but no magic in the numbers.

A father's occupation and wealth were important, but not definitive indicators of a judge's social origins. When fathers held multiple occupations, the highest ranking occupation was used. The ranking of occupations is presented in Table 11; it is related to the scheme developed by Aronson.[43] Data on father's wealth was gleaned from a variety of sources, including estate records, tax lists, state censuses, and the federal censuses of 1850, 1860, and 1870. Although invaluable, these sources have significant limitations. Estate inventories are perhaps the most accurate, but they come at the end of a man's life and often deal only with personal property holdings instead of real property holdings. Tax lists invariably understate the actual value of property, and it is often impossible to determine the degree of underestimation.[44] The federal manuscript census offers the most comprehensive source of wealth data, but it covers only the middle years of the nineteenth century. Recent studies by Lee Soltow, Robert Gallman, and Alice Hanson Jones provide the most explicit statements of wealth distribution.[45] In all but two cases, the data taken from these sources were used at face value. First, estimates of the real property holdings of individuals in the 1850 census were assumed to constitute 80 percent of total wealth. An additional 20 percent was added to arrive at a figure of wealth. Second, when fathers held slaves who were not included in the specific wealth record, such as a tax list, an additional $500 for each slave was added to the value of his holdings. The $500 figure was considered to be an average of the value of a prime field hand and the worth of children, the sick, and the aged.[46] When multiple values were found in either one or several sources, the highest value was used.

Estimates of occupational prominence and family importance were based on four sources: genealogies, obituaries, county histories, and the voluminous letters of application and recommendation in the National Archives. Although often uneven in quantity and accuracy, these sources offered invaluable clues to a father's occupational prominence and family importance. If a source or sources identified a father's occupation but failed to identify his prominence in it, the father was arbitrarily deemed to have been of local importance. This judgment was predicated on the assumption that if a man's calling were known to a county historian, genealogist, obituary writer, or supporter of an applicant, then the father must have been at least locally prominent.

Paternal education, political activism, and religious affiliation were also important indicators of a judge's social-origins. Only a fraction of the population ever went to college in the eighteenth and nineteenth centuries, and college attendance was associated with elevated social status. So, too, was public officeholding, especially in state and national government.[47] Although religious diversity has been an integral aspect of American history, nonevangelical Protestant denominations have been associated with high status, whereas evangelical and non-Protestant denominations have commanded less social prestige.[48]

In an effort to impose order on the various elements comprising social origins, they were ranked on a scale from one to ten (one being the lowest). The ranking attempted to take account of not only internal differences within a variable, but also the relative importance of variables to one another. Such ranking is fraught with hazards; it assumes a historical continuity among variables in social status. The technique has the value of making explicit implicit assumptions about status, but the numbers themselves are, and should be treated as, approximations. The values assigned to a judge's father in each category were summed, providing a cumulative score for social origins. Elite fathers had between thirty-five and fifty-one points; prominent fathers had between eighteen and thirty-four points; and modest fathers had between four and seventeen points. The breaking points in these divisions represented the sums of the high, middle, and low values for each indicator. When information was missing, two conditions had to be met in order to estimate social origins: first, at least four of the seven indicators had to be known; second, one of these four indicators had to be either father's wealth or occupation. When some variables could not be established, a score was obtained by dividing the number of known variables into total points. The quotient was then compared with the quotient obtained by dividing the total number of indicators (seven) into the sums of the highest and lowest values for each indicator.

Elite, prominent, and modest social origins assigned to the judges did not correspond exactly with high, middle, and low status. Modest probably corresponded to the bulk of the population in the late colonial and nineteenth centuries. The evidence leaves no doubt that the lowest elements of that era's social order—slaves, free blacks, Indians, and white laborers—did not contribute offspring to the territorial courts. Elite and prominent origins suggest that a judge's background offered exceptional advantages, although significant differences existed between judges in the two categories. If the lowest elements of society provided no judges, there were also few from the top end of the social order. Until historians know more about the specific contours of early American society, efforts to relate precisely the social origins of the judiciary to the broader social context necessarily must remain speculative.[49]

## NOTES

1. Finley Peter Dunne, *Mr. Dooley's Opinions* (New York, 1901), 127.

2. James Willard Hurst, *The Growth of American Law: The Lawmakers* (Boston, 1950), 143.

3. For a listing of the major works in political science and judicial administration, see Philip L. Dubois, *From Ballot to Bench: Judicial Elections and the Quest for Accountability* (Austin, 1980), 257–62. For the relevant historical literature, see Kermit L. Hall, "The Judiciary on Trial: State Constitutional Reform and the Rise of the Elected Judiciary, 1846–1860" *The Historian* 45 (May 1983): 337–54.

4. Evan Haynes, *The Selection and Tenure of Judges* (Newark, N.J., 1944), 27–50, 80–135.

5. Morton Keller, *Affairs of State: Public Life in Late Nineteenth Century America* (Cambridge, 1977), 358–59; Hurst, *Growth of American Law*, 138–46; and Lawrence M. Friedman, *A History of American Law* (New York, 1973), 593.

6. Simon Fleischmann, "The Influence of the Bar in the Selection of Judges throughout the United States," *American Law Review* 30 (May–June 1905): 350–51.

7. Ibid.

8. Morton Keller, "The Politics of State Constitutional Revision, 1820–1930," in Kermit L. Hall, Harold M. Hyman, and Leon V. Sigal, eds., *The Constitutional Convention as an Amending Device* (Washington, 1981), 72–73.

9. Friedman, *History of American Law*, 332–35; Keller, *Affairs of State*, 358–70.

10. The midwestern states embraced popular election of appellate court judges in the following order: Illinois (1848), Wisconsin (1848), Michigan (1850), Indiana (1851), Ohio (1851), Minnesota (1857), Iowa (1857). Haynes, *Selection and Tenure of Judges*, 101–35.

11. Hall, "The Judiciary on Trial."

12. Ibid. The specific constitutional provisions treating the judiciary are set forth in

Francis N. Thorpe, *The Federal and State Constitutions, Colonial Charters, and Other Organic Laws*, 7 vols. (Washington: Government Printing Office, 1909). These formal rules governing the size and operation of the courts and the conduct of judicial elections were important for two reasons. First, they suggest that, apart from informal and personal considerations, there were other significant variables capable of shaping the character of the bench, of which tenure, ease of removal, and salary would seem most significant. Second, differences in the formal rules from state to state underscore the potential hazards of generalizing on the basis of experiences of particular jurisdictions. See, for example, the contradictory assessments of Hurst and Friedman about the extent of competition for judicial office: Hurst, *Growth of American Law*, 143; Friedman, *History of American Law*, 323–24. However, on the significance of regional variations in the backgrounds of appellate judges, see Bradley C. Cannon, "The Impact of Formal Selection Processes on the Characteristics of Judges—Reconsidered," *Law and Society Review* 6 (May 1972): 579–93.

13. See, for example, James M. Love, "The Election of Judges by the People for Short Terms of Office," *Southern Law Review* 3 (n.s., 1877): 20; Samuel F. Miller, "Address of Samuel F. Miller," *New York State Bar Association Reports, 1878*, 31–40; Charles Hartshorne, "The Boss and the Bench," *New Jersey Law Journal* 23 (1900): 141; *Albany Law Journal* 23 (1880–1881): 66; and ibid. 36 (1887): 505.

14. Keller, *Affairs of State*, 359; Friedman, *History of American Law*, 322–26.

15. Friedman, *History of American Law*, 334.

16. Cooley's *Treatise on the Constitutional Limitations Which Rest upon the Legislative Power of the States* (1868) was a strong, sinewy legal text with powerful political ramifications. It was also better and more forcefully written than many of Cooley's opinions. See Alan Jones, "Thomas M. Cooley and 'Laissez-Faire Constitutionalism,' " *Journal of American History* 53 (March 1967): 751–71.

17. Friedman, *History of American Law*, 334–35.

18. Hurst, *Growth of American Law*, 277–81.

19. Of the thirty-four state appellate judges with law school training, seven (approximately 20.6 percent) had been to an Ivy League institution. More than one-half (52.9 percent) of the state judges who had attended law school had done so at a Big Ten institution, primarily the University of Michigan. On the other hand, slightly more than two-fifths (41.3 percent) of lower federal judges had attended Ivy League law schools.

20. The figure overstates by about 10 percent the judicial experience of federal judges. This is so because it counts the experience of district judges who were subsequently appointed to the federal circuit court bench. While this was a separate appointment, it also constituted continuing federal service.

21. See, for example, *Albany Law Journal* 18 (July 1873): 11–12; Glenn R. Winters, "The Merit Plan for Judicial Selection and Tenure—Its Historical Development," *Duquesne University Law Review* 7 (1968): 63–67.

22. Angus Campbell et al., *The American Voter* (Chicago, 1976), 169–87. There is, however, evidence for the period of the so-called third-party system that suggests the electorate responded to economic and ethnocultural as well as partisan cues in voting. See Paul Kleppner, *The Third Electoral System, 1853–1892: Parties, Voters, and Political Cultures* (Chapel Hill, 1979). Whether this had an impact on voting for judges remains unexplored.

23. Dubois, *From Ballot to Bench*, 243–44, 251.

24. See *Guide to Resources and Services, 1980–1981* (Ann Arbor, 1980).

25. There is a good deal of evidence that points, at least on state and federal courts in the mid-twentieth century, to the salience of partisan affiliation to the direction of judicial voting. See, for example, S. Sidney Ulmmer, "The Political Party Variable in the Michigan Supreme Court," *Journal of Public Law* 11 (Spring 1963): 352–62. The connection between other background factors and voting seems more tenuous. See, for example, Ulmmer, "Dissent Behavior and the Social Backgrounds of Supreme Court Justices," *Journal of Politics* 32 (August 1970): 580–98.

26. The various provisions governing the filling of interim vacancies are set forth in Haynes, *Selection and Tenure of Judges*, 101–35.

27. Of course, this means that more than three-fifths (62.2 percent) of interim appointees did win election.

28. See, for example, James M. Love, "The Election of Judges by the People for Short Terms of Office," *Southern Law Review* 3 (n.s., 1877): 20, 28–29; "Is There Danger in an Elective Judiciary?" *Western Jurisprudence* 8 (1874): 524; Dorman B. Eaton, *Should Judges Be Elected?* (New York, 1873), 8–20, 51–87.

29. Haynes, *Selection and Tenure of Judges*, 110–35.

30. Kermit L. Hall, "The Children of the Cabins: The Lower Federal Judiciary, Modernization, and the Political Culture, 1789–1899," *Northwestern University Law Review* 75 (October 1980): 459–62.

31. See, for example, Eric Wolf, "Kinship, Friendship, and Patron-Client Relations in Complex Societies," in Michael Banton, ed., *The Social Anthropology of Complex Societies* (New York, 1966), 214–30.

32. *Albany Law Journal* 8 (July 1873): 18.

33. Mark Tushnet, "A Marxist Analysis of American Law," *Marxist Perspectives* 1 (January 1978): 99.

34. Hurst, *Growth of American Law*, 138–46; Friedman, *History of American Law*, 335.

35. For a discussion of social-class origins, see the Appendix to this essay.

36. Hall, "Children of the Cabins," 467–69.

37. Friedman, *History of American Law*, 334.

38. Fleischmann, "The Influence of the Bar in the Selection of Judges throughout the United States," 360–62.

39. James Bryce, *The American Commonwealth*, abridged ed. (New York, 1906), 353.

40. Carl Bridenbaugh, *The Colonial Craftsman* (New York, 1950), 156.

41. Ralph Dahrendorf, *Class Conflict in Industrial Society* (New York, 1959), 118–222; Edward Pessen, *Riches, Class, and Power Before the Civil War* (Lexington, Mass., 1973), 47, 49–52, 74–75.

42. Sidney Aronson, *Status and Kinship in the Higher Civil Service* (Cambridge, Mass., 1964), 53–83; Pessen, *Riches, Class, and Power*, 74; Joseph Schneider, "Fame and Social Origin," *Social Forces* 14 (March 1936): 354–61; Charles F. Westoff, Marvin Bressler, and Philip C. Sagi, "The Concept of Social Mobility: An Empirical Inquiry," *American Sociological Review* 25 (June 1960): 375–85.

43. Aronson, *Status and Kinship*, 55–66; P. K. Whelpton, "Occupational Groups in the United States, 1820–1920," *Journal of the American Statistical Association* 21 (September 1926): 328–42.

44. Wealth and family data were collected at the Genealogical Society Library of the Church of Jesus Christ of Latter-Day Saints. On the value of these holdings, see Larry

Wimmer and Clayne Pope, "The Genealogical Society Library of Salt Lake City: A Source of Data for Economic and Social Historians," *Historical Methods Newsletter* 8 (April 1975): 51–59. On probate records, see Gloria L. Main, "Probate Records As a Source of Early American History," *The William and Mary Quarterly* 32 (January 1975): 89–99.

45. The value of the census and patterns of wealth holding in the nineteenth century are discussed in Lee Soltow, *Men and Wealth in the United States, 1850–1870* (New Haven, Conn., 1975), 2–6. See also Robert Gallman, "Trends in the Size Distribution of Wealth in the Nineteenth Century: Some Speculations," in Lee Soltow, ed., *Six Papers on the Size Distribution of Wealth and Income* (Athens, Ohio, 1969), 1–22.

46. Kenneth M. Stampp, *The Peculiar Institution: Slavery in the Ante-bellum South* (New York, 1956), 201–2, 388, 402, 414–17.

47. Schneider, "Fame and Social Origin," 354–61.

48. Liston Pope, "Religion and the Class Structure," *Annals of the American Academy of Political and Social Sciences* 56 (March 1948): 84–91.

49. For contradictory assessments of the nineteenth century social order, see Rowland Berthoff, *An Unsettled People: Social Order and Disorder in American History* (New York, 1971); and Stephan Thernstrom, *Poverty and Progress: Social Mobility in a Nineteenth-Century City* (Cambridge, Mass., 1969).

*ROBERT W. GORDON*

# *"The Ideal and the Actual in the Law": Fantasies and Practices of New York City Lawyers, 1870–1910*

## THE CLASSICAL IDEAL AND ITS RELATION TO PRACTICE

My title is taken from that of a speech that James C. Carter gave to the American Bar Association in 1890.

> If we examine ourselves closely, we shall find that, associated with much thankfulness there is yet a feeling of discontent, a feeling that we are not individually, nor collectively as a profession, all that we ought to be, a consciousness of unsatisfied desires, . . . a dream if you please, that there is for us as lawyers a higher condition and a higher life that we nowhere see realized; in short, we find ourselves moved by the everlasting contrast, everywhere exhibited, between the ideal and the actual; and by that longing—the noblest which inhabits the human breast—of lifting up the actual to a nearer approach to the ideal.[1]

The speaker was well chosen to convey elevating themes. A founding partner of a firm that still survives as Carter, Ledyard & Milburn, he was a leader of the New York City corporate bar and nationally famous. Cleveland had almost appointed him to the U.S. Supreme Court in 1888. He appeared often before the court, notably to argue for the constitutionality of the income tax in 1895, and was chief counsel for the United States in the international arbitration (1892) over fur seals in the Bering Sea. In 1870, he served on the organizing committee of the first modern bar association, the Association of the Bar of the City of New York, and in 1897 became its president. In between, he played a dominant role in important movements for the reform of New York City governments: the Tilden Commission of 1877, the anti-Tammany Committee of Seventy (1894), the founding of the National-Municipal League, Citizens Union, City Club (a social club for patrician reformers), and Good Government Clubs. A leading

Mugwump in the '80s, Carter turned into a leading, though relatively conservative, Progressive in the '90s, joining some 48(!) other Wall Street lawyers to help form the Committee of One Hundred that, in 1896, campaigned to remove the city's public schools from political and neighborhood control and to bring them under centralized professional administration.[2] Active in Harvard Law School affairs as a fund raiser, donor of a chair in general jurisprudence, and head of the alumni association, he was a legal intellectual in his own right who, in 1905, wrote, at Harvard's invitation, some painfully turgid lectures that confirmed his reputation as the chief interpreter of German historical jurisprudence in America.[3] When New York's law reformers split in the 1880's between proponents and opponents of David Dudley Field's draft Civil Code, Carter headed the anticodification attack that ultimately sunk the code in New York State.[4] As an advocate, Carter was known for grounding his case on fundamental legal "principles": indeed "so masterly," as Joseph H. Choate rather maliciously put it,

> was his independence of mind and character, that he was not always willing to admit or recognize the binding force of precedents, however numerous, which failed to run the gauntlet of his own reasoning powers. One of his favorite maxims was that nothing was finally decided until it was decided right, and so no amount of so-called authorities was sufficient to dissuade him from maintaining the contrary view.[5]

In one way or another, then, this rigid, aloof, and humorless personality was connected to nearly every one of the projects through which New York's late nineteenth century elite lawyers sought to make good their commitment to what they liked to call the Ideal: the development of a legal "science" consisting of general "principles" derived from philosophical reflection and historical scholarship; the application of the principles to training law students, to proposing changes in procedure or substantive law, to settling international disputes through arbitration, and, above all, to arguing or deciding cases; and the sponsorship of "reform"—meaning the purification of legislation, judicial decisions and appointments to office of corrupt influence; and the displacement of politics in some fields altogether by expert professional (or nonpartisan amateur) administration.

Of course, only a minority of practicing lawyers ever spent much time promoting legal science, law reform, or any other public cause. But since this minority was large in absolute numbers, included many of the lawyers of the highest professional standing in the city, and dominated all the bar organizations, its members were effectively able to take on the role of articulating the aspirations of the profession's elite, to occupy by default its symbolic high ground.[6] And, of course, as Carter's example shows, these lawyers did much more than make speeches at bar meetings. They played a major role in building the organizational forms that were intended to house their conceptions of the Ideal: schools of law and political science, bar associations, law reform committees; merit selection of judges; commissions to investigate legislative corruption or Tammany finances; reform political clubs; actual reform administrations (city and state); commissions regulating railroads, public utilities, securities, and insurance; professionalization of civil service appointments at the city, state, and federal levels; and even some international organizations.

Disenchantment with some of the results of all this busy activity has given us a historical literature that is quick to spot the motives of interest that got this activity started and made it work. Reform in the name of scientific professionalism was among other things an ideology of middle-class, native-born whites. They could invoke it to impose training or certification requirements to exclude riffraff, or to create and control new markets for their services, or to assert that it gave them title to cultural dominance over immigrant groups, since only scientists could know the "one best system" for running cities or schools.[7] Scientific reform could also be, and often was, a convenient slogan for advancing the interests of business clients: "legal science" was deployed to attack labor unions or protective labor laws, scientific public administration of rates or service to restrict competition.[8]

Without disputing the validity of these critical insights, I still think it will be helpful to look at the lawyers' version of the general late nineteenth century elite ideology of scientific reform from a different angle, one that tries to see what they were thinking and doing more or less as they themselves saw it. This means to see them as having "ideal interests" as well as material ones, and as struggling to work out a relationship between their beliefs and their practices—between the ideal and the actual—with which they could live in comfort. Lawyers are perhaps especially interesting objects of this kind of study because they are double agents. They have obligations to a universal scheme of order, "the law," understood as some fairly coherent system of rules and procedures that are supposed to regulate social life in accordance with prevailing political conceptions of the good.

The law, to put this another way, is an artificial utopia of social harmony, a kind of collectively maintained fantasy of what society would look like if everyone played by the rules. But lawyers are also supposed to be loyal toward and advance the interests of clients pursuing particular ends. The lawyer's job, thus, is to mediate between the universal vision of legal order and the concrete desires of his clients, to show how what the client wants can be accommodated to the utopian scheme. The lawyer, thus, has to find ways of squeezing the client's plan of action into the legally recognized categories of approved conduct. Of course, the law's view of the client's reality is often a highly distorted one, since its categorizing forms are administratively manageable only if they drastically abstract and simplify from that reality, and legitimate only if they seem to be part of the system of universal normative order. Even so, the lawyer's job is selling legitimacy: reassurance to the client and its potential regulators, investors, or business partners that what it wants to do is basically all right; and the lawyer cannot deliver unless she can make plausible arguments rationalizing her client's conduct within the prevailing terms of legal discourse. She must, in short, be able to understand the day-to-day world of the client's transactions and deals as somehow approximating, in however decayed or imperfect a form, the ideal or fantasy world of legal order.

Reform-minded lawyers of 1870 had no trouble perceiving that their world was, from this point of view, in lots of trouble. The articulate ones are most easily described as modified or pragmatic classical liberals, that is, their ideal society was one in which (adult male) individuals were left free to pursue self-interest within a framework of property rights, exchange rules, and public order guaranteed by law—rules of general application, treating individuals as formally equal, and impartially and predictably applied. They assumed most of this law would be derived from the common law, but were by no means hostile to legislation that fit their formula, and actively promoted certain legal restrictions on property and liberty for community benefit, such as public health laws, occupational licensing, regulation of education and morals, and taxation for public improvements. Within their ideal scheme of order, all participants had definitely bounded rights and powers—the individual vis-à-vis other individuals and the state, the states vis-à-vis one another and the federal government, the separate branches of government vis-à-vis one another—which it was the role of the judiciary, the natural arbiter of the system as well as a player in it, to enforce.[9]

Yet this scheme had for some years—since the '50s or '60s, depending on whether one blamed the railroads or Reconstruction—been in a process of total breakdown. Liberal lawyers analyzed the breakdown much as other reformers did, except that they were more prone to see it as the result of *legal* failure that was remediable by legal reform. The present evils could be summed up as lack of generality in framing laws, and lack of predictability and impartiality in applying them. Southern black codes, debtor's stay laws, legislation relieving municipalities from contracted bond obligations, handouts of subsidies, exemptions, and privileges to railroad corporations—all had in common the vice of *particularly* favoring or disfavoring special classes of citizens. Impartiality of application had been subverted by patronage appointments or machine-controlled election of corrupt judges or officials. Predictability was undermined by the same factors, as well as by sloppiness in statutory draftsmanship, judicial decision making, and administration of procedural rules, and by the wild variety of law-making jurisdictions.[10]

The lawyers proposed to restore all this unruly mess to the dominion of the rule of law. The short-term program and most urgent priority was the reclamation of the state and law from their capture by private interests and the restoration of their capacity for general, neutral definition of rights and duties: this was the task of legislation against corrupt electioneering and lobbying practices, and in favor of merit selection of judges, reform or ''Fusion'' political candidacies, and establishment of a professional civil service. The long-term and more interesting program was that of setting up a practical system for reaching correct legal results—i.e., rules, procedures, and institutions that would function to keep all the legal actors in society within their proper boundaries, but make them as free as possible within those boundaries. On the whole, lawyers did not treat this as a problem in political economy, but as one of scientific reform of the case law of common law and the Constitution. That is to say, lawyers believed that the existing common law, scientifically understood and expounded, already contained the fundamental principles necessary to maintain a liberal social order; they simply assumed the consonance of these principles with those of (as they somewhat vaguely understood it) classical political economy. Thus, the common law of restraints of trade, properly interpreted, would operate to prohibit bad competitive practices, but leave good ones alone.[11] This helps to explain why the lawyers of the 1870s and 1880s should have invested most of their public energy in what may seem to us a relatively sterile and peripheral activity: the improvement of legal science.

Corporate lawyers were not antagonistic during this period (though, as will be seen, many became so later) to social science; some of them belonged to the American Social Science Association; others helped found and staff the first important political science department at Columbia University. They encouraged and on occasion conducted publicly funded studies whose mission was to come up with scientific (i.e., maximizing but noncoercive) solutions to problems such as railroad rates or factory conditions, and supported the institution of expert administrative commissions to handle such problems.[12] Nonetheless, the institutions they really counted on to regenerate society were those devoted to the scientific exposition of legal principles and to making these nationally effective: "national" law schools like Harvard's, federal general common law, uniform state laws, and legal treatises and articles. The elite bar may have split on the codification issue, but they were united on the ideal of scientific law that codes were supposed to promote.

Now the issue that chiefly interests me is this: What was the relationship between these lawyers' work on behalf of the ideal—the project to both construct a unified science of law and apply it through reformed institutions—to their practical tasks on behalf of clients? One possible answer, though I think it is mostly incorrect for the period between 1870 and 1890, is that there was *no* effective relationship and no serious idea of one; the cultivation of science was a prosperous lawyer's hobby like the opera or collecting Japanese finger bowls, or was adopted to give the profession a little European tone or polish. Some doubtless saw legal science in exactly that light, if they did not think it a complete waste of time; but this cannot plausibly have been the view of men like Carter who poured half their careers into science and reform. A more likely account would stress the interest of the elite in setting themselves up as a special caste, distinct from both the common run of lawyers, and, perhaps even more important, from their business clients.[13] Still another account would emphasize the fondness, indeed the enthusiasm, for hypocrisy characteristic of middle-class Victorians, who endlessly projected visions of the ideal that they repeatedly violated in practice with no sense of incongruity or bad faith.[14] One who took this view would be inclined to see the Harvard Law School, the *American Law Review*, and the Committee on Jurisprudence and Law Reform of the American Bar Association as displacements, perhaps occasioned by guilt feelings, onto another and separate sphere, of longings for respectability and order that lawyers knew could never be realized in practical affairs. Those who engaged full-time in science and reform, like the woman in the Victorian family, would radiate moral influence at the cost of exclusion from the masculine worlds of politics and business. Evidently there is something to this. Lawyers *did* think of science and reform as belonging to a separate and "higher" plane from that of ordinary life; they spoke of science as a semisacred calling and invested those who practiced it with an aura of monastic purity. They created or adopted specialized vocations of the law teacher or law reformer, to be added to the existing vocation of the judge, as practices whose whole meaning consisted in their insulation from everyday preoccupations and pressures; for this reason, regular politicians and practical lawyers contemptuously labeled these vocations feminine pursuits.[15]

Yet none of these accounts to my mind pays enough attention to the fact that high-minded lawyers were embarked on a practical program of reform. As leaders of the bar, they belonged to a tradition, communicated through endless reiteration in formal speeches, of patrician Whig aspirations to play a distinctive role in American society as a Third Force in politics (in fact the role of "the few" in classical republican theory), mediating between capital and labor, between private acquisitiveness and democratic redistributive follies; thus, they kept looking for social stages on which to enact the role of Tocqueville's lawyer-aristocrats.[16] If anything, their ambition for roles of public virtue was intensified by the fact that, in background, they were not really aristocrats at all, but rather, the sons of the Protestant, back-country gentry, the ministers, doctors, and lawyers of small New England and upstate New York towns.[17] Their picture of the ideal tended to call on images of the communities they had left; and they themselves were often men of high, not to say rigid, personal rectitude with a mission to reform a world ensnared in sin. Moreover, the means for reformation were at hand in the techniques of science; there was as yet no reason not to be as confident as the rest of the American intelligentsia at this time that science would not fail them.

There was a special urgency to realizing the ideal in the fact that most of the reform lawyers were not set apart from the actual, but were deeply implicated in it, that is, in the very practices that they wanted to reform. One of the motives behind the formation of the City Bar Association was concern over some leading lawyers' roles in the efforts of Fisk and Gould to keep control of the Erie Railroad from Vanderbilt and to corner the market in gold.[18] Counsel were accustomed to rough tactics and to compliant judges to execute them: the favorite seemed to be to obtain ex parte injunctions to throw corporations into receiverships, to get one's friends appointed as receivers, and to serve arrest orders on opponent's counsel or executives just as they were needed at a stockholder's meeting. The lawyers involved were all lions of the New York City bar: Charles O'Conor,

David Dudley Field, John Shearman. Shearman and his partner John Sterling, cofounders of one of the grandest of present-day firms, helped Gould and Fisk evade their purchase contracts on gold, after their attempt to corner the market had failed, by getting a judge to throw the Gold Exchange bank into receivership. (The lawyers accomplished this by making out blank affidavits for cooperative plaintiffs to sign to the effect that the plaintiffs had heard officers of the bank were insolvent.) For some reason, Field was later picked out as the worst offender among these lawyers, and almost disciplined by the new City Bar Association.[19] But none of the lawyers involved could have been ignorant of the fact that the judges who granted their injunctions had been paid off by the Tweed Ring. This was an unusually well-publicized scandal that, like the Armstrong Committee insurance investigations of 1905, produced an exposure of corruption in rare detail, as well as a public occasion for moralizing. It is quite impossible to estimate its representativeness of the general ethical standard among practitioners at that time. It is clear that legislative favors, municipal franchises, and judicial decisions could sometimes be bought—and in the case of municipal franchises, may have only been available if bought. Eminent lawyers often acted as counsel for the corporate favor-seeker. They may have done the buying; more likely, however, they just knew about it.

Anyway, the point is that the lawyers at the center of these scandals were prominent voices in science and reform. Field was, of course, the leading law reformer of his day and often wrote against political corruption.[20] Shearman was the coauthor of the leading treatise on negligence as well as the author of a polemic against judicial corruption, and later even joined the single-tax movement.[21] O'Conor, at the new City Bar Association's insistance, was chosen special state attorney general to prosecute Tweed. It is difficult to escape the conclusion that the reformers' program was partially embraced as a cure for their own condition. An impartially administered, scientific legal order would bridge the gulf between the ideal and the actual, the lawyers' high-minded and public-regarding selves, and their activities on behalf of clients. Lawyers could help clients pursue their particular interests within a general framework (like that of a competitive market) that harmonized that interest with the whole. The reform instrument of first importance was science; if legal rights could be made *certain* and procedurally *effective*, the advantages accruing from illegitimate tactics would simply disappear, and lawyers could keep their clients within the law. The gulf was huge, but it could be closed. Yet by 1910, though the gulf seemed smaller, it also seemed more unbridgeable, and the elite of the city's profession had lost its unified commitment to the reform of private practice through the project of legal science.

## LAWYERS HELP UNDERMINE THEIR OWN IDEAL, 1885–1910

The 1870–90 legal elite's vision of the ideal was an integrated whole, in the sense that if all of its projects could have been carried through, they would all have *fit together*: Lawyers in their public roles would perfect the system for defining rights that lawyers in private roles would apply to the affairs of clients. What is irretrievably lost in the late nineteenth century is the wholeness of the vision, the possibility of seeing an effective synthesis of all its parts. Lawyers were far from passive spectators of this process of disintegration. Though they usually attributed it to evolutionary forces beyond their control, they were truly zealous servants of those forces.

## SOURCES OF FRAGMENTATION

### *The Corporation Breaks Its Bounds*

The most obvious of the destabilizing forces was the refusal of corporate clients to remain within the framework of competitive individualism marked out for them by liberal-legal science. The chief legal devices for restricting them to that framework had been (a) state charter policy, setting limits to corporate purposes and capitalization, and the public (*quo warranto*) and private (*ultra vires*) remedies against their transgressing those limits; (b) the power to exclude foreign corporations; (c) a variety of remedial devices for stockholder and creditor control of management powers; (d) state prohibitions on one corporation's owning another's stock; and (e) the common law of unfair competition.[22] Several of the corporate lawyers of New York City were, of course, the principal architects of the legal forms that by the late 1880s to the more discerning, and by 1903 even to the obtuse, had made it impossible for state-enforced law to contain corporate consolidation: the "trust" form (S. C. T. Dodd),[23] The New Jersey Holding Company Act (James Dill)[24] and organization under the Act (W. N. Cromwell for the Cotton Oil Trust; John Dos Passos for the Sugar Trust, etc.);[25] erosion in the courts of *ultra vires*, "trust fund" and shareholder approval doctrines that had set at least formal limits to the exercise of management powers;[26] the flowering of doctrines licensing the exercise of management's discretionary "business judgment";[27] and the stonewalling, through defensive litigation, of state antitrust enforcement.[28] Evidently, the old understanding, which to the extent it did not assimilate corporations to the general private-law scheme of individual rights and duties, assumed adequate state power to regulate them, required revision by the end of the merger movements of the '90s.[29]

### *Neutrality of Legal Science Placed in Doubt*

I have emphasized that the distinguishing feature of the vision of the ideal was the *generality* of legal science—meaning the phrasing of legal rules in broadly and abstractly defined categories (i.e., categories, so far as possible, of juristic concepts such as sellers, buyers, offerers, offerees, stockholders, creditors, directors, rather than of particular classes, industries, or, worst of all, individual parties) and the impartial and uniform application of these rules.[30] At century's end, influential state courts (including New York's) and federal courts had gravely jeopardized the claims to neutrality of legal science by pressing the claims so vigorously in the context of invalidating state social reform legislation and enjoining strikes that even conservative lawyers began to worry that judges would be perceived to be taking political sides in the class struggle.[31] At the same time, in a more subtle series of developments whose long-run effects are much harder to evaluate, the notion of all specific common law and Constitutional legal rules as derivable from general legal conceptions was beginning to be subjected to intellectual critiques that would ultimately reduce to ruins the possibility of ever actually being able to articulate the principles of legal science; this was, in brief, the critical position that one could never reason from principles to concrete cases without assuming some additional set of premises concerning what were desirable social "purposes" or "policies." If the critique were accurate, even such root concepts as "private property" or "contract" could have *no content* independent of their constitutive public policies.[32]

### *Changing Character of Practice*

Perhaps the most dramatic evidence of the inadequacy of the old ideal was its increasing irrelevance to the principal preoccupations of corporate practice. The legal elite of the 1870s, as has often been pointed out, was still predominantly one of trial practitioners who, at least in theory, were hired by the case. First insurance, and then bank and railroad retainers had already begun the erosion of such freelance practices;[33] but even lawyers whose fees derived increasingly from writing opinion letters on railroad bond issues and drafting mortgages to secure such bonds made their public reputations from trial work and appellate argument. By the mid-1880s, the locus of the most elite practice had decisively shifted from the courtroom to the law office and conference room.[34] The main work of this practice was to serve as legal brokers and intermediaries between large American corporations trying to attract new capital in the process of consolidation or of reorganization after bankruptcy, and the investment banking communities of Wall Street and Europe that supplied most of the capital. Nominally representing these corporations, banking houses, or committees of security holders in bankruptcy proceedings, lawyers invented for themselves liaison roles in building or rebuilding the financial structures of American corporations that ensured the prosperity of the largest New York City law firms and came to seem indispensable to their clients.[35]

It is not easy to explain how *lawyers* were able to carve out these roles and do so well at them since many of the jobs they did are not done by lawyers in any other advanced industrial society. An attempt at explanation that tried to go beyond the usual clichés about the legalism of American culture might do well to focus on such factors as the following.

1. By the late nineteenth century, the job of producing the basic legal forms for the carrying on of the corporate enterprise had become by comparison to European standards a remarkably decentralized one. Lawyers for individual enterprises drafted the documents they needed to build governance and capital

structures to settle the rights, duties, and discretionary authority of the participants in the enterprise and, if necessary, had them approved by a legislature or a court. The deterioration of the ante-bellum tradition of state-supported "public" and "mixed" enterprise had left a vacuum of centralized form-drafting capacity:[36] there were no bureaucratic staffs who might have done it, as there were in the European countries where governments had assumed a much more extensive role in building and supervising major enterprises, especially railroads.[37] In the United States, not only contractual agreements such as mortgages securing corporate debts or leases on other companies' property, but the fundamental legislative frameworks of general corporation law were mostly products of the private corporate bar.

2. Corporations needed favors—the grants of sovereignty that gave them their existence, gifts of public lands, franchises to run cars on public streets or supply city services, eminent domain powers, etc.—from multiple levels of government. Lawyers commonly served as the broker-dealers for these favors. They were well placed to do this because the law has been the preferred corridor of access to political office in this society. A company's lawyer always knew, or knew someone who knew a brother at the bar who was strategically placed to influence the granting of favors.

3. Until the appearance of economists in the present century, occupations that in other societies have dominated the market for the services of generalist-intermediaries—such as civil servants, financial specialists, engineers, or classically trained gentlemen—failed to develop much of a competitive threat to the legal profession. In particular, despite the efforts of Anglo- and Germanophilic reformers, the civil service never attained the prestige it would have needed to attract high-achieving men to exchange the income of private practice for the influence of office.[38]

4. The dominant American political ideologies—liberal individualism and "republicanism"—though friendly to "free enterprise," have recurrently taken forms that are extremely hostile to corporate power. Liberals have attacked corporations as anticompetitive conspiracies; republicans have insisted that corporate powers be granted only if they serve the public ends of the "commonwealth." The persistence of these ideologies has made it easy throughout most of our history for conflicting interest groups, competitive rivals, and genuine populists to mobilize popular constituencies behind legislation trying to control or restrain concentration of corporate power.[39] The demand for corporate legal services is at least partially a function of these ideologies: corporations want lawyers to fend off or neutralize such restrictions, or to invent or lobby for new legal forms that circumvent the restrictions, or, perhaps most important, to find ways of writing the restrictions so as to reassure people that corporate conduct within them is safe and legitimate.

The demand for legitimating forms became particularly acute in the late nineteenth century as a result of the lawyers' success, already referred to, in eroding the old forms of state control: they had helped bring on the crisis of legitimacy that they now proposed their services to relieve. To the extent that they could not, as increasingly they could not, rationalize the power and freedom of the new corporate giants by assimilating them to the same legal status (entitled to the same freedom of action and security against state restraints) as that of private individuals, they had to create a whole new body of law for public utilities.[40]

However one explains the demand for these new jobs, my point for present purposes is that their performance severed the income sources of the legal elite from their profession's traditional raison d'être as the repositories and oracles of legal science. They were now doing essentially business jobs, selling stocks and bonds, directing tactical maneuvers in intercorporate warfare, and brokering deals among security holders of bankrupt corporations; they almost invariably were on the boards of their major clients; and quite frequently left outside firm practice to become their principal client's chief executive or general counsel.[41]

One of the chief signs of their response to these new practices is the extraordinary outpouring of rhetoric, from all the public pulpits of the ideal—bar association and law school commencement addresses, memorial speeches on colleagues, articles and books—on the theme of the profession's "decline from a profession to a business." Richard Hofstadter, among others, noticed some of these speeches and used them as evidence of his "status anxiety" thesis.[42] Their significance is hard to assess, for in what sense could the profession have been said to have declined? The general ethical standards of practice among both businessmen and lawyers were almost certainly significantly higher, if measured by the personal engagement of high-level corporate officials in plainly illegal conduct, after 1890 than in the '60s and '70s. After eliminating their competitors and devising receptive legal forms in state corporation statutes, consolidated enterprises were grateful for the chance to be respectable, and their counsel was grateful for the chance to preach respectability.[43] Indeed, the new roles of counsel made them in some ways much *more* independent of their clients than trial lawyers are of theirs. As intermediaries between corporate clients and powerful outsiders—investors, creditors, and stockholders as well as local, national, and foreign governments—and as cosmopolitans attuned to popular and foreign public opinion, corporate lawyers were frequently in a position to tell their clients that some proposed action would have adverse long-run effects. A bond lawyer's opinion is of no use to his client unless investors think it represents an independent judgment.[44] Also, they were organized in independent firms, rather than in the legal departments within the managerial hierarchies of clients.[45] Lawyers, therefore, were probably no less ethical, in crude terms, or more dependent on clients; they were certainly much richer, since the new practice not only brought in large fees, but opened up inside tracks to shares of corporate wealth in the form of undervalued stock or investment opportunities; and they were recognized to be powerful and influential people, as classic accounts such as those of both Bryce and Croly point out.[46]

The laments about "decline" are about something else. (Often, of course, they are about *someone* else, as Auerbach has emphasized,[47] about grubby immigrant lawyers who are lowering the standard of practice, or about the take-over of old legal fields such as conveyancing by nonlegal businesses such as title insurance companies.[48] But I am talking here about leading lawyers' descants upon their *own* fall). They are about the decay of the ideal—about the loss of opportunities to exemplify *through private practice* the public roles demanded by conceptions of republican virtue. Right after the Civil War, the elite's collective hope was to reconstitute the professions' virtue on the foundation of legal science, made effective through reform. But that conception of the ideal had worn thin.

## NEW STRATEGIES OF ADJUSTMENT

How did the corporate elite reconceptualize the relationship between its practice tasks and its notions of universal order, in the face of the old conception's obsolescence?

### *Three Roads Not Taken*

One way to understand what the corporate elite did was by reference to what they did not do. There were at least three options readily available to them—in the sense that they were proposed and debated in the United States or exemplified in the contemporary practices of lawyers elsewhere—that they did not take up.

The first option would have been to try to preserve the profession's traditional ideal by withdrawal into purified zones of practice. In concrete terms, this would have meant isolation of a separate career path for a barrister caste, trained in legal science at a handful of elite schools, and confined to an advocacy—even, perhaps, an appellate advocacy—practice. Everything outside the purified zones—corporate finance, rate regulation, industrial organization, administrative law, legislation—would be labeled "not law" and hence none of this specialty's business. This strategy would also presumably have entailed the courts' distancing themselves from the more obviously political kinds of decision making—deferring to legislative competence and administrative expertise, surrendering the power of judicial review, reading statutes narrowly and literally.[49]

A second option would have been to differentiate the legal elite into a public bar, trained and recruited to service in government bureaucracies, and a private bar, groomed for careers in the managerial hierarchies of large corporations. (A traditional bar would, of course, have continued to handle the problems of small businesses and individual clients.) This option would have tried to eliminate the potential for conflict between lawyers' public and private roles by devolving them onto separate specialties. It would also have eliminated the traditional basis for their claims to occupy an independent status as mediators between the particular desires of their clients and the universal interests of society that are expressed in law; a profession with pretensions to "autonomy," to put this in another way, would have become "heteronomous," absorbed into the bureaucracies of state and corporation, indistinguishable as a career from that of business or civil service.[50]

Yet a third option would have been to try to reconstitute a vision of the ideal on the foundation of the actual conditions of the bar's new practice jobs, through a conception of science and reform that would attempt to integrate the performance of these jobs with a conception of law as a public calling. Aspects of this option were given especially articulate form by such lawyers as Louis D. Brandeis and Adolf A. Berle, Jr.: it is the Progressive vision of the corporate lawyer as technocrat and fiduciary.[51] His knowledge of social "facts" gives him special insight into the morality of the long run, the efficient resolution of social conflict; his primary duty as a fiduciary is to that long-run public interest, which is inevitably the true interest of his client as well. This vision represents an attempt to formalize into a professional-ethical standard the new corporate lawyer's intermediary position as "lawyer for the situation"—he is to have not just the opportunity (which, presumably, he has already) to serve the "situation," but the duty to do so. The curriculum to train such a practitioner would naturally stress public policy subjects and the "facts" of industry, finance, and society as well as traditional private law.[52]

None of these options was ever taken up in pure form. Instead, the bar proceeded schizophrenically down all these roads at once, and so gave up on the practical attempt to unify its public and private roles.

### *The Ideal and the Actual, New Style*

Evidently corporate lawyers did not withdraw from business practice into traditional advocacy roles in order to reaffirm their connection with the dogmatic basis of the profession and their social independence. (Indeed, they relinquished their old dominance of the trial bar to less prestigious practitioners.) But they did not allow themselves to be absorbed by their business clients either; they continued to be organized in independent firms rather than solely as members of the legal departments of corporations, and they held on to at least a symbolic attachment to an ideal of science and reform that supposedly continued to define the profession's special identity.

Many elite lawyers, for example, retained the nineteenth century's conception of legal science, but resisted any attempt to relate it to the concerns of ordinary practice. The invocation of science in the twentieth century becomes more abstract, remote, and dreamlike, a "heaven of juristic conceptions," in Jhering's famous phrase.[53] In the hands of such teachers as Langdell and Dwight, legal science had been a *substantive* discipline, a way of organizing legal principles in order to arrive at correct answers.[54] By the 1890s, the law schools had stopped trying to communicate anything about the legal system as a whole, and were plugging the case system as a method of skills training.[55] At the same time, they kept up a running and largely successful battle to exclude subjects, such as administrative law or corporate finance, that might have provided relevant substantive training for actual corporate practice tasks.[56] The result was the preservation of an ideal conception of legal order that had not lost any of its power as a critical and reformist force. One is tempted to conclude that in the early twentieth century, the bar and the schools had struck an implicit bargain much like that Fritz Ringer found between the German university mandarinate and Bismarck's state: the bar would support the schools by hiring their graduates, giving them money, and recognizing their claims to special stewardship of the ideal; the schools, in turn, would keep their research and teaching on topics safely removed from the actual.[57] It was, of course, precisely this distancing, this refusal to juxtapose, in the work of the law academies and such bar-sponsored projects as the "Restatements" of the 1920s, that inspired by reaction the movement we now call Legal Realism. The Legal Realists were driven by the urge to reconnect legal norms and practices by reconstructing legal science on the basis of empirical knowledge (or, at any rate, hunches) about what officials, lawyers, and clients actually did.[58] As one might have expected, the law reform establishments of the corporate bar greeted the products of this movement with hostility and indifference.[59]

Cultivation of the sterile gardens of classical legal science was not, however, the only project by which the twentieth-century corporate elite sought to vindicate its conception of the ideal. Some lawyers also went part-way down the other road, that of the Progressive program of institution building in the service of "efficiency and uplift."[60] The involvement of such lawyers in Progressive municipal reform movements is well documented;[61] what is of special interest is their relation to causes that touched in some way upon the interests of their corporate clients. Did they manage to find new ways of unifying public projects and private practices?

The most promising candidate for such a synthesizing ideology would have been one of the varieties of corporate liberalism that flourished in the early part of this century and was institutionalized in such ventures as the program of the National Civic Federation, Theodore Roosevelt's New Nationalism, the War Industries Board, the efforts of Secretary Hoover's Commerce Department to coordinate the activities of trade associations, and the National Industrial Recovery Act. This ideology partially fused private and public interests in the aspiration for a national industrial policy set by a partnership between big businesses (represented by their trade associations or by the most enlightened vanguard firms), and the government. Corporatists sought recognition of industrial concentration as inevitable and desirable, a flexible approach to the legal regulation of competition through selective enforcement of or exemption from the antitrust laws, and a positive—if largely noncoercive—role for the state as collector and analyst of economic statistics as well as draftsman, negotiator, and policeman of cartel agreements. As a legal entity, the corporation in this vision gladly trades its status as a "private" person for a share of delegated public authority entitling it to "industrial self-government."[62]

Occasionally, influential segments of the New York City bar would act as if they thought lawyers could develop a new sense of ideal identity and mission by promoting corporatist positions. There was, for example, a brief flurry of interest among counsel (Elihu Root and James Beck) for large insurance enterprises in seeking national regulation of the insurance business.[63] Other corporate lawyers, most prominently James B. Dill, floated proposals (of a type recently revived by Ralph Nader) for the federal chartering of corporations doing a national business;[64] others promoted a more active governmental role in policing securities markets.[65] Still others helped to design corporatist experiments at the local level, such as the Rapid Transit Act of 1894, which authorized municipal construction of New York City's first subway, but under the supervision of a commission set up to ensure the domination of members chosen from the Chamber of Commerce, the exclusion of labor and Tammany interests, and administration by a Wall Street lawyer (Edward M. Shepard).[66]

Yet this group of practitioners never developed any stable set of commitments to the policies of corporatism. They could talk business clients into accepting an active state regulatory role in their affairs if there were some evident benefit to the client, but not if the state fell into what the clients thought were hostile hands, excessively devoted to antitrust enforcement, inclined to push for coercive administrative sanctions instead of judicial remedies, publicity, or negotiated deals, or too hospitable to labor. Governor Hughes's proposed public utility regulation of 1907, for example, giving the public service commission sweeping enforcement powers and precluding judicial review of its orders, drew opposition testimony on behalf of the utilities from the leading lions of the bar: Joseph Choate, Paul Cravath, DeLancey Nicoll, and Edward Shepard,[67] even though this was exactly the kind of measure they could have represented to their clients as protecting their long-term interests (as those clients, in fact, quickly came to realize[68]). Not only the lawyers' clients, but the other main source of the political opinions of the upper bar, namely, high court judges, inhibited the fuller articulation of novel theories of channeling corporate power in the public interest: The U.S. Supreme Court, despite concessions of its own to the spirit of corporate liberalism and the regulatory state,[69] notoriously retained its commitment to the sharp separation of public and private spheres of legitimate power that had been characteristic of classical liberalism, and struck down both probusiness and antibusiness regulatory schemes that, in its view, transgressed that separation.[70]

In default of a new unifying ideology, the bar leadership split along (roughly) three divergent paths. One was simply reactionary, reverting to the now discredited and irrevelant principles of classical legal science, incongruously combining an insistence upon the inevitability of corporate concentration with the old rhetoric of individualism and the inviolable rights of property. James Beck and William D. Guthrie were probably the best-known lawyers who took this position.[71] A second path was what might be called institutionalized schizophrenia. This position held that lawyers should take some time off from private practice to engage in public service, but that the two roles were antagonistic; consequently, it was appropriate for lawyers in one role to do the utmost to undo their accomplishments in the other. This perspective, which is, of course, familiar to us today, represents an uneasy compromise between the Progressive notion of law as a tool for the efficient management of the social order in the public interest, and the classical notion that the structure of the legal-regulatory framework as a whole automatically guarantees ultimate harmony through agonistic contest. Some notable representatives of this approach were lawyers such as Elihu Root, George Wickersham, and Samuel Untermyer.[72] The third path was probably the most common of all, namely, the path of withdrawal altogether from issues of public concern and retreat into the role of apolitical technician with no ideology save that of craftsmanlike client service.[73] This sort of lawyer treats both client desires and the framework of legal regulation as wholly exogenous givens for which he has no responsibility; his is merely the technical role of maximizing the one in view of the constraints dictated by the other. Although, in fact, the corporate lawyer has a major part in framing the client's desires—by translating them into the legal categories that constitute important forms of public discourse, ways of specifying what it is legitimate to want—and also a major part in specifying the day-to-day practical operational content of legal rules through thousands of discrete acts of interpretation, application, manipulation, and resistance; he nevertheless avoids responsibility for the profession's impact on its clients or the state of the law simply by denying, in the teeth of ordinary experience, that it has any impact.[74]

In the 1870s and 1880s, readers who wanted informed treatment of public affairs, especially the local affairs of New York City, were more likely than not to find them in writings of the city's bar.[75] Even between 1890 and 1910, not only the law reviews and bar journals, but also political science and economics journals as well as semipopular magazines devoted to discussion of serious subjects had articles written by leading lawyers on "The Trust Problem," or "Federal Regulation of Commerce," and other issues of major concern to their corporate clients.[76] By the 1920s, most of this literature had disappeared, to be replaced by a steady diet of pieces on narrowly technical law reform. Of course, increasing specialization is part of the reason for all this: real economists and real urban planners took over where lawyers once fecklessly trod;[77] and the job of (relatively) large-scale thinking about law itself and its reform devolved increasingly onto the academic wing of the profession.[78]

Specialization, however, is surely inadequate as an explanation of the failure of the entire profession to develop a theory of its public purposes that would rationalize, make sense of, and give normative direction to its practice tasks, that could even approach in integrity and coherence the classical legal science that began to collapse in the 1890s. Materials for a fuller explanation may be implicit in the story just related, that is, the profession could have preserved the classical-liberal ideal only at the cost of losing most of its business, influence with clients, and political power. For various reasons, the profession was not able to synthesize a new ideal; the Brandeis/Berle notion was too liberal-reformist politically, and even the conservative versions of corporate liberalism were sometimes unacceptable to leading clients and the courts. The real obstacle to a new synthesis, however, surely has deeper roots than this. Lawyers have slid into the modes of reaction, schizophrenia, and privatistic denial of any public role not from any innate depravity of the profession, but from the poverty of modern liberalism. The categories of contemporary thought still commit them to the classical opposition of public and private spheres of action, to the notion that private practice is one thing, and public power is another, though corporate lawyers, more than most people, have occasion to recognize how all "private" action is "publicly" constituted, and has "public" consequences. But this must be a subject for another occasion.

## NOTES

This essay is part of a larger work-in-progress on the ideas and practices of the American legal elite, 1870–1910. The work has been supported by the American Council of Learned Societies (through a grant from the National Endowment for the Humanities), the American Bar Foundation, and the Graduate School of the University of Wisconsin–Madison. An earlier version of this essay was presented to the annual meeting of the American Historical Association, December 1982.

1. James C. Carter, Jr., "The Ideal and the Actual in the Law," *American Bar Association Reports* (1890): 3–31.

2. Details of Carter's career in reform politics may be found in George W. Martin, *Causes and Conflicts: The Centennial History of the Association of the Bar of New York City* (Boston, 1970); Gerald W. McFarland, *Mugwumps, Morals, and Politics* (Amherst, 1975), 41, 94, 130; David C. Hammack, *Power and Society: Greater New York at the Turn of the Century* (New York, 1982), 224, 286, 310.

3. James C. Carter, Jr., *Law: Its Origin, Growth, and Function* (New York and London, 1907).

4. See, for example, James C. Carter, Jr., *The Proposed Codification of Our Common Law* (New York, 1884).

5. Quoted in Joseph S. Auerbach, *The Bar of Other Days* (New York, 1940), 158.

6. In connection with this project, I have been compiling biographical data on 1,150 lawyers who entered practice in New York City between 1860 and 1910. Out of this sample, I have made a further selection for more detailed study of 200 lawyers who by various criteria (e.g., partnership in one of the larger firms, partnership in a firm noted by contemporaries as a leading firm, reputation among contemporaries as a leader of the bar, length of memorial notices and obituaries, and officership in the Association of the Bar of the City of New York) might be identified as a superelite. At least sixty-seven members of this superelite (probably an undercount, since a lawyer was only counted for this purpose if the biographical sources happen to mention it) were active in reform politics or law reform (or, as was often the case, both). Perhaps the most prominent among these, besides Carter himself, were George F. Canfield, Joseph H. Choate, Bainbridge Colby, Frederic Rene Coudert (Sr., and Jr.), Lewis Livingston Delafield, John F. Dillon, Dorman B. Eaton, William M. Evarts, David Dudley Field, Samuel Greenbaum, William D. Guthrie, William B. Hornblower, Charles Evans Hughes, Joseph Laroque, Edward Lauterbach, Louis Marshall, S. Stanwood Menken, John G. Milburn, Victor Morawetz, Dwight Morrow, DeLancey Nicoll, Charles O'Conor, William W. Niles,

Peter B. Olney, John E. Parsons, Wheeler H. Peckham, William Gibbs Peckham, Elihu Root, Edward M. Shepard, Simon Sterne, Albert Stickney, Henry L. Stimson, Henry W. Taft, Samuel Tilden, Samuel Untermeyer, Everett P. Wheeler, Edward B. Whitney, and George W. Wickersham.

7. See Jerold S. Auerbach, *Unequal Justice: Lawyers and Social Change in Modern America* (New York, 1976); Magali Sarfatti Larson, *The Rise of Professionalism: A Sociological Analysis* (Berkeley, 1977); David B. Tyack, *The One Best System: A History of American Urban Education* (Cambridge, 1974).

8. See Arnold M. Paul, *Conservative Crisis and the Rule of Law: Attitudes of Bar and Bench, 1887–1895* (Ithaca, 1960); Samuel Haber, *Efficiency and Uplift: Scientific Management in the Progressive Era, 1890–1920* (Chicago, 1964); David F. Noble, *America by Design: Science, Technology, and the Rise of Corporate Capitalism* (New York, 1977); Gabriel Kolko, *Railroads and Regulation, 1877–1916* (Princeton, 1965).

9. I have tried to give a fuller description of this worldview in "Lawyers and Legal Thought in the Age of Enterprise," Gerald Geison, ed., *Professions and Professional Ideologies in America* (Chapel Hill, 1983). For other general accounts, see David Montgomery, *Beyond Equality: Labor and the Radical Republicans, 1862–1872* (New York, 1967), especially 379–86; Stephen Skowronek, *Building a New American State: The Expansion of National Administrative Capacities, 1877–1920* (Cambridge, England, 1982), 41–59, 132–50; Geoffrey Blodgett, *The Gentle Reformers: Massachusetts Democrats in the Cleveland Era* (Cambridge, Mass., 1966); Gerald W. McFarland, "Partisan of Non-Partisanship: Dorman B. Eaton and the Genteel Reform Tradition," *Journal of American History* 54 (1968): 806–22; John G. Sproat, *The Best Men: Liberal Reformers in the Gilded Age* (New York, 1968); Geoffrey Blodgett, "Reform Thought in the Genteel Tradition," in H. Wayne Morgan, ed., *The Gilded Age: A Reappraisal*, rev. ed. (Syracuse, 1970), 55–76; and Sidney Fine, *Laissez-Faire and the General Welfare State* (Ann Arbor, 1956). The most illuminating account of legal thought during this period is Duncan Kennedy's seminal work, "Towards an Historical Understanding of Legal Consciousness: The Case of Classical Legal Thought in America, 1850–1940," in Stephen Spitzer, ed., *Research in Law and Sociology* (1980), 3:3–41.

10. See, in addition to the works cited in n. 9, Morton Keller, *Affairs of State: Public Life in Late Nineteenth Century America* (Cambridge, Mass., 1977), chap. 9; Harold M. Hyman, *A More Perfect Union: The Impact of the Civil War and Reconstruction on the Constitution* (New York, 1973), 347–66.

11. See William Letwin, *Law and Economic Policy in America: The Evolution of the Sherman Antitrust Act* (New York, 1965), 77–99.

12. R. Gordon Hoxie, et al., *A History of the School of Law, Columbia University* (New York, 1955); Thomas L. Haskell, *The Emergence of Professional Social Science: The American Social Science Association and the Nineteenth Century Crisis of Authority* (Urbana, Ill., 1977); Lee Benson, *Merchants, Farmers, and Railroads: Railroad Regulation and New York Politics, 1850–1887* (Cambridge, Mass., 1955), 120–22, 205–7; John Foord, *The Life and Public Services of Simon Sterne* (New York, 1903); William E. Nelson, *The Roots of American Bureaucracy, 1830–1900* (Cambridge, Mass., 1982), 119–33; Martin J. Schiesl, *Municipal Administration and Reform in America: 1880–1920* (Berkeley and Los Angeles, 1977), chaps. 3, 5, and 6; Hammack, *Power and Society in Greater New York*, chaps. 8, 9.

13. Larson, *Rise of Professionalism*, chaps. 6, 7.

14. Walter Houghton, *The Victorian Frame of Mind, 1830–1870* (New Haven, 1957) 394–430.

15. On the "feminizing" of reform and intellectual cultures, see, for example, Alan Trachtenberg, *The Incorporation of America: Culture and Society in the Gilded Age* (New York, 1982), 163–64.

16. See Gordon, "Law and Lawyers"; Samuel Haber, "The Legal Profession among the others at the End of the Nineteenth Century" (paper presented at the annual meeting, American Society for Legal History, October 1979).

17. This is a rough generalization from my card file of lawyers, supra, n. 6. A detailed breakdown of the sample by geographical origin and father's occupation will be published when the project has been completed.

18. The classic account of this episode is Henry Adams, "The New York Gold Conspiracy," in Frederick C. Hicks, ed., *High Finance in the Sixties* (New Haven, 1929), 120–55. I owe the description of the role played by Shearman and Sterling to the biography-in-progress of Benjamin Cardozo by Professor Andrew Kaufman of the Harvard Law School.

19. On the City Bar Association's role in prosecuting Tweed, see Martin, *Causes and Conflicts*, 91–103.

20. David Dudley Field, "Political Corruption," in A. P. Sprague, ed., *Speeches, Arguments, and Miscellaneous Papers of David Dudley Field*, 3 vols. (New York, 1884), 2: 128–49.

21. Thomas Shearman and Amasa A. Redfield, *A Treatise on the Law of Negligence* (New York, 1868); Shearman [? commonly attributed], "The Judiciary of New York City," *North American Review* 105 (1867): 148–76.

22. Useful summaries of corporate control devices and the process of their erosion are in James Willard Hurst, *The Legitimacy of the Business Corporation in the Law of the United States, 1780–1970* (Charlottesville, 1970), 65–86; and Charles W. McCurdy, "The Knight Sugar Decision of 1895 and the Modernization of American Corporation Law, 1869–1903," *Business History Review* 53 (1979): 304–42. On the evolution of the general legal structures of the megacorporation, see also Alfred D. Chandler, Jr., *The Visible Hand: The Managerial Revolution in American Business* (Cambridge, Mass., 1977), 315–39.

23. Allan Nevins, *Study in Power: John D. Rockefeller, Industrialist and Philanthropist*, 2 vols. (New York, 1953) 1: 388–95.

24. James B. Dill, *The Statutory and Case Law Applicable to Private Companies under the General Corporation Act of New Jersey*... (New York, 1899); E. Merrick Dodd, Jr., "Statutory Developments in Business Corporation Law, 1886–1936," *Harvard Law Review* 50 (1936): 27–59.

25. Arthur H. Dean, *William Nelson Cromwell, 1854–1948: An American Pioneer in Corporation, Comparative, and International Law* (New York, 1957), 98–101; Alfred S. Eichner, *The Emergence of Oligopoly: Sugar Refining as a Case Study* (Baltimore, 1959), 76–78.

26. Adolf A. Berle, Jr., and Gardiner C. Means, *The Modern Corporation and Private Property* (New York, 1932), 127–287. For a skeptic's views expressing doubts about whether shareholders had ever exercised enough control over large American corporations for their control to have been eroded, see Walter Werner, "Corporation Law in Search of Its Future," *Columbia Law Review* 81 (1981): 1611–60.

27. Harold Marsh, Jr., "Are Directors Trustees?" *Business Lawyer* 22 (1966): 35–57.

28. McCurdy, "Knight Sugar Decision"; Bruce Bringhurst, *Antitrust and the Oil Monopoly: The Standard Oil Cases, 1890–1911* (Westport, Conn., 1979); Chestler M. Destler, *Roger Sherman and the Independent Oil Men* (Ithaca, 1967).

29. For unusually prescient statements, see William W. Cook, *The Corporation Problem* (New York, 1891); Frederic J. Stimson, "Trusts," *Harvard Law Review* 1 (1887): 133–34. After a brief decline in the early 1890s, the number of books and articles devoted to corporate concentration suddenly exploded. See Charles J. Bullock, "Trust Literature: A Survey and Criticism," *Quarterly Journal of Economics* 15 (1901): 167–216.

30. See text at n. 9, above.

31. See generally Paul, *Conservative Crisis*. Paul argues, however, that the general effect of the labor struggles of the 1890s was to drive moderate legal opinion that had formerly been critical of judicial activism into supporting hard-line conservative judicial policies intended to protect corporate property against Progressive legislatures, administrative commissions, and labor unions.

32. For examples of this form of critique, see Wesley N. Hohfeld, "Some Fundamental Legal Conceptions as Applied in Judicial Reasoning," *Yale Law Journal* 23 (1913): 16–59; Morris R. Cohen, "Property and Sovereignty," *Cornell Law Quarterly* 13 (1927): 8–30; Richard T. Ely, *Property and Contract in Their Relations to the Distribution of Wealth* (New York, 1914); Oliver Wendell Holmes, Jr., "Privilege, Malice, and Intent," *Harvard Law Review* 8 (1894): 1–14.

33. The beginnings of the "modern" style of American law office business, which emphasized drafting, planning, negotiating, and giving advice about possible hazards of the client's projects rather than litigation, may be traced back at least as far as the marine insurance practice of New York and Philadelphia in the first decades of the nineteenth century. See Julius Goebel et al., eds., *The Law Practice of Alexander Hamilton: Documents and Commentary*, 5 vols. (New York, 1969) 2: 406.

34. The best general account of the changing character of law practice in the late nineteenth century remains James Willard Hurst, *The Growth of American Law: The Lawmakers* (Boston, 1950), 295–313.

35. See, for example, Robert T. Swaine, *The Cravath Firm and Its Predecessors, 1819–1947* (New York, 1946–1948) 1: 369–71; Henry W. Taft, *A Century and a Half at the New York Bar* (New York, 1938) 191–201.

36. Louis Hartz, *Economic Policy and Democratic Thought: Pennsylvania, 1776–1860* (Cambridge, Mass., 1948), chaps. 1–4; Wallace D. Farnham, "The Weakened Spring of Government: A Study in Nineteenth-Century American History," *American Historical Review* 68 (1963): 662–80.

37. Alfred D. Chandler, Jr., "The United States: Seedbed of Managerial Capitalism," in Chandler and Herman Daems, eds., *Managerial Hierarchies: Comparative Perspectives on the Rise of the Modern Industrial Enterprise* (Cambridge, Mass., 1980), 36.

38. Cf. the constant struggles, never more than partially successful, to develop the Foreign Service into a career that would be professional enough to attract an "aristocracy of talent" and well-enough paid to compete for that talent among ambitious men who were not independently wealthy. Warren F. Ilchman, *Professional Diplomacy in the United States* (Chicago, 1961).

39. For a useful survey of differences between American and European ideologies influencing public policies toward the corporation, see Morton Keller, "Regulation of

Large Enterprise: The United States in Comparative Perspective," in Chandler and Daems, *Managerial Hierarchies*, 161–81.

40. For a more elaborate argument that much corporate law practice consists of the production of ideology, see Gordon, "Lawyers and Legal Thought."

41. Preliminary biographical data on my "superelite" of 200 lawyers indicates that at least 69 of them served as directors of corporations (a figure that probably drastically undercounts). See also William Miller, "American Lawyers in Business and Politics—Their Social Backgrounds and Early Training," *Yale Law Journal* 60 (1951): 66–76.

42. Richard Hofstadter, *The Age of Reform* (New York, 1955), 154–63.

43. For some examples, see Nevins, *Study in Power*, 2: 389; Morton Keller, *The Life Insurance Enterprise, 1885–1910: A Study in the Limits of Corporate Power* (Cambridge, Mass., 1963), chap. 16; Philip C. Jessup, *Elihu Root*, 2 vols. (New York, 1938) 1: 185–86. Root's most notorious client, the promoter Thomas Fortune Ryan, said about him:

> Root was always keeping me out of trouble and prevented me from doing many things that I wanted to do. . . . In those days we generally issued bonds for the property but in the case of common stock and even preferred stock it was not considered necessary to have anything but water behind it—good will. Root always wanted to have value put in and to have the stock represent property. (Ibid., 186)

Root's own view, writing in 1907, was that the standards and legal and business ethics had risen considerably since thirty years before: Elihu Root, "The Citizen's Part in Government," in *Addresses on Government and Citizenship* (Cambridge, Mass., 1916) 66–68.

44. The new practice required a different approach. Litigation deals with events of the past. The advocate's duty to his client requires him to cull from existing facts those which support his client's position, and so to color and arrange them as to paint the picture his client wants. He must urge that concept of the legal principles involved which will support the client. Few are the advocates who are able, despite their necessary zeal for their client's cause, to weigh, with complete objectivity, either the true facts or the true legal doctrine. In handling a security issue, a consolidation or a reorganization, counsel build a structure which must be designed to withstand future attack. The exact truth of all present facts must be discovered and the principles of the governing law ascertained, free in each case from color or bias. In creating a capital structure, counsel make the facts inherent in that structure, but must make them with strict regard to the extrinsic facts and with strict conformity not only to legal precedent but also to legal trends. Whatever may be their personal views or those of the client as to the merits of relevant decisions of the courts of last resort, or of changing legal concepts foreshadowed in changing personnel on such courts, counsel in a creative corporate matter are more rigidly controlled by those decisions and trends than is any judge sitting in a court of first instance. (Swaine, *Cravath Firm* 1: 371–72)

45. In contrast to American engineers, for instance, who by the turn of the century were overwhelmingly salaried employees of corporations; see Edwin T. Layton, Jr., *The Revolt of the Engineers* (Cleveland, 1971).

46. James Bryce, *The American Commonwealth*, rev. ed. (New York, 1913), 2:307; Herbert Croly, *The Promise of American Life* (New York, 1909), 131–37.

47. Auerbach, *Unequal Justice*, 102–29.

48. See, for example, Theron G. Strong, *Landmarks of a Lawyer's Lifetime* (New

York, 1914), 348–49; George W. Bristol, "The Passing of the Legal Profession," *Yale Law Journal*, 22 (1913): 590–613.

49. This roughly describes the path taken by English barristers and judges.

50. Dean Roscoe Pound was one of the many notable lawyers to express fears that lawyers were in danger of losing their autonomy to bureaucratic careers: Pound, *The Lawyer from Antiquity to Modern Times* (St. Paul, 1953), 353–62. For a general discussion of the relation of the professions to bureaucratization, see Larson, *Rise of Professionalism*, chap. 11. For an interesting comparative view of German lawyers, concluding that they are *less* inclined than their American counterparts to see themselves as members of an autonomous profession when they work for public bureaucracies, but *more* inclined to define themselves as distinct from business clients in their private practices, see Dietrich Rueschemeyer, *Lawyers and Their Society: A Comparative Study of the Legal Profession in Germany and in the United States* (Cambridge, Mass., 1973), 77–78, 109–22.

51. Louis D. Brandeis, "The Opportunity in the Law," in *Business—A Profession* (Boston, 1933), 313–27; Adolf A. Berle, Jr., "Modern Legal Profession," *Encyclopedia of the Social Sciences* (1933) 9: 340–46; idem, "For Whom Corporate Managers *are* Trustees," *Harvard Law Review* 45 (1932): 1371–72. A splendidly fleshed-out account of this vision may be found in William Simon, "The Ideology of Advocacy: Procedural Justice and Professional Ethics," *Wisconsin Law Review* 1978 (1978): 62–91.

52. Proposals for such curricula have surfaced periodically in American legal education. Woodrow Wilson had something of the kind in mind for the law school projected, but never built, at Princeton; Ernst Freund taught and hoped to increase offerings in legal public-policy courses at the University of Chicago Law School; reformers at Columbia Law School in the 1920s tried to remake the curriculum to stress a "functional" and "institutional" approach to law that would emphasize the study of the social effects of legal rules, and carried this approach into some of their research and writing at Yale Law School in the 1930s.

53. The scientific reform activity that came more than any other to engage the attention of the early twentieth century legal elite was that of producing "Restatements" of the common law under the auspices of the American Law Institute (ALI), an august gathering of distinguished practitioners, judges, and law professors organized for this purpose. For a brief, caustic account of the projects of the ALI, see Lawrence M. Friedman, *A History of American Law* (New York, 1973), 580–82. Leaders of the New York City bar—James Byrne, C. C. Burlingham, George W. Wickersham, Edward J. McGuire, John G. Milburn, George Welwood Murray, Elihu Root, Henry W. Taft, Charles A. Boston, Frederic R. Coudert, Jr., John W. Davis, R. C. Leffingwell, William D. Guthrie, and Victor Morawetz—made up the largest single contingent of the forty lawyers on the ALI's first organizing committee: American Law Institute, *An Account of the Proceedings at the Organization of the Institute* (Philadelphia, 1923), 3–4. It is not easy to imagine anything more removed from their ordinary practices than the subjects these men sat gravely discussing at ALI sessions devoted to Restatements—e.g., whether a promise by Uncle to pay Johnny $1,000 on his 21st birthday if he refrained from smoking were enforceable, and, if so, what the damages should be for its breach. Thurman Arnold understood better than any other contemporaries the ritual and symbolic nature of these meetings. See Arnold, "Institute Priests and Yale Observers—A Reply to Dean Goodrich," *University of Pennsylvania Law Review* 84 (1936): 811–24.

54. On Langdellian legal science, see especially Thomas C. Grey, "Langdellian Orthodoxy," *University of Pittsburgh Law Review* (forthcoming, 1984).

55. Robert Stevens, "Two Cheers for 1870—The American Law School," *Perspectives in American History* 5 (1971): 440–41.

56. See Gordon, "Lawyers and Legal Thought"; William L. Chase, *The American Law School and the Rise of Administrative Government* (Madison, Wisconsin, 1982), chaps. 1–2.

57. Fritz Ringer, *The Decline of the German Mandarins* (Cambridge, Mass., 1969), 116.

58. For insight on these aspects of Legal Realism, see John Henry Schlegel, "American Legal Realism and Empirical Social Science: From the Yale Experience," *Buffalo Law Review* 28 (1980): 459–586.

59. Schlegel tells an especially revealing story of a body of eminent practitioners' rejection of a Yale study of plea bargaining, probably on the grounds that they did not wish it to be true: idem, "American Legal Realism," 504. For an unusually candid diatribe by a Wall Street lawyer against social science, see Henry W. Taft, "Law and the Sciences," in Henry W. Taft, *Legal Miscellanies: Six Decades of Changes and Progress* (New York, 1941), 98–111.

60. The phrase is, of course, Samuel Haber's: *Efficiency and Uplift: Scientific Management in the Progressive Era, 1820–1920* (Chicago, 1964).

61. Several studies of the Progressive movement have identified lawyers as the largest occupational group within the movement. Alfred D. Chandler, Jr., "The Origins of Progressive Leadership," in Elting E. Morison, ed., *The Letters of Theodore Roosevelt*, 8 vols. (Cambridge, Mass., 1954) 8: 1462–65; Otis L. Graham, Jr., *An Encore for Reform: The Old Progressives and the New Deal* (New York, 1967), 203; McFarland, *Mugwumps, Morals and Politics*, 201–5.

62. On American corporatism generally, see Ellis W. Hawley, "The Discovery and Study of a Corporate Liberalism," *Business History Review* 52 (1978): 309–20, and the works cited therein.

63. Keller, *Life Insurance Enterprise*, chap. 14; idem, *In Defense of Yesterday: James M. Beck and the Politics of Conservatism, 1861–1936* (New York, 1958), 75–78.

64. James B. Dill, "National Incorporation Laws for Trusts," *Yale Law Journal* 11 (1902): 274–85; Samuel Untermyer, *The Lawyer-Citizen—His Enlarging Responsibilities* (New York, 1916), 11–12.

65. Paul Cravath, for example, did so, although he was not normally much interested in reform: Swaine, *Cravath Firm* 2: 95–99.

66. Hammack, *Power and Society*, chap 8.

67. Robert F. Wesser, *Charles Evans Hughes: Politics and Reform in New York, 1905–1910* (Ithaca, 1967), 159.

68. Richard L. McCormick, *From Realignment to Reform: Political Change in New York State, 1893–1910* (Ithaca, 1981), 238.

69. For example, *New York Central Railroad Co. v. White*, 243 U.S. 188 (1917) (upholding workmen's compensation scheme); *Appalachian Coals Inc. v. United States*, 288 U.S. 377 (1921) (upholding cartel arrangement).

70. For example, *Lochner v. New York*, 198 U.S. 45 (1905) (statute limiting bakers' hours of labor); *Carter v. Carter Coal Co.*, 298 U.S. 238 (1936) (invalidating, as excessive delegation of public power to private organizations, statute that authorized coal producers and their employees to fix hours and wages, binding on the entire coal industry).

71. Keller, *In Defense of Yesterday*, 80–84; William D. Guthrie, *Magna Carta and Other Addresses* (New York, 1916).

72. On institutionalized schizophrenia, the best account is the description of Root's practice in Hurst, *Growth of American Law*, 368–69.
73. Ibid., 369–70.
74. Simon, "Ideology of Advocacy," 52–61, stresses the lawyer's role in *defining* the ends of clients.
75. Hammack, *Power and Society*, 53–54.
76. For bibliographies, see Hans B. Thorelli, *The Federal Antitrust Policy: Origination of an American Tradition* (Baltimore, 1955), 617–39.
77. Hammack, *Power and Society*, 54.
78. Berle, "Modern Legal Profession," 342.

*JOHN A. MATZKO*

# *"The Best Men of the Bar": The Founding of the American Bar Association*

On a cool but sunny Wednesday morning, August 21, 1878, nearly one hundred lawyers gathered in the narrow courtroom behind the Saratoga Springs town hall to organize the American Bar Association. There was some risk of embarrassment to the elite members of the bar who had lent their names and respectability to the affair; a majority of those who had signed the call for the organizational meeting were not even in attendance. The establishment of a national legal organization might well have seemed premature in a era of weak or nonexistent state and local bar associations. In fact, these leading lawyers had no reason to fear that their half-hearted confidence had been misplaced. During its more than one hundred years of existence, the American Bar Association has become one of the most influential private interest groups in American political life.[1]

Curiously, there has been little scholarly study of the founders and their motives for organizing the association. The official, organizational *History of the American Bar Association* (1953) says only that the "proposal to organize a nationwide association of members of the American bar originated with Simeon E. Baldwin of Connecticut."[2] In the absence of such studies, it has been suggested that the ABA was organized in reaction to the movement for liberal reform in the 1870s and as a means of promoting that variety of radical conservatism usually denominated laissez-faire. Even a recent ABA president characterized the founders of the association "as conservatives very much linked with big business.... [The] 'good' which the Association was designed to foster throughout the land had a rather specific meaning which had to do with railroads and banks and all the forces which changed our country [into] the mightiest industrial empire on the face of the earth, with all its concomitant rape of the earth, pollution and political corruption."[3]

This theory attracted the noted constitutional historian, Edward S. Corwin, and first appeared in the dissertation of Benjamin Twiss, one of his students.[4] Twiss was somewhat vague about the influence of the ABA in the promotion of laissez-faire economics and contented himself with demonstrating that a number of conservative lawyers were indeed members of the association. However, Corwin, in the introduction to Twiss's *Lawyers and the Constitution*, stated flatly that "the development of American Constitutional law during the period from 1875 to 1935 was. . . the work primarily of a small group of lawyers whose clients were great financial and business concerns—in short, of the aristocracy of the American bar, the founders and principal figures of the American Bar Association."[5] Even before this work appeared, Corwin had developed the thesis further in *Constitutional Revolution, Ltd.* The ABA, he wrote, "organized in the wake of the decision in *Munn v. Illinois*. . . soon became a sort of juristic sewing circle for mutual education in the gospel of *Laissez-Faire*."[6] Corwin then cast subtle inference aside in a series of lectures published as *Liberty against Government*. Here the birthplace of the ABA became Chicago, "a fact reflecting the animus of some of its founders toward the 'barbarous' decision in *Munn v. Illinois*."[7] Finally, C. Herman Pritchett, citing Corwin, transformed the theory into textbook certainty: "The Association was founded in Chicago in 1878, and a principal purpose of its organization was to fight the 'barbarous' decision of *Munn v. Illinois*."[8]

Aside from the difficulty of geography, the most obvious flaw in the Corwin thesis is its anachronism. Corwin's "founders," except for William M. Evarts and Edward J. Phelps, were not, in fact, founders of the American Bar Association, though they *were* influential turn-of-the-century lawyers. (Besides, as Arnold Paul has demonstrated, "the general hardening of conservative attitudes began only in 1892."[9]) Certainly the belief that the American Bar Association was "from its foundation embarked on a deliberate and persistent campaign of education designed to reverse the [Supreme] Court's broad conception of legislative power" would have surprised the little band who met behind Saratoga's town hall in 1878.[10] Powerless to control entrance into their own profession, they were hardly in a position to lecture the Supreme Court.

In reality, the impetus for organizing a national lawyers' organization sprang more from professional than political or economic motives. Far from opposing the reform spirit of the age, the organization of the American Bar Association was itself a manifestation of that spirit, a spirit to which its founders were highly sympathetic.

During most of the nineteenth century, professional legal organizations had experienced a slow if sporadic decline in both numbers and influence. A number of lawyers' clubs and library societies were snuffed out after the Revolution when the normal unpopularity of lawyers was heightened by their attempts to enforce the repayment of debts and to protect Tory property.[11] Other associations fell before Jacksonian democracy with its distrust of an elite, faith in a natural right to follow any calling, and a fear that a recognition of professionals would create a privileged class.[12]

Across the nation standards for admission to the bar were lowered or abolished altogether. In 1800, a definite period of preparation for entering the legal profession was required by fourteen of nineteen states; by 1840, such preparation was required by eleven of thirty states; in 1860, only nine of thirty-nine states had any educational requirements. Several states adopted constitutional provisions similar to that of Michigan which permitted "every person of the age of twenty-one years, of good moral character" to practice law.[13] Virtually every legal memoir of the early nineteenth century seems to include a half-humorous illustration of the casual manner in which prospective lawyers were certified to practice in ante-bellum America. L. E. Chittenden, chairman of a committee on bar admission in Vermont of the 1850s, questioned two young men who wanted to go west:

> Of any branch of the law, they were as ignorant as so many Hottentots. . . . I frankly told them that for them to attempt to practice law would be wicked, dangerous, and would subject them to suits for malpractice. They begged, they prayed, they cried. . . . I, with much self-reproach, consented to sign their certificates, on condition that each would buy a copy of Blackstone, Kent's Commentaries, and Chitty's Pleadings, and immediately emigrate to some Western town.[14]

To Roscoe Pound, such instances buttressed a belief that the period between the demise of the Suffolk [Boston] Bar Association in 1836 and the organization of the Association of the Bar of the City of New York in 1870 represented an "Era of Decadence" for the American legal profession, a decadence from which it was rescued only with difficulty by the elite leadership of resurgent bar associations.[15] However, as Maxwell Bloomfield has pointed out, "this moral drama of light and shadow," places too much emphasis upon "formal organization as the appropriate yardstick by which to measure the strength of professionalism within the bar."[16] In a small community, and especially while riding the judicial circuit, lawyers and judges could more easily and informally discipline a colleague than can the grievance committee of a modern bar association. Furthermore, such notables as Oliver Wendell Holmes, Jr., Charles Francis Adams, Elihu Root, Joseph H. Choate, Salmon P. Chase, and John Peter Altgeld began their distinguished careers during this period with almost as little legal knowledge as Chittenden's western exiles. Finally, in an era when high geographic and social mobility was combined with the relatively mudane tasks of the frontier lawyer, the old professional standards would have been difficult to maintain with or without bar associations. "*Formal* restrictions disappeared; but the market for legal services remained, a harsh and efficient control. It pruned away deadwood; it rewarded the adaptive and the cunning. Jacksonian democracy did not make everyman a lawyer. It did encourage a scrambling bar of shrewd entrepreneurs."[17]

A "scrambling bar" did not encourage strong bar associations, however. Although little research has been done into the records of these organizations, now scattered among state libraries or destroyed by fire and neglect, it seems that far from enforcing an aristocratic monopoly over the legal profession, most ante-bellum bar associations were ineffective in maintaining even a modicum of ethical and disciplinary standards. Indeed, this was not often their intention. Many were engaged solely in the establishment of a law library, whereas others, perhaps the majority, were chiefly social. In some cases, their only surviving publications are banquet menus.[18]

Renewed interest in bar associations after the Civil War stemmed from changes both within the profession of law and in American society as a whole. Although the cities had grown enormously between 1850 and 1870, the number of urban lawyers had grown even faster. No longer could the elite at the bar expect to maintain their informal and at least partly successful control over the profession. Having forsaken the courthouse for the law office, the most affluent lawyers were unlikely even to know the members of the lower caste "police-court lawyers." Therefore, unlike ante-bellum societies, the new bar associations generally restricted membership to the "decent part" of the profession, "primarily well-to-do business lawyers, predominately of old American stock."[19] Elite lawyers had once controlled admission to the legal profession itself; they now hoped to restrict membership in the bar association in order to distance themselves, in the words of a New York bar leader, from the men "seen in almost all our courts, slovenly in dress, uncouth in manners and habits, ignorant even of the English language, jostling and crowding and vulgarizing the profession."[20]

It was also clear that although the elite of the bar had gained great wealth by its alliance with corporate capitalism, it had lost much of its traditional influence upon political life.[21] Even in the ante-bellum period, young lawyers had been warned not to leave "the broad highway of an honorable and profitable profession, for the fitful and exciting pursuits, and the unsubstantial rewards of the mere politician."[22] At least in the 1840s, the myth of the office seeking the man might seem possible; by the 1870s it was not even lawyerly fiction. The *American Law Review* complained that a "great democratic flood" had filled "the bench with political partisans, the minor legal offices with political hacks, and the bar with an indiscriminate herd of camp followers" and had "spread its waters over the whole country."[23] Bar associations seemed to be one solution. Although the elite of the bar, unable to "afford the business sacrifice of serving in the General Assembly," might continue to disdain politics, a bar association organized for their "protection and self-preservation" could "secure the results of all the. . .experience of the entire bar of the State in recommendations for reform in the law."[24]

Some elite lawyers were also concerned with the decline in the status of their profession, clearly evident in the last decades of the nineteenth century. More than a hundred years before, law had supplanted theology at the apex of public influence. Lawyers were fond of quoting de Toqueville's famous dictum that the "American aristocracy" was not to be found "among the rich who are bound by no common tie" but among "the judicial bench and bar."[25] By the 1870s, this rang somewhat hollow. The status of the lawyers had obviously eroded in relation to the rich, who had grown vastly richer with the advent of financial capitalism. Whereas the lawyer had once been an independent policy-maker in the public forum, he had since become a wealthy but dependent servant of some corporate chieftain. Furthermore, his former status was also being eroded by the rise of scientifically based professions such as medicine, engineering, and chemistry. "Thus," wrote W. G. Hammond in 1875, "the bar has lost its privileged position, and its members stand on the same broad social platform with the rest of that great army who earn their bread by the labor of their brains, rather than their hands."[26]

Finally, the organization of bar associations was, in part, a manifestation of the upsurge in the formation of all types of voluntary associations after the Civil War—professional, humanitarian, and fraternal. This "habit of forming associations" was spurred by improved transportation and communication and especially by the increase in leisure time provided by the success of American capitalism.[27] Bar association leaders represented that segment of the profession which could give attention to the more theoretical aspects of law in the same way that the Founders of the Republic had studied government. The more affluent the lawyer, the greater the possibility that he would engage in social activities which had at least an aura of serious purpose about them. And what better way to separate the elite from the "scrambling bar" than by sponsoring an expensive bar association banquet? Lawyers, no less than other groups, understood the value of organizing for purposes which crisscrossed the civic, professional, and social sphere. "If it were for nothing more than to be in the fashion and to protect their class interests," wrote the editor of the *Albany Law Journal*, "it would be proper for lawyers to formally unite."[28]

The varied motives for organizing bar associations were evident in the formation of the Association of the Bar of the City of New York (1870). Usually credited to a "battle of lawyers against the Tweed Ring,"[29] the association was actually organized for other reasons as well. In 1868, the leaders of the New York City bar had begun a shifting fratricidal struggle on behalf of Cornelius Vanderbilt, Daniel Drew, Jay Gould, and Jim Fisk, who were attempting to gain control of the Erie Railroad. When judges as well as legislators and lawyers proved for sale to the highest bidder, the legal system nearly collapsed into anarchy. Soon after an armed conflict between two hired gangs on the Erie tracks outside Binghamton was halted by the state militia, a call for an organization of the New York City bar began to circulate.

While the Tweed Ring did have some interest in the Erie scandal, the Association of the Bar did not move immediately against either Tweed or Fisk, the erstwhile employers of most of its members. Instead, the association purchased a brownstone building for $43,000 and installed a full-time librarian, rare books, busts of eminent lawyers, and a punch bowl filled with a beverage "brewed according to a special recipe furnished by the nearby Century Club." When the association did get around to prosecuting Tweed in 1873, one of the most influential lawyers of the city and a maverick member of the association, David Dudley Field, defended the boss.[30]

The speeches of association organizers like Dorman Eaton, William Evarts, James Emott, and Henry Nicoll make it clear that the major thrust of the new association was to be directed at restoring "the honor, integrity, and fame of the profession in its two manifestations of the Bench and Bar." This Nicoll believed could be achieved by gathering together "all that is intelligent, all that is honest, all that is honorable in this Profession."[31] (The latter was pretty nearly defined by an entrance fee of $50 and annual dues of $40.) "We have become simply a multitude of individuals, engaged in the same business," said Emott. "And the objects and the methods of those engaged in that business are very much dictated by those who employ them. . . . Power is one thing we are first to aim at. The use of it we are to determine afterwards."[32]

But most of the new bar associations of the seventies were not as successful in gaining power as they had hoped. A few were able to have corrupt judges replaced. Others suggested to their state legislatures legal reforms both politically inoffensive and dull. Most continued the older social tradition of the ante-bellum societies. One convened only at funerals—"not much life in our organization," the secretary commented.[33]

The formation of the American Bar Association, then, was not, except in a metaphorical sense, the capstone of a pyramid of state and local bar associations.[34] In 1878, there were probably no more than seven city and eight state bar associations in twelve states. Had the organization of the ABA awaited the formation of bar associations in only half of the United States, it could not have been organized until after the turn of the century.[35]

That it was organized as early as 1878 must be largely credited to the energy and foresight of Simeon Baldwin. But it does his successful effort no injustice to note that others had previously conceived of a national organization of lawyers. Isaac Grant Thompson, editor of the *Albany Law Journal*, had suggested as early as 1875 that the lawyers of the nation "should be combined in an organic whole."[36] Two years later, he published, anonymously, a letter that proposed a "legal congress of a week's duration," composed of two to four delegates from each state, at which would be discussed

> questions of inter-state commerce and national control of railroads; extradition; naturalization; citizenship; suffrage; uniform divorce laws, etc., etc. I believe the Federalist and Elliott's debates and the like might be put completely in the shade and a mine of legal political wisdom be thus supplied from which half-educated congressmen and legislators might thereafter draw with great profit to themselves and the people. . . .[37]

Gustave Koerner may have antedated both of these gentlemen by suggesting in the *Chicago Legal News* that the Chicago Bar Association assist the organization of a representative national association.[38]

Ironically, an actual attempt to organize a national bar association in 1876 failed so miserably that it seems doubtful that the founders of the American Bar Association were even aware of its putative existence. The movement began among leaders of the "United States Law Association," a lawyer referral service of 2,500 members who frequently engaged in the collection of debts on commission.[39] When state legislatures began to discriminate against out-of-state creditors in favor of resident debtors, the lawyers found themselves frustrated by the long delay and prohibitive costs from taking the matter to the Supreme Court. In May 1876, the Law Association announced a "Congress of Lawyers" to be convened in Philadelphia on June 20, to discuss "the assimilation or unification of the laws of the several states, especially in those particulars most directly interesting to the commercial world."[40] Leaders of the movement, such as Orlando F. Bump of Baltimore and Charles S. Ullman of New York, clearly hoped to organize a permanent association that might have influence in Washington as well as in state legislatures.

The actual meeting of the "Congress" in the Philadelphia Merchant Exchange was a comedy of errors. The invitations had been mistakenly printed with a July date rather than a June date, so that fewer than sixty lawyers arrived for the session. Half of these then wandered off to view the nearly completed Centennial Exhibition. When Bump and Ullman presented their plans for the new organization to the handful of lawyers in attendance, their ideas were immediately labeled "impracticable" and "impossible." Even the elected president of the "Congress," one M. F. Slocum of Boston, was scarcely encouraging, fearing that the "work was of such magnitude that, if the Congress attempted it at all, nothing would be accomplished."[41] So dispirited was Ullman that he moved an adjournment of the assembly until a committee could arrange another meeting "in the early autumn." The *Albany Law Journal* hailed the United States Law Association as "the pioneers in attempting to form a national [bar] association," but the "Congress of Lawyers" nonetheless disappeared without a trace.[42]

The fact of the matter was that the wrong strata of lawyers had been assembled in 1876. As a rule, the elite of the bar did not collect debts on commission, and it was the elite of the bar which was necessary to the success of a national bar association in the late nineteenth century. Even then, the establishment of the American Bar Association might have been delayed many years had it not been for the catalyst of a young Connecticut lawyer, Simeon E. Baldwin (1840–1927).[43]

Baldwin was the youngest and most precocious of nine children born to a prominent New Haven family. One of his great-grandfathers was Roger Sherman, a signer of the Declaration of Independence. His grandfather had been an influential Federalist and founder of an antislavery society, and his father, who had served both as a senator and governor of Connecticut, argued the famous *Amistad* slave case in association with John Quincy Adams. Because poor eyesight prohibited service in the Civil War, Baldwin was able to continue the study of law at both Yale and Harvard before returning to New Haven in 1863 to practice in his father's law office. He wisely specialized in corporate practice, gained the New York and New England Railroad as a client, and soon took his place among the most distinguished (and wealthy) members of the Connecticut bar.

Though Baldwin eventually became Chief Justice of the Connecticut Supreme Court and, still later, governor of the state, his importance lies only partially in a political career studded with as many defeats as successes. Beginning in childhood with the organization of a "corporation" and a secret order called the "Clio Society," Baldwin remained throughout life an avid organizer and joiner. Probably no one else in American history has held the presidencies of as many different professional societies. Between 1890 and 1910 he was president of the American Bar Association, the American Historical Association, the American Social Science Association, the International Law Association, the American Political Science Association, and the Association of American Law Schools. Vice-president of a number of other organizations, notably the American Association for the Advancement of Science, Baldwin retained membership in such diverse groups as the YMCA (president, 1884–1886), the New Haven Colony Historical Society (president, 1884–1896), the Board of Park Commissioners of New Haven, the American Economic Association, the New England Tariff Reform League, the Union International de Droit Penal, the General Hospital Society of Connecticut, the Conference of Congregational Churches of Connecticut (moderator, 1881), and the Sons of the American Revolution.

Despite his organizational proclivities, Baldwin was hardly a hail fellow well met. To those outside his immediate family he projected an image of aloof formality. His capacity for work was enormous, a characteristic indicative not only of his personality and patrician upbringing, but of tragedy as well. After 1872, when his wife became completely insane and his oldest daughter died, Baldwin submerged himself in work. "There are those to whom hard work brings its daily blessing as a banisher of sorrow," he once said. "Melancholy is a foe to be expelled at any cost, and preoccupation is often the only thing that avails to shut it out."[44]

In great part, Baldwin's consuming energy was directed toward the concerns of Gilded Age reform. Baldwin was, in fact, the epitome of "The Best Men," "the men of breeding and intelligence, of taste and substance," who saw themselves standing between the two extremes in American political life—the robber barons, whose greed for gain seemed to threaten traditional moral principles, and the radicals, whose desire to tamper with basic economic standards threatened American prosperity.[45] On the national level, "The Best Men" included such academicians as Mark Hopkins and Charles Eliot Norton; men of letters William Dean Howells and Thomas Wentworth Higginson; influential journalists like E. L. Godkin of the *Nation* and Horace White of the *Chicago Tribune*; and politicians of the caliber of Carl Schurz, Samuel J. Tilden, Dorman B. Eaton, George F. Edmonds, Grover Cleveland, the young Theodore Roosevelt, and Henry Cabot Lodge.

"The Best Men" viewed themselves as independents, reformers whose goals would be acceptable to their colleagues in either party. They sought to purge the political system of its corruption—bosses in the North, carpetbaggers in the South—but they had no desire to make sweeping changes in society. Moderate reform, "safe, careful, and deliberate reform," in the words of Grover Cleveland, was their objective.

> For the abuses that offended them they proposed the simple remedies of "good government," economic orthodoxy, and moral rejuvenation. Put "good men" into positions of responsibility and power, they urged, revive the Jeffersonian regard for limited government; respect and defend the tested Christian moral precepts and apply them to everyday affairs, as well as to government; trust in the "natural laws" of political economy to right the economic wrongs of the day.[46]

Throughout his long life, Baldwin was able to touch all the conventional bases of Gilded Age reform and some unconventional ones as well. One of his longest and most unsuccessful struggles was an attempt to rid Connecticut of the grossly misapportioned electoral districts that favored rural areas of the state. (Not surprisingly, he organized a New Haven County Constitutional Reform Association in attempting to achieve this purpose.) In 1880, Baldwin wrote Senator George Edmunds of Vermont requesting that crusty New Englander to run for the Republican presidential nomination in order to thwart the ambition of the bête noir of reformers, James G. Blaine. The following year, Baldwin mobilized support for the establishment of a civil service system in state government and organized Connecticut's Civil Service Reform Association. When the Republican Party nominated Blaine in 1884, Baldwin bolted the party, organizing and becoming president of the Connecticut Independent Republicans. Most of these Mugwumps eventually returned to the Republican fold, but Baldwin became a Democrat.

As might be expected, many of Baldwin's reform interests were intimately connected with the law. At twenty-seven, he tackled the ambitious task of preparing a digest of Connecticut law, persuaded the legislature to purchase 183 copies of the finished product, and gained an instant reputation when *Baldwin's Connecticut Digest* became a standard reference work for lawyers of his state. From 1877 to 1879, Baldwin worked with several committees that finally abolished the obsolete distinction between suits at law and suits at equity, and at the end of the nineteenth century, he joined penologists in advocating what seems at first glance to be an odd assortment of criminal reforms directed against the penitentiary system: probation, parole, indeterminate sentences, the reintroduction of the whipping post, and castration for rape. Baldwin was also one of the first American lawyers to suggest laws prohibiting the use of heroic methods to preserve the lives of terminally ill patients.[47]

Baldwin devoted much of his energy to the improvement of legal education. Improbable as it may seem considering his other activities, Baldwin was a professor at the Yale Law School from 1869 to 1912—including two years when he was also governor of the state. At Yale, he successfully advocated the lengthening of the law school course from two to three years and introduced the first graduate law program in the United States. Throughout his life, Baldwin remained unenthusiastic about the major contemporary innovation in legal education, the case book method introduced by Christopher C. Langdell at Harvard Law School in 1870. In a sense, Baldwin was ahead of his time, for he criticized the pseudoscientific nature of this pedagogical method because it ignored "the human element in whatever judges may say or do" and "the power of circumstances to affect their conclusions."[48]

In September 1877, Baldwin explained both the Yale plan for graduate study in law and the need for a longer course of study for the professional degree to the American Social Science Association (1865–1909), which, at the time, was the only national organization providing a forum for the discussion of legal topics. The ASSA had been founded by a group of philanthropists and social Don Quixotes whose urge for reform had led them to a quest for knowledge. Believing in an absolute truth, in natural laws which governed human conduct, and in man's ability to discover these laws by piling up empirical data, society members earnestly hoped that social science would become "the science of the age," that it would produce "an earthly paradise—an enchanted ground."[49] The interest of the association was divided into four departments: education, public health, social economy, and jurisprudence. To the fourth department was assigned the task of considering

> the absolute science of Right; and second, the Amendment of laws. This department should be the final resort of the other three; for when the laws of Education, of Public Health, and Social Economy are fully ascertained, the law of the land should recognize and define them all. Under this head shall be considered all questions of the justice, the expediency, and the results of existing statutes, including their bearing on Suffrage, Property, Privilege, Debt, Crime, and Pauperism. Here, then will come up the vexed questions of Prison Discipline and Capital Punishment.[50]

As time passed, the utopian overtones of the ASSA program seemed less and less in harmony with the prevailing notions of reform, and the association collapsed—though not before it had served as the matrix from which emerged such professional organizations as the American Economic Association, the American Political Science Association, the American Historical Association, and the American Bar Association.

After Baldwin read his paper, "Graduate Courses in Law Schools," to the ASSA Department of Jurisprudence, a discussion occurred in which three future leaders of the ABA took part. On the motion of Carleton Hunt, dean of the University of Louisiana [Tulane], the assembly adopted a vague resolution commending "the care, future encouragement, and future development" of law schools "to the members of the legal profession and to the friends of learning in general."[51] A year later, at the opening of the conference that launched the American Bar Association, Baldwin claimed that the idea for such an organization had sprung from a resolution passed by the Department of Jurisprudence. Since no such resolution has been discovered, it is probable that Baldwin conveniently confused the resolution on legal education with an informal conversation in which he had engaged with wealthy Louisiana lawyer, Felix P. Poché.[52]

In any case, Baldwin seems to have considered organizing such a professional group almost immediately following the ASSA convention, for he broached the idea to a former college classmate soon afterward. When his friend responded with an encouraging reply suggesting that the proposed organization would encourage legal reform, Baldwin began the task of gaining the support of his seniors in the profession.[53] At the annual meeting of the Connecticut State Bar Association in January 1878, he moved "that a committee of three be appointed to consider the propriety of organizing an association of American lawyers: with power to issue a circular on the subject." The association—a more active and businesslike organization than most of its counterparts—approved the motion and appointed Baldwin, Gov. Richard D. Hubbard, and William Hamersley as committee members. A favorable assessment by the committee was assured since both the governor and Hamersley, a personal friend of Baldwin and a founder of the Connecticut Bar Association, were sympathetic to legal reform.[54]

Baldwin then traded on the reputation of the governor to obtain approval of the new association by "a small number of leading lawyers in different parts of the country," who were asked to sign "a circular recommending the matter to the favorable consideration of the profession."[55] On April 29, Baldwin sent a letter requesting such signatures to thirteen prominent attorneys: Judge Charles Devens of Massachusetts, Governor Hubbard of Connecticut, Charles O'Conor of New York, Secretary of State William M. Evarts (New York), S. Teakle Wallis of Maryland, former Senator Charles R. Buckalew of Pennsylvania, Alexander R. Lawton of Georgia, Carleton Hunt of Louisiana, former Senator John B. Henderson of Missouri, former Senator Lyman Trumbull of Illinois, Governor George Hoadly of Ohio, Judge Thomas M. Cooley of Michigan, and Senator Stanley Matthews of Ohio.[56]

When six of these gentlemen—namely, Devens, O'Conor, Wallis, Buckalew, Henderson, and Cooley—either refused to permit their names to be used or did not respond, Baldwin addressed another letter to those who had agreed to sign the call, advising them that the committee was "inviting a few others to add their names." These included Senator Benjamin Bristow of Kentucky, Henry Hitchcock of Missouri, Richard McMurtrie of Pennsylvania, John K. Porter of New York, Charles Train of Massachusetts, J. Randolph Tucker of Virginia, and Edward J. Phelps of Vermont.[57]

Excepting Evarts and Cooley, these twenty men are remembered today only by specialists. Yet, in the late nineteenth century, they were prominent members of their respective state bars; fifteen were of sufficient note to warrant a sketch in the *Dictionary of American Biography*. A composite portrait reveals striking similarities in both the background and viewpoint of these Gilded Age lawyers.

Although nine of the twenty were Democrats, eight were Republicans, and the political affiliation of three is unknown, virtually all were political moderates. Typical of their Civil War attitudes are those of Charles Devens and Stanley Matthews, both of whom defended the Fugitive Slave Laws to their political detriment before becoming colonels in the Union army. On the opposing side were men like Carlton Hunt who, with strong Union sympathies, fought for the Confederacy. After the war, the twenty, almost to a man, opposed the Radicals. O'Conor, Tucker, and Hoadly represented Jefferson Davis or his estate; Trumbull and Henderson were two of the famous seven Republicans who saved Andrew Johnson from conviction at his impeachment trial. Some of the twenty switched from one party to another, an oddity in Gilded Age politics. Henderson and Cooley went from Democrat to Republican, Matthews from Democrat to Republican to Liberal Republican, and Hoadly and Trumbull from Democrat to Republican to Liberal Republican to Democrat.

Unlike most lawyers of the period, fourteen of the twenty had attended college, and a majority had either attended law school (seven), or served an apprenticeship in another lawyer's office (seven), or both. Only a few had "read law" privately in the manner of Abraham Lincoln. Significantly, of the six who did not sign the call, only two had attended college, and only one had attended law school.

In 1878, the average age of the twenty was fifty-seven, and fifteen were born between 1816 and 1826. They were at the height of their careers, and most had already served in some state or federal office. As might be expected, the twenty were, on the whole, very prosperous gentlemen doing a substantial amount of corporation work, though none were corporation lawyers in any modern sense of the term.

It is as liberal reformers, however, that they exhibit their most striking similarity. O'Conor and Evarts were the chief prosecutors of Boss Tweed; Wallis was president of the Civil Service Reform Association of Maryland; Buckalew reformed the penal code of Pennsylvania; Hunt became city attorney of New Orleans under a reform administration; Bristow and Henderson investigated and prosecuted the Whiskey Ring; Cooley later became an important member of the Interstate Commerce Commission under Grover Cleveland; Train, as a congressman, served as manager of impeachment proceedings against a corrupt judge; and even McMurtrie, an apolitical legal monomaniac, had one outside interest—hospital reform. John K. Porter, who had defended President Grant's venal private secretary Orville E. Babcock, was something of an exception. Yet he was the president of the newly organized New York State Bar Association and was included on the call at the request of O'Conor, who suggested that his former legal apprentice replace him.[58] Conspicuously absent from the call was the name of that brilliant individualist of the New York City bar, David Dudley Field, whose aforementioned defense of Boss Tweed had not endeared him to his professional colleagues, already offended by his combative personality and self-righteousness.[59]

Only four of the fourteen who signed the call—Bristow, Hitchcock, Phelps, and Hunt—actually attended the organizational meeting of the American Bar Association. The remainder, except for Randolph Tucker and Alexander Lawton, never played a significant role in the affairs of the ABA. Their places were taken by another similar, though slightly younger group that included Baldwin, Luke Poland of Vermont, James Broadhead of Missouri, George Wright of Iowa, John

H. B. Latrobe of Maryland, Thomas Jenkins Semmes of Louisiana, William Allan Butler of New York, and Francis Rawle of Pennsylvania.[60]

This "Saratoga clique," which was to direct the association for at least the first decade from "the hotel porch after lunch," was also reform minded. Broadhead had acted as special counsel for the government in the Whiskey Ring scandal, and Poland was noted for his congressional investigations of both the Crédit Mobilier, the carpetbag government of Arkansas, and the Ku Klux Klan. The most significant difference between the gentlemen asked to sign the call and the "Saratoga clique" was the number of legal educators in the latter group. Thus, these men might have been expected to emphasize not only the more theoretical aspects of the law, but also professional, rather than political, reform.[61]

After Baldwin had acquired consent for the use of their names from fourteen bar leaders, he printed the call for organization which had circulated in handwritten form for several months. The call proposed "an informal meeting at Saratoga, N.Y., on Wednesday morning, August 21, 1878, to consider the feasibility and expediency of establishing an AMERICAN BAR ASSOCIATION," and Baldwin represented himself as a secretary to the fourteen worthies who would report the views of the call's recipients to the August meeting.[62]

Baldwin clearly indicated that the call was to be sent only to a select group of lawyers "whom such a project might interest." Discovering these gentlemen seems to have been fairly difficult in 1878. Baldwin was forced to rely a great deal on personal acquaintance or word of mouth. He kept a large notebook with a record of all lawyers to whom the call had been sent, and of the 607 names listed, one-third were residents of either Connecticut or the two neighboring states, New York and Massachusetts. Baldwin also sent copies of the call to most of the original sponsors for them to distribute judiciously.[63]

With the call circulating throughout the country, Baldwin made arrangements for group rates at Congress Hall, the largest resort hotel in both Saratoga and the nation. Saratoga Springs was chosen because more wealthy lawyers were likely to vacation at this prestigious spa than at any other in the country. It was also central to the East, the section from which the ABA was to draw most of its members, and its cool temperatures and race track attracted large numbers of Southerners. More than usual of the latter were residing in Saratoga that summer because a yellow fever epidemic was ravaging the lower Mississippi Valley. It is not surprising, therefore, that Louisiana had the largest representation at the organizational meeting.[64]

The responses that Baldwin had requested in the call were not forthcoming in the numbers he might have hoped. Fully four-fifths of the recipients ignored it, sixty-four expressed approval of the organization, but said they could not attend the August meeting, and fifty-four replied that they would be present. On the other hand, it seems that Baldwin received only one negative reply from a recipient unfriendly to the notion of a national bar association.[65]

These responses to the call for organization as well as the few speeches and resolutions of the Saratoga convention itself provide substantial evidence that the impetus for founding the American Bar Association sprang from a desire to promote professional reform rather than to thwart political or economic reform. In fact, the varied facets of this reform interest may be grouped under the four purposes adopted by the Saratoga assembly as Article I of its constitution: "to advance the science of jurisprudence, promote the administration of justice and uniformity of legislation throughout the Union, uphold the honor of the profession of the law, and encourage cordial intercourse among members of the American Bar."[66]

Though advancing "the science of jurisprudence" seems a glittering generality in our own day, "in an age which honored science above other sources of wisdom, it became clear that people who established their ability to study. . . scientifically would command attention and influence the course of events."[67] Judge Koerner, who claimed to have suggested a national bar association in the *Chicago Legal News*, reflected the mild utopianism of the ASSA in his reply to Baldwin. He hoped—and was undoubtedly disappointed—that the meetings of the bar association would be "*scientific conferences of Jurists*, working in sections and preparing at each session material to be discussed at subsequent sessions. Judges, law writers, and members of the Bar. . . should all participate in such discussion and assist in laying practical measures of reform before the National and State legislatures."[68] Although the first meeting was not of primary importance to the founding of the Association, it did authorize a committee on jurisprudence and another on international law, thus providing a forum for the discussion of the more theoretical aspects of legal practice. Of course, it also produced a measure of intellectual detachment from the overriding practical concerns of the "scrambling bar."[69]

The promotion of "uniformity of legislation throughout the Union" was, on the other hand, perhaps the greatest concern of Baldwin's correspondents, as it had been for the United States Law Association, a concern which could not be met by local or state bar associations. With the growth of national corporations and the expansion of trade across state boundaries as a result of advances in transportation and communication, lawyers found "the diversity existing in our commercial law" frustrating and inefficient. "Defects of existing statues. . . might be pointed out and proper remedies suggested," said one correspondent, if lawyers from one state were well acquainted with the legislation and judicial decisions of another.[70] At the first meeting of the association, a committee on commercial law was authorized with the particular task of examining laws concerning negotiable paper, "looking toward further uniformity in the law on that subject."[71]

"Uphold[ing] the honor of the profession" was the euphemism for raising standards of legal education and admission to the bar, one of the primary motivations for founding the ABA. A number of Baldwin's correspondents feared that the organization might flounder unless its membership was restricted to those of "high standing in the profession." Only gentlemen could inaugurate and carry forward "such true reforms as [were] in harmony with the progressive spirit of the age." At the organizational meeting, Baldwin and Henry Smith of Albany "argued forcibly" that the new association admit no men who would not be worthy members.[72]

Baldwin hoped to de-emphasize the final objective of the ABA: the establishment of "cordial intercourse among members of the bar." In the constitution and the preliminary circular, he listed it last, though in the call itself "comparison of views and friendly intercourse" appeared first. But even sociability could be viewed in the more serious light of the restoration of national harmony after the bitterness of the Civil War and Reconstruction. A national bar association, in the words of Gustave Koerner, would have "a most powerful tendency to weaken mutual prejudices, to produce harmonious and fraternal feelings amongst an influential and leading class of men, and would be a means of cementing our Union, so lately disrupted."[73] The timing of the convention could hardly have been improved, following as it did, the Compromise of 1877 and occurring in the midst of a Southern yellow fever epidemic which brought immediate organized relief efforts from the North and expressions of gratitude from the South.[74] Lawyers as a professional group, moderate in political stance and representing the interests of national economic development, might have been expected to stand in the vanguard on the "road to reunion," and, indeed, from its inception, the American Bar Association successfully fostered friendly relations among late enemies both publicly at open sessions and privately at the annual banquet.[75]

Perhaps Senator Charles Jones of Florida best summarized the motives of the founders of the American Bar Association in his reply to the call: "[W]hen innovation and change are demanded in every quarter, there ought to be found somewhere in our system a calm conservative power which can expose fallacies, point out abuses, and suggest reforms without violence or shock to our government."[76] This was the objective of the "best men of the bar": safe, conservative reform.

Because of Baldwin's extensive planning, the actual organizational meeting on August 21 proved somewhat dull. There was much convention harmony and little controversy or dissent, although "an animated discussion arose on the point whether all lawyers present should take part in the organization, or only those to whom invitations had been sent." In the end, only the latter were considered as the founders of the ABA. A committee to report a constitution returned with a completed draft only hours after its appointment. Baldwin had actually written it during his summer vacation in the Adirondacks, and it was adopted by the association with only a few minor alterations.[77]

The unanimous election of James O. Broadhead (1819–1898) as the first president of the Association—at the time a largely honorary post—symbolized both the strengths and the weaknesses of the new organization. Broadhead was dwarfed intellectually by many men in attendance at the meeting, but he was the epitome of the "best men of the bar." A native of Charlottesville, Virginia, he had gone west to Missouri as a young man. Though he had attended the University of Virginia for only a single session, he later became a lecturer at

St. Louis Law School [Washington University]. Broadhead was "a rather old-fashioned country practitioner. . .careless about details, sometimes slipshod in his work, "who, nevertheless, had successfully represented the railroad interests before the United States Supreme Court. A strong Union man during the Civil War, he was in great part responsible for preventing the fall of Missouri to the Confederacy. Then, after the war, disgusted with the "test-oath" act and the "Force Bills," he became a Democrat. He also took a former Confederate officer as a law partner. Broadhead had acquired a reputation as a reformer from his fierce prosecutions of the Whiskey Ring, a notorious Collector of Internal Revenue in St. Louis, and the venal Chief Clerk of the Treasury Department. "Broadhead was a lion," said one unknown contemporary, "when he was awake."[78]

Baldwin and the other founders of the American Bar Association were not disheartened by the absence of most of the signatories of the call nor by the small attendance. "What they lacked in numbers they made up in quality and that proved to be decisive."[79] The *Albany Law Journal* reported that the "business in hand was discussed by the best men present, and with an obvious desire to secure the best organization—the best results possible. This we believe has been done."[80] And Baldwin returned to New Haven to confide in his journal, "The American Bar Association, which is really my child, was born nicely—full weight, and good prospects."[81]

## NOTES

1. Albert P. Melone, *Lawyers, Public Policy, and Interest Group Politics* (Washington, 1977); see especially 207–13; Gerald Carson, *A Good Day at Saratoga* (Chicago, 1978), 3.

2. Edwin R. Sunderland, *The History of the American Bar Association* (New York, 1953), 3. The ABA commissioned two popular articles on the founding of the association for its centennial in 1978, one by Baltimore attorney Walker Lewis, "The Birth of the American Bar Association," *American Bar Association Journal* 64 (July 1978):996–1002 (hereafter cited as *ABAJ*); and another, published as a fifty-nine page book, by noted freelance writer Gerald Carson, *A Good Day at Saratoga* (Chicago, 1978). Both are good examples of their genre, nicely written and illustrated. The implication for academic historians should be obvious.

3. Robert Meserve, "The American Bar Association: A Brief History and Appreciation" (Paper delivered to the Massachusetts Dinner of the Newcomer Society, New York, March 28, 1973), 12.

4. Benjamin R. Twiss, "Lawyers against Government: Their Assertion and Defense of Laissez Faire as a Constitutional Doctrine" (Ph.D. diss., Princeton University, 1938), published posthumously as *Lawyers and the Constitution: How Laissez Faire Came to the Supreme Court* (Princeton, 1942). The topic has been thoroughly analyzed by Norbert Brockman in both "The Politics of the American Bar Association," (Ph.D. diss., the Catholic University of America, 1963), 15–20; and "Laissez-Faire Theory in the Early American Bar Association," *Notre Dame Lawyer* 39 (1964):270. The discussion of Corwin in this essay relies heavily upon Brockman's research.

5. Twiss, *Lawyers and the Constitution*, x.

6. Edward S. Corwin, *Constitutional Revolution, Ltd.* (Claremont, Calif., 1941), 85.

7. Edward S. Corwin, *Liberty against Government* (Baton Rouge, 1948), 137–38.

8. C. Herman Pritchett, *The American Constitution* (New York, 1959), 538. Actually, the first public mention of the Granger cases at an ABA meeting occurred in 1884; see Andrew Allison, "The Rise and Probable Decline of Private Corporations in America," *American Bar Association Report* 7 (1884):241, 253–54 (hereafter cited as *ABA Rep*).

9. Arnold M. Paul, *Conservative Crisis and the Rule of Law: Attitudes of Bar and Bench, 1887–1895* (Ithaca, N.Y., 1960), 4, 76–81.

10. Alpheus T. Mason and William M. Beaney, *American Constitutional Law* (Englewood Cliffs, N.J., 1954), 383.

11. Anton-Hermann Chroust, "The Dilemma of the American Lawyer in the Post-Revolutionary Era," *Notre Dame Lawyer* 35 (1959):48.

12. Roscoe Pound, *The Lawyer from Antiquity to Modern Times* (St. Paul, Minn., 1953), 180–83; Anonymous, "Bar Associations," *Southern Literary Messenger* 4 (1838):583; W. Raymond Blackard, "The Demoralization of the Legal Profession in Nineteenth Century America," *Tennessee Law Review* 16 (1940):314.

13. Pound, *The Lawyer*, 225.

14. L. E. Chittenden, "Legal Reminiscences," *Green Bag* 5 (1893):309. The candidate was often expected to bring cigars and some liquid refreshment to his examination; Lincoln is supposed to have examined an applicant while taking a bath. Questions ranged from the quantity and nature of law books read to the date of the Magna Carta to the difference between whiskey and brandy. One A. H. Nelson was admitted while his examiners continued to argue over the correct answer to a question they had posed. William Tecumseh Sherman was admitted to the bar without any examination on "the ground of general intelligence"; Walter Hill said that it was common knowledge in Georgia that one man had secured admission to the profession though he had signed his name with his mark! Oliver A. Harker, "Fifty Years with Bar and Bench of Southern Illinois," *Transactions of the Illinois State Historical Society* 27 (1920):41–53; Albert Woldman, *Lawyer Lincoln* (Boston, 1936), 153–54; John Prentiss Poe, "Remarks," *ABA Rep* 20 (1897):438; A. H. Nelson, "Remarks," *ABA Rep* 20 (1897):424; Max Radin, "The Achievements of the American Bar Association," *ABAJ* 26 (1940):19; unsigned review of Sherman's Memoirs, *American Law Journal* 11 (1875):360; Walter B. Hill, "Bar Associations," *Georgia Bar Association Reports* 5 (1888):80.

15. Pound, *The Lawyer*, 225.

16. Maxwell Bloomfield, *American Lawyers in a Changing Society, 1776–1876* (Cambridge, Mass., 1976), 137; see Wayne Karl Hobson, "The American Legal Profession and the Organizational Society, 1890–1930," (Ph.D. diss., Stanford University, 1977), 216–17; William R. Johnson, *Schooled Lawyers: A Study in the Clash of Professional Cultures* (New York, 1978), 25–31.

17. Lawrence M. Friedman, *A History of American Law* (New York, 1973), 278; J. Willard Hurst, *The Growth of American Law: The Law Makers* (Boston, 1950), 286.

18. Pound, *The Lawyer*, 246; Philip J. Wickser, "Bar Associations" *Cornell Law Quarterly* 15 (1930):401; Albert P. Blaustein, "New York Bar Associations Prior to 1870," *American Journal of Legal History* 12 (1968):50. The latter typifies the paucity of our knowledge regarding these early societies. On the other hand, Gerard Gawalt, in his exhaustive study of Massachusetts lawyers, suggests that in some cases bar associations in that state were able to maintain high educational standards and that the percentage of

lawyers holding liberal arts degrees actually increased in the early nineteenth century; Gerard W. Gawalt, *The Promise of Power: The Emergence of the Legal Profession in Massachusetts, 1760–1840* (Westport, Conn., 1979), see especially 140–48.

19. Friedman, *History of American Law*, 561; Wickser, "Bar Associations," 396; James Bryce, "The Legal Profession in America," *McMillan's Magazine* 25 (January 1872):214.

20. Samuel Hand, "Annual Address of the President," *New York State Bar Association Proceedings* 3 (1880):71. Walter B. Hill wrote that a "zealous, conscientious, and fearless scrutiny of the qualifications of persons proposed for membership is of supreme importance" (Hill, "Bar Associations," 63).

21. James Bryce, *The American Commonwealth*, 2 vols. (London, 1888), 2:490; Audra L. Prewitt, "American Lawyers and Social Ferment," (Ph.D. diss., Northwestern University, 1973), 16–17.

22. "The Hon. John Holmes," *Monthly Law Reporter* 1 (1839):275, quoted in Bloomfield, *American Lawyers*, 148.

23. "Summary of Events," *American Law Review* 5 (1871):556.

24. "Professional Organization," *Albany Law Journal* 6 (1873):233; Hill, "Bar Associations," 75.

25. Alexis de Tocqueville, *Democracy in America* (1835) [Reeve-Bowen translation, ed., Phillips Bradley], 278. "During the early part of the nineteenth century the bar came nearer to constituting an exclusive privileged class in the new republic than any other group in the community" (Harlan Fiske Stone, "The Lawyer and His Neighbors," *Cornell Law Quarterly* 4 [1919]:179).

26. W. G. Hammond, "The Legal Profession—Its Past, Its Present, and Its Duty" (paper delivered before the Iowa State University Law Department) *Albany Law Journal* 11 (1875):114. Hammond added, however, that "it is untrue, unjust, un–American, to infer thence that the bar is degraded." See Joseph Katz, "The Legal Profession, 1890–1915," (M.A. thesis, Columbia University, 1954), 18–21.

27. Arthur Schlesinger, "Biography of a Nation of Joiners," *American Historical Review* 50 (1944):16–18; Howard Mumford Jones, *The Age of Energy: Varieties of American Experience, 1865–1915* (New York, 1970), 166–70; Bryce, *American Commonwealth*, 2:239–40. "[In] the crowded urban centers, humanitarians intensified their earlier efforts and discovered many new outlets for reform zeal. Representative of these multifarious interests were the American Prison Association, the National Conference of Social Work, the Women's Christian Temperance Union, and the Society for the Prevention of Cruelty to Children, all formed in the 1870s, and the American Red Cross Society, the National Divorce Reform League, the National Arbitration League, and the Indian Rights Association, which came along in the 1880s" (Schlesinger, "Nation of Joiners," 17–18).

28. *Albany Law Journal* 13 (June 17, 1876):423.

29. Hurst, *The Growth of American Law*, 286; James Grafton Rogers, "The American Bar Association in Retrospect," in Alison Reppy, ed., *Law: A Century of Progress*, 3 vols. (New York, 1937), 173.

30. George Martin, *Causes and Conflicts: The Centennial History of the Association of the Bar of the City of New York* (Boston, 1970), 3–86; see *American Law Review* 5 (1871):556.

31. Speeches of William M. Evarts and Henry Nicoll, *Association of the Bar of the*

*City of New York Report* 1 (1870):8, 26; quoted in Martin, *Causes and Conflicts*, 33–34.

32. "Lawyers in Council," *Albany Law Journal* 1 (March 19, 1870):219.

33. Hill, "Bar Associations," 65; Friedman, *History of American Law*, 561–63. For a list of bar associations and their dates of organization, see Wickser, "Bar Associations," 117–18.

34. Robert Wiebe, *The Search for Order* (New York, 1967), 117.

35. Wickser, "Bar Associations," 396, 417.

36. *Albany Law Journal* 13 (March 11, 1875):171.

37. Ibid., 16 (October 13, 1877):268.

38. Koerner to Simeon Baldwin, August 3, 1878, printed in Simeon Baldwin, "The Founding of the American Bar Association," *ABAJ* 3 (1917):680. Gustave Koerner (1809–1896), a German émigré and former justice of the Illinois Supreme Court, was appointed minister to Spain in 1862 by his friend Abraham Lincoln. Koerner became a Liberal Republican after the war and supported Tilden against Hayes in 1876. He remained influential in the German-American community till his death. It is not improbable that Koerner's advocacy of "scientific conferences of Jurists" sprang from his study of jurisprudence at the University of Jena.

39. The United States Law Association was an unrelated successor to the American Legal Association (1849–1854), the first such national referral service; Bloomfield, *American Lawyers*, 154–55. Information regarding the "Congress of Lawyers" has been gleaned from the *Albany Law Journal* and the *Philadelphia Inquirer*, *Public Ledger*, and *Press* of June 21–22, 1876.

40. *Albany Law Journal* 13 (May 27, 1876):375.

41. *Philadelphia Inquirer*, June 22, 1876, 2. The improbably named Orlando F. Bump (1841–1884) was a graduate of Yale and a prolific writer of legal works on commercial topics; his *Law and Practice of Bankruptcy* went through ten editions. Bump, who had little time for politics or organized religion, worked himself to death at the age of forty-three. "Orlando F. Bump," *American Law Review* 18 (1884):307.

42. *Albany Law Journal* 13 (June 24, 1876):440.

43. The only scholarly biography of Baldwin is by Frederick H. Jackson, *Simeon Eben Baldwin* (New York, 1955). See also Frederick H. Jackson, "Simeon E. Baldwin: Father of the American Bar Association," *ABAJ* 39 (1953):686; James Grafton Rogers, *American Bar Leaders: Biographies of the Presidents of the American Bar Association, 1875–1928* (Chicago, 1932), 61–65. Charles C. Goetsch, *Essays on Simeon E. Baldwin* (West Hartford, Conn., 1981), makes excellent use of the Baldwin diaries and other newly discovered correspondence. The diaries, however, contain little of importance directly relating to the American Bar Association.

44. Frederick C. Hicks, *Yale Law School, 1895–1915: Twenty Years of Hendrie Hall* (New Haven, 1938), 84. Baldwin said this "at the memorial exercises to William K. Townsend, June 18, 1907." Baldwin's friend Lyman Brewster told him that his "astounding and continuous power of work and that of most tedious description and of detail and minutiae" made him seem like "a calculating machine" (Jackson, *Baldwin*, 79). For the morbid details of Susan Baldwin's insanity, see Goetsch, *Essays on Simeon E. Baldwin*, chap. 3. Baldwin's attempt to use work as "a banisher of sorrow" was only partly successful. Frederick Hicks called Baldwin "lonesome and heartsick" (85), an assessment easily confirmed by a reading of his journals.

45. John G. Sproat, *"The Best Men": Liberal Reformers in the Gilded Age* (New

York, 1968), 4–10; see also Gerald W. McFarland, "Partisan of Nonpartisanship: Dorman B. Eaton and the Genteel Reform Tradition," *Journal of American History*, 54 (March 1968):806–22.

46. Sproat, "*The Best Men*," 6.

47. Jackson, *Baldwin*, 82ff., 139–40, 134.

48. Ibid., 94–95, 106, 125–32, 136, 214; Simeon E. Baldwin, "Education for the Bar in the United States," *American Political Science Review* 9 (August 1915):437–48.

49. Carrol Wright, "The Growth and Purpose of Bureaus of Statistics," *Journal of Social Science* 25 (1888):2–3; Daniel Coit Gilman, "Opening Address," ibid., 12 (1880):xxiii, quoted in Mary O. Furner, *Advocacy and Objectivity: A Crisis in the Professionalization of Social Science* (Lexington, 1975), 21.

50. "Principal objects of the American Social Science Association," *Journal of Social Science* 1 (1869):3–4; "The American Social Science Association," ibid., 6 (1874):1.

51. Baldwin, "The Founding of the American Bar Association," 658.

52. Ibid.; Rogers, "The American Bar Association," 173. "[The ABA] is a great achievement of mine. A casual remark of Judge Poché as we sat chatting at a Social Science Assn. meeting in Saratoga, in 1877, that we ought to have a national association of lawyers, led me to bring the matter before our state bar assn in 1878. . ." (Simeon E. Baldwin diary, July 12, 1916, Baldwin Family Papers, Yale University). Felix Pierre Poché (1836–1895) made $15,000 in his first year of law practice, mostly through war-related liquidations and settlements. He was appointed to the Louisiana Supreme Court in 1880 after a long personal fight against carpetbag government in his state. Apparently, his idea for a national bar association was stimulated by knowledge of "L'Ordre des Batonniers de France" (*Biographical and Historical Memoirs of Louisiana* 2 [1892]:314–16; and *ABA Rep* 18 [1895]:505–6).

53. Anthony Higgins to Simeon Baldwin, October 16, 1877, Baldwin Family Papers, Yale University.

54. Jackson, *Simeon E. Baldwin*, 80; Baldwin, "The Founding of the American Bar Association," 659; "William Hamersley," *National Cyclopaedia of American Biography*, 19:371; "Richard Dudley Hubbard," ibid., 10:342. Hamersley, who was instrumental in improving the jury system and procedural rules in Connecticut, later sat with Baldwin on the state supreme court. Baldwin's method of organizing the American Bar Association seems similar to Hamersley's previous organization of the Connecticut bar in 1875; see Victor M. Gordon, ed., "A History of the First One Hundred Years of the Connecticut Bar Association, 1875–1975," *Connecticut Bar Journal* 49 (1975):201–26.

55. Baldwin, "The Founding of the American Bar Association," 659. Although Baldwin did the lion's share of the work, Hubbard and Hamersley were not complete ciphers; each wrote to the "leading lawyers" with whom they had some acquaintance. See Hamersley to Baldwin, June 1, 1878, Baldwin Family Papers, Yale University.

56. "Charles Devens," *Dictionary of American Biography*, 5:260 (hereafter cited as *DAB*); "Charles O'Conor," *DAB*, 13:620; "William Maxwell Evarts," *DAB*, 6:215; "Severn Teackle Wallis," *DAB*, 19:385; "Charles Rollin Buckalew," *DAB*, 3:225; "Alexander Robert Lawton," *DAB*, 11:61; "Carleton Hunt," *DAB*, 9:382; "John Brooks Henderson," *DAB*, 8:527; "Lyman Trumbull," *DAB*, 19:19; "George Hoadly," *DAB*, 9:84; "Thomas M. Cooley," *DAB*, 4:392; "Stanley Matthews," *DAB*, 12:418. There are internal discrepancies within Baldwin's reminiscences regarding the names and numbers of lawyers to whom requests for signatures were sent.

57. "Benjamin Helm Bristow," *DAB*, 3:55; "Henry Hitchcock," *DAB*, 9:75; "J.

Randolph Tucker," *DAB*, 19:34; "Edward John Phelps," *DAB*, 14:528; "John K. Porter," *National Cyclopaedia of American Biography*, 3:252; "Charles R. Train," *Who Was Who*, 1:608; [Richard C. McMurtric], *The Law Association of Philadelphia: 1802–1902* (Philadelphia, 1906), 55–70; *American Law Register* 33 (1894):845–48.

58. Charles O'Conor to Richard Hubbard, May 14, 1878, in Baldwin, "The Founding of the American Bar Association," 663–65; Wayne K. Hobson, "The American Legal Profession and the Organizational Society," 221.

59. For an excellent discussion of Field's running controversy with the Association of the Bar of the City of New York, see George Martin, *Causes and Conflicts*, 55–60, 88–103.

60. "Luke P. Poland," *DAB*, 15:33; "James Overton Broadhead," *DAB*, 3:58; "George Grover Wright," *DAB*, 20:551; "John Hazlehurst Boneval Latrobe," *DAB*, 11:27; "Francis Rawle," *DAB*, 15:400; "Thomas Jenkins Semmes," *DAB*, 16:582; "William Allan Butler," *DAB*, 3:369. Lawton, Hunt, Hitchcock, and Tucker either were members of the ASSA or had attended the 1877 meeting of the Judicial Department at which Baldwin had spoken. Members of the "Saratoga clique" are identified by James Grafton Rogers in "The American Bar Association in Retrospect," 176–78, though Rogers's informal sources probably overrated the importance of the clique in the early direction of the association.

It is interesting to note that at the Centennial Celebration of the Supreme Court of the United States on February 4, 1890, the four major addresses were given by Butler, Hitchcock, Semmes, and Phelps. By 1890, all were past presidents of the ABA (*ABA Rep* 13 [1890]:345).

61. Richard Hofstadter, *The Age of Reform: From Bryan to F.D.R.* (New York, 1955), 158: "In the movement for broader conceptions of professional service, for new legal concepts and procedural reforms, for deeper professional responsibility, for criticism of the courts, the teaching side of the profession now became important." Of course, Hofstadter had reference to the Progressive Era, but his comments are accurate, to a lesser extent, for this period as well.

62. "Call for a Meeting to Form an American Bar Association," *ABA Rep* 1 (1878):4.

63. Francis Rawle, "How the Association Was Organized," *ABAJ* 14 (1928):375; Baldwin, "The Founding of the American Bar Association," 671–72.

64. For amusing anecdotes about Saratoga, see contemporary guidebooks such as R. F. Dearborn, *Saratoga and How to See It* (Albany, 1873); Hugh Bradley, *Such Was Saratoga* (New York, 1940); and Carson, *A Good Day at Saratoga*. Rawle, "How the Association Was Organized," 375; Rogers, "The American Bar Association in Retrospect," 175; *New York Tribune*, August 22, 1878, 1.

65. Rawle, "How the Association Was Organized," 375; John C. Ropes to Baldwin, July 9, 1878, in Baldwin, "The Founding of the American Bar Association," 672. John C. Ropes (1836–1899), a distinguished and reform-minded Boston lawyer, had "no doubt that the meetings of such a body of gentlemen would be very pleasant"; however, he doubted that their association would be of "any practical benefit." Significantly, Ropes was afflicted with a spinal deformity which prevented a much desired military career. He remained a bachelor, retired from the courtroom to the office, and is remembered, when remembered at all, as the author of a military history of the Civil War.

The responses in reply to the call were systematically removed from the Baldwin Papers, probably by Baldwin himself in April 1917, while he was preparing his article for the *ABAJ*. Most are now lost, although the Cromwell Library of the American Bar Foundation has twenty-four such letters.

66. *ABA Rep* 1 (1878):16.

67. Furner, *Advocacy and Objectivity*, 1.

68. Koerner to Simeon Baldwin, August 3, 1878, in Baldwin, "The Founding of the American Bar Association," 680; italics in original.

69. Occasionally mentioned in the replies to Baldwin was the belief that the bar association might provide "a new field of professional activity... in which the temptations that beset the mental labors and habits" of an attorney would be sublimated in the search for justice in the abstract. The quote is from Hill, "Bar Associations," 86.

70. Koerner to Baldwin, August 3, 1878; and Senator Charles Jones to Baldwin, August 10, 1878, in Baldwin, "The Founding of the American Bar Association," 680, 682.

71. *ABA Rep* 1 (1878):27.

72. Judge E. W. Stanley to Baldwin, July 24, 1878; and Chief Judge William C. Ruger to Baldwin, August 1, 1878, in Baldwin, "The Founding of the American Bar Association," 677, 679. Another of Baldwin's correspondents wrote requesting action upon the "licensing of incompetent practitioners. This is an evil, the magnitude of which, one cannot appreciate, unless brought in actual contact with it. These raters of good moral characters have brought a discredit upon the profession, that it will take years to eradicate, even with the help of merited reforms [*sic*]" (Green Durbin to Baldwin July 23, 1878, in Baldwin, ibid., 688). "Upholding the honor of the profession" was of great importance to Baldwin himself. He queried his diary: "Why am I with my scholarly tastes and capabilities groveling among ants... when my mind might find more congenial occupation in other fields? But is there any aim higher than that of raising the standard of your profession?" (Simeon Baldwin diary, February 8, 1874, Baldwin Family Papers, Yale University).

73. Koerner to Baldwin, August 3, 1878, in Baldwin, "The Founding of the American Bar Association," 680; Rogers, "The American Bar Association," 180; *New York Tribune*, August 22, 1878, 1.

74. Paul H. Buck, *The Road to Reunion, 1865–1900* (Boston, 1937), 140–41.

75. "Current Topics," *Albany Law Journal* 18 (August 24, 1878):141; Jacob Weart, "The American Bar Association: Its History for the First Sixteen Years of its Existence and its Impress Upon the Thought of the Nation," *New Jersey Law Journal* 27 (1904):338. "We come together from all parts of our country—our common country—from the scenes of desolation and sorrow on all hands, that God alone can estimate.... Let it all pass. We come to bury the armed Caesar, not to praise him" (Edward J. Phelps, "Chief Justice Marshall," *ABA Rep* 2 [1879]:191); see Walter Hill, "Bar Associations," 71.

76. Jones to Baldwin, August 10, 1878, in Baldwin, "The Founding of the American Bar Association," 682.

77. Ibid., 691–93; *ABA Rep* 1 (1878):10–11; *ABA Rep* 33 (1908):54.

78. Rogers, *American Bar Leaders*, 123; "James O. Broadhead: A Subject for Reappraisal," *Missouri Historical Society Bulletin* 27 (January 1971):125–28.

79. Carson, *A Good Day at Saratoga*, 4.

80. "Current Topics," *Albany Law Journal* 18 (1878):141.

81. Simeon Baldwin diary, August 31, 1878, Baldwin Family Papers, Yale University; and his diary for September 4, 1881 and April 7, 1917. Baldwin was never excessively modest, especially in private.

*GERARD W. GAWALT*

# *The Impact of Industrialization on the Legal Profession in Massachusetts, 1870–1900*

In the second half of the nineteenth century, Massachusetts completed its shift from a largely homogeneous society of British ancestry centered in small towns and commercial centers to a heterogeneous society of increasingly variant ethnic stock concentrated in urban areas and industrial-commercial centers. Statistical and documentary evidence indicates that the legal profession not only adjusted to this transformation, but adopted many aspects of industrialization for use in the teaching and practice of law. Rather than opposing the rise of this new dominant group in society, the legal profession joined the business community in many forms and, as a result, shared in its socioeconomic advances at the expense of professional and individual autonomy.

This essay will examine the impact of this emerging industrial society on the profession's patterns of recruitment, marriage, geographic mobility, wealth, income, and education. The variations between urban and rural regions and between law school graduates and the profession as a whole will be stressed. The growing emphasis on corporate and business law and the adaptation of industrial techniques of mass production for both law school education and legal practice in corporate law firms will be discussed.

Prosopographic and census studies of the legal profession help demonstrate how the learned professions adjusted from a homogeneous, rural-small community society with pockets of commercial urbanization to a heterogeneous, urban-industrial society with pockets of rural-small community life. In Massachusetts, this shift was well underway by 1840, and the change was virtually accomplished by 1870.

Lawyers became heavily concentrated in urban areas such as Boston, Lowell, Cambridge, and Worcester. As these industrial areas burgeoned during the nineteenth century, they drew large numbers of professionals to service them. In 1800, there were only 200 lawyers in Massachusetts of which thirty-three were in Suffolk County, i.e., in Boston. By 1840, there were 640 lawyers in the state and 215 in Suffolk County; in 1870, there were 1,270 lawyers in the state and 301 living in Suffolk County, but nearly as many living in neighboring counties, such as Norfolk and Middlesex, commuted to work in Boston. Moreover, there were thirty-eight lawyers in Lowell—a Middlesex County city that was virtually created by the industrial revolution in textiles—and forty-seven in Worcester, which had grown from a small rural county seat to a massive transportation and industrial center. At the end of the century 3,412 lawyers practiced in Massachusetts; 992 practiced in Boston, 191 practiced in Cambridge, and 131 practiced in Worcester.[1]

Not only were lawyers numerically concentrated in urban areas, but the largest number of both wealthy and apparently propertyless lawyers were also to be found there. Using the 1870 census data (see Table 6), it is clear that the highest percentages of property-holding (both real and personal) lawyers were to be found in the rural counties—in, for example, Berkshire (91.8 percent), Hampshire (87.5 percent), and Nantucket (100 percent). At the same time, urbanized and industrialized regions had a remarkably lower percentage of property-holding lawyers—see, for example, Suffolk (44.2 percent), Middlesex (65.7 percent) and Essex (76.4 percent). However, in Worcester County, where rural small towns surrounded an industrial center city, 86 percent of the lawyers in both the county and the city of Worcester were property-holders. These same tendencies were also evident for the medical and ministerial professions. For the entire state, 69 percent of the lawyers were property-holders as compared to 71.3 percent of the doctors and 70.4 percent of the ministers.

Moreover, all of the indices for the wealth of property-holding lawyers show that the most prosperous lawyers lived in the urban areas (see Table 6). In Suffolk County, the average wealth of all lawyers was only $22,858, but the average for property-holding lawyers was more than double—$51,731—and the average for the ten wealthiest lawyers was $329,800. Compare this to Berkshire where the average wealth of all lawyers was $20,042, and for all property-holding lawyers $21,824, and for the ten wealthiest, $70,460. Except for the urban counties of Suffolk, Middlesex, Essex, and parts of Worcester, great disparities did not exist within the legal profession in this statistical sense. The average wealth of all lawyers in the state was $21,316, and for all property-holding lawyers, $32,053. The comparable figures for doctors were $10,148 and $14,232, and for ministers $5,097 and $7,236. Of the three professions, law definitely offered the best chances both for acquiring great wealth and for failure.

As is to be expected, age and its concurrent factor of length of practice had important effects on the accumulation of wealth. As can be seen in Table 7, propertyless lawyers were consistently younger in average age than property-holding attorneys. And the average age of the ten wealthiest lawyers in each county was consistently higher than the average age of all other property-holders. Another study of forty-seven lawyers practicing in Worcester in 1870 shows that nearly 75 percent of the lawyers who continued practicing in 1900 owned more property in 1890 than in 1870, and more in 1900 than in 1890.[2] Nevertheless, in an age when the average mill hand lived in rental property, owned less than $100 in personal property (and, therefore, was not recorded as a property-holder in the 1870 census), and the average shoe worker, for example, made less than ten dollars a week in 1890, the great disparity between lawyers and workingmen, so apparent five decades before, had expanded.[3]

Even though court practice was becoming a less important part of legal practice, an examination of the Massachusetts Supreme Judicial Court reports for the post–Civil War period reveals the same pre–1840 pattern of a few lawyers in each county dominating court practice. But more and more lawyers appeared in court for a single case. For example, in Worcester County only six lawyers—G. F. Verry, H. B. Staples, F. P. Goulding, P. E. Aldrich, F. A. Gaskill, and T. L. Nelson–dominated court cases between 1870 and 1875. These six lawyers handled 256 out of 507 reported cases during this five-year period. Twenty-six lawyers had just one case, and only fifteen lawyers had two or more cases in the October 1871 term. In Middlesex County during this same period, only five lawyers handled more than fifteen cases—T. Wentworth, G. Stevens, D. S. Richardson, T. H. Sweetser, and G. A. Somerby—and they handled 132 out of 627 cases. Again, most lawyers handled only one case—in the January 1874 term, sixty-two lawyers handled just one case, and thirty-one handled two or more cases. Even the limited court-circuit following of the 1800–1840 period had dissipated. There was little intercounty practice except between bordering counties, and in Suffolk County where lawyers often maintained an office in Boston and one in their town of residence.[4]

Despite wide variations, it seems clear that $5,000–$10,000 in annual legal fees would have been considered an above average law practice and $2,000–$3,000 would have been a good average income in post–Civil War Massachusetts. The Boston patent law firm of Wright, Brown, and Quimby shows both the potential wealth and the rapid rate of growth in the new, industrial fields of law. The firm began in 1881 with 31 clients, but within twenty years their ledgers listed 580 active clients. Their income was substantial—in 1898–1899, C. H. Brown drew $5,010.33; William Quimby drew $6,127.98, and, after $14,290.21 in expenses were paid, there remained $23,055.82. In 1900–1901, although Brown and Quimby drew about the same amount and expenses had only risen $1,200, there was a balance of $48,083.51. The firm's fees ranged from $1.50 for recording a patent to several hundred dollars for overseas applications. Even though their clients were numerous, the firm's court cases were few—ten in 1894 and fourteen in 1900. Other Boston lawyers, such as F. O. Prince, made $4,000 to $5,000 a year. On the other hand, the Boston law firm of George S. Hale and Charles S. Wolcott divided $4,063.68 of which Hale got $2,844.57 and Wolcott got $1,219.11.[5]

Members of the bar in other areas of the state were aware that lawyers in Boston were able to obtain higher fees—often for identical work. In 1861, the Fitchburg firm of Wood and Torrey doubled its $3,000 income when George A. Torrey convinced Nathaniel Wood to bring his fees in line with Boston lawyers.

As Worcester lawyer John R. Thayer wrote: "I have continued the practice of my profession here in Worcester doing an immense amount of work for what lawyers in New York or Boston would think a very small sum." In support of his claim, the assessors records show that Thayer had accumulated only $9,000 in real property by 1900 after 18 years of practice. Nevertheless, lawyers in other urban areas also prospered. The Salem firm of Stephen Ives and Solomon Lincoln reportedly made $7,000 to $8,000 in 1869. Henry Bacon, as a junior member of the Worcester firm of Hopkins and Bacon received a $2,000 annual salary in 1875. John H. Clifford of New Bedford reported a professional income of $4,000 in 1866, but a total income of $13,192. In 1871, Clifford reported a professional income of $1,500, but a total income of $21,079. Not surprisingly, Clifford became president of the Anti–Income Tax Association in 1871.[6]

The growth of industrial centers accentuated the traditional divergence between the incomes of urban and rural lawyers, and, with few exceptions, modern industrial society improved the market situation of the professions. Lawyers were able to capitalize on opportunities available through the rise in the complexity of society, the growth of population, the expansion of education, the growth of government and laws, and the rise of living standards with increased disposable income for services. Lawyers were able to generate higher incomes and they were able to restrict their roles as the errand boys of the commercial community by increased specialization in the management of legal affairs and business expansion. Entire branches of the legal profession were created in response to industrial demands—patent law, corporate law, trust and estate planning, government regulation, and tax law. These were the newest and most profitable areas of legal practice; they were responses to the needs of industrial society and required different skills than those of trial-oriented advocates.

As large law firms replaced one- or two-man firms as the most prestigious and profitable, lawyers lost individual autonomy. These institutionalized firms can be seen as law factories with assembly-line handling of cases and staffs; firms were divided into partners, associates, clerks, trial and brief specialists, business getters and conveyancers, secretaries and office boys. Such large firms were made possible by vital aspects of industrial mechanization—typewriters, telephones, railroads, telegraph, and electric lighting. Just as industry escaped the bounds of master craftsmen, the urban legal profession first began to move beyond the bounds of solitary practitioners. In the process, some lawyers lost autonomy, general legal skills, and economic opportunities, but others acquired broader powers and managerial skills, and generated higher incomes. Massachusetts lawyer Joseph H. Choate zeroed in on the new commercialism when he wrote, on the verge of joining a New York City corporate law firm: "An established law office in New York is like a mercantile establishment anywhere offering a sure reward to any one who gets into it." And Choate was right—within twenty years he was making over $100,000 per annum.[7]

Boston attorney Louis D. Brandeis epitomized the emerging industrial lawyer. Son of a successful businessman, Brandeis graduated from law school and then founded his own vertically organized, specialized law firm that concentrated on corporate law in the broadest sense of offering business advice as well as legal advice. Brandeis became a staunch advocate of large-scale law firms which he said offered the best chances for monetary and professional success. When confronted by complaints from his young law associates that he received all the credit for their work, Brandeis made this August 19, 1896, reply to William H. Dunbar, a young associate in his firm:

> The organization of large offices is becoming more and more a business—and hence also a professional necessity—if properly planned and administered—it must result in the greatest efficiency to clients and the greatest success to the individual members both pecuniary and in reputation.
>
> Second: In such an organization the place of each man must be found—not prescribed. The advantage of the large field is that every man has the opportunity of trying himself at everything or anything—and by the natural law comes to do those things that on the whole he does most effectively.

Eventually, Brandeis, who, by 1890 was well on his way to becoming a millionaire and by 1902 had an annual income of $45,116 from his legal practice, concluded that business, law, and reform politics had to be amalgamated to the benefit of society.[8]

Corporate lawyers were most often found in urban areas because in those areas they could capitalize on the advantages offered, as W. Oakey Hall wrote in 1899, by "the increase in variety of litigation" made available through the "expansion of commerce and business" and also through direct opportunities in commerce and industry. Being a house counsel was one very common way. Judge Augustus L. Soule, for example, resigned from the Massachusetts Supreme Judicial Court in 1881 to become counsel for the Boston and Albany Railroad at $9,000 per annum, replacing another Boston lawyer, George S. Hale. In another instance, Francis A. Houston, a graduate of Harvard and Harvard Law, began as a Boston general practitioner in 1883. In two years, he entered the law office of the New England Telephone and Telegraph Company, successively serving as attorney, counsel, general manager, vice-president, and treasurer before resigning in 1918. These are just two of many examples that could be given. Becoming an industrialist was another direct option. A good example is Frank B. Smith, son of a cotton manufacturer, banker, and railroader. After attending Harvard and Harvard Law, he entered the Worcester firm of Hopkins and Bacon before becoming a cotton mill operator and founder of the Worcester Bank and Trust Company.[9] The evidence leaves no doubt that the large, urban law firm, like its business counterpart, offered the best opportunities for professional profit and prestige in late nineteenth-century Massachusetts.

Let us now turn from the differences between urban and rural lawyers to an examination of the composition of the legal profession throughout the state based on an examination of biographical data for 1,806 lawyers admitted to practice in the state between 1870 and 1890. These prosopographic studies will show not only divergences within the state at that time, but also alterations in the profession since 1840 (the ending point for my earlier investigation of the Massachusetts legal profession, which was published as *The Promise of Power: The Emergence of the Legal Profession in Massachusetts, 1760–1840*).

Reflecting the intensive internal development within the state, few lawyers moved out of state after their admission to practice. (See Table 1.) Although more than 21 percent of the lawyers were born in other states (compared to less than 15 percent before 1840), only slightly more than 3 percent were foreign-born. There was a noticeable decline in postadmission mobility from the pre–1840 period. Nearly 90 percent of the lawyers admitted between 1870 and 1890 practiced in one town or city for their entire career, and less than 5 percent moved out of state. By way of comparison, about 70 percent of the lawyers admitted before 1840 practiced in only one town, whereas nearly 18 percent moved out of state. Geographic mobility was apparently low before 1840, and for lawyers admitted between 1870 and 1890 geographical immobility became nearly universal. In part, this may have reflected the increasing opportunities in industrial Massachusetts; it may also have been a result of technological advances (such as the telegraph and telephone) and improved transportation that widened the geographic scope of a centrally located law office. Moreover, improved transportation systems made commuting into core cities practical during the post–Civil War period and, therefore, either precluded the necessity of moving one's practice when a lawyer moved his residence, or offered the opportunity to operate two offices.[10]

A dramatic shift in the recruiting patterns of the legal profession is indicated by studies of the occupations of the fathers of lawyers. (See Tables 2 and 3.) This does not appear to show that the legal profession had become more of a vehicle for vertical mobility (i.e., social and occupational ascendency at the expense of others), but the legal profession, reflecting changes in society, began to attract many more offspring of businessmen and white-collar workers than it had in the pre–1840 period. Whereas before 1840, more than 70 percent of the lawyers who studied were found to have had fathers who were doctors, ministers, judges, or lawyers, only slightly more than 40 percent of the college-educated lawyers and 30 percent of the noncollege-educated lawyers admitted between 1870 and 1890 were the children of professionals. On the other hand, children of businessmen rose dramatically from about 10 percent before 1840 to about 35 percent for lawyers admitted between 1870 and 1890.[11]

This same shift occurred in the marriage patterns of lawyers. (See Table 4.) Whereas before 1840, most lawyers had married daughters of professionals, only slightly more than 35 percent of those admitted between 1870 and 1890 married daughters of professionals, and more than 45 percent married children of businessmen.[12] Such definite shifts in recruiting and marriage patterns demonstrate the profession's basic adjustment to societal changes. This lateral broadening of membership in the legal profession broke down the inbred professional class that was so evident and so disliked in Jacksonian America and gave the profession a more business oriented background.

By 1900, the Massachusetts legal profession had accepted the reality of the admission of women, blacks, and foreigners by providing for the regular admission of women through the bar examination procedure and by allowing (in contrast to twenty-three other states including New York, New Hampshire, Pennsylvania, Illinois, and Michigan) citizens and "an alien who has declared his intentions of becoming a citizen" to be admitted to the bar.[13]

Even in Boston, ethnic lawyers remained a small part of the legal profession as late as 1900. The heterogeneous nature of the population—a result of the industrialization of America and Europe—did not fully impact on the professions until after 1900. When it did, many of the colleges and professional schools moved to exclude or establish quotas for Jewish, Catholic, and East European enrollment.[14] Before 1900, Irishmen were the dominant ethnic group of lawyers in Massachusetts. In 1870, there were only 40 (3.3 percent) foreign-born lawyers in Massachusetts; 50 percent were Irish, with only a single Eastern or Southern European. In a study of 1,806 lawyers admitted to practice between 1870 and 1890 (see Table 7), only 59 (3.2 percent) were foreign-born, and most of these were Irish. In comparison, 9.1 percent of the doctors and 14.4 percent of the clergy in 1870 were born in a wide variety of foreign countries. There were, however, more Irish lawyers than the figures for foreign-born lawyers would indicate. There were, for example, 110 lawyers of Irish ancestry listed in Boston in 1889. Even so, in 1896, the Irish represented less than 1 percent of Boston's lawyers, doctors, dentists, engineers, and architects.[15] But ethnic lawyers were on the increase. By 1890, there were 57 foreign-born lawyers in Boston as well as 107 who had foreign-born parents; there were 7 foreign-born lawyers in Lowell and 22 who had foreign-born parents.[16] Most foreign-born lawyers were living and practicing in urban industrial areas, where, of course, most of their fellow countrymen lived and worked and provided lawyers a ready made ethnic clientele.

Evidence seems to indicate that many of the foreign-born lawyers had less education and low-status parents. For example, James Farley, who was born a laborer's son in Ireland, had become a Boston lawyer by 1870. Edward F. Jenkins, a Londoner, was the son of a porter and became a lawyer in 1881. In a study of 110 Irish lawyers in Boston in 1889, sufficient biographical data was found for seventy-two. Fifty-five were born in Massachusetts and just thirteen in Ireland. Thirty had attended college, and fifty-three had attended law school (thirty-six at Boston University Law School).[17] Although the level of collegiate education among Irish lawyers was considerably lower than for the profession as a whole, the level of professional education was similar to the profession. If anything, many Irish lawyers went to law school because they had difficulties obtaining apprenticeships.

There is considerable doubt that Irish lawyers were fully accepted by native-born, elite lawyers. George A. Torrey, a Fitchburg lawyer, recalled that Matthew J. McCafferty had been the only Irish lawyer in Worcester in the 1860s and his "practice was mainly confined to criminal cases." This assessment was confirmed by my own research of the Supreme Judicial Court reports. Boston attorney G. S. Hilliard spurned appearing with "McCafferty, who is, I suppose, a native of the Emerald Isle" until it became apparent that he would not win the liquor license case and get "paid well." Hilliard then attempted to retain McCafferty as co-counsel, but he in turn was refused by McCafferty.[18]

Foreign-born lawyers did acquire property at only a slightly lower rate than native-born lawyers—62.5 percent for foreign-born lawyers to 70.9 percent for native-born lawyers—but they accumulated less. (See Table 5.) The aforementioned McCafferty, for example, owned $7,000 in property in 1870, but this was far below the $28,424 owned by the average property-holding lawyer in Worcester County in 1870. A few other random examples make the same point; Adam Mackie, a fifty-eight-year-old New Bedford lawyer born in Scotland—$500; Patrick E. Cronin, 27, born in Ireland and practiced in Lawrence—zero; John E. Tatlock, 61, born in England and practiced in Pittsfield—$7,500; Michael Norton, 37, Brighton, born in Ireland—$4,400.[19] Admission to practice was one thing; parity with the professional elite was clearly quite another, more distant objective.

Few black lawyers practiced in Massachusetts during the post–Civil War period—only three were listed in the 1870 census—and little could be found out about them. (See Table 7.) Robert Morris was the first black lawyer in Boston in 1847, and his son Robert also became a Boston lawyer in the 1870s. George Ruffin, the first black law student at Harvard Law School in 1869, apprenticed at the Irish firm of Jewett and Gaston and, in 1878, became the first black judge in the North, serving in the Charlestown Municipal Court, 1878–1886. Their property holdings were small: in 1870, George Ruffin of Boston had none; Robert Morris of Chelsea had $17,500; and William H. Johnson of New Bedford had $500. Black lawyers in Massachusetts were out of the mainstream of the legal profession and, like their counterparts elsewhere, apparently represented chiefly a black clientele.[20]

Lelia Robinson Sawtelle, the first woman graduate of Boston University Law School in 1881, won the right to admission to the bar through a court test and a consequent legislative act in 1882. But this did not open the gates to large numbers of female lawyers before 1900. Sawtelle only practiced for two years before marrying and moving to Seattle, Washington. Alice Parker, a daughter of Dr. Hiram Parker, had a large probate business in Lowell in the 1890s. Anna Christy, a Boston University Law School graduate of 1891, practiced law in Boston and married a fellow Boston lawyer, George H. Fall. Prior to Lelia Sawtelle's breakthrough, some women had become conveyancers—Mary E. Stephen, for example, was a Cambridge conveyancer in 1870 and owned $3,000 in property. A later study indicated that by 1920, women who had been admitted to the bar between 1890 and 1900 had an average income of $4,075 and a median income of $3,925.

Women, like blacks, were not a significant part of the legal profession in

Massachusetts before 1900, even though there were forty-seven female lawyers at that time, most of whom practiced in urban areas—sixteen in Boston alone. Still, most women did not practice in the prestigious fields such as corporate or commercial law, or in large urban firms, but instead handled civil and real estate law in small firms. Professionally, women were much stronger in medicine (729 women, 13.2 percent, in Massachusetts in 1900, up sharply from 3.8 percent in 1870). In medicine, at the time, women were at a peak; although they did not know it, the future lay ahead in the legal profession. Even in 1920, women were still only 3 percent of the professions, even though nearly 50 percent of the college graduates were women. However, compared to other countries, such as England, where women were not admitted to practice until after World War I, the Massachusetts legal profession was a model of progress.[21] But the admission of women had been reluctant, and their full inclusion and acceptance in the profession awaited future events.

Lawyers were not the only professional group that failed to provide an available route for vertical mobility. Even the relatively new profession of engineering was predominantly the preserve of middle-class and upper-class men—white males who were overwhelmingly Anglo-Saxon or North European Protestants. The great majority were sons of prosperous businessmen, managers, lawyers, doctors, ministers, farmers, or engineers. Although very few came from extremely wealthy families, in contrast to lawyers, fewer still were born in poverty. Attaining professional competence, despite massive aid from industry and the federal government through the 1862 Morrill Act, required family financial and social support. The professions were not different from society as a whole. Stephan Thernstrom found that in Boston during the decade from 1880 to 1890, 88 percent of the workers remained in the same social class. Joseph Kett argues that by the 1870s there was "a sharp difference between the opportunities available to middle-class and working-class youth"; as formal education became more important, this divergence of opportunity became "much more pronounced as America moved toward the status of a mature industrial society."[22]

Along with the increased diversification of the legal profession's pattern of recruitment came a decline in collegiate education and an increase in law school training. (See Table 12.) In a study of 1,806 lawyers admitted to the bar between 1870 and 1890, only 1,050, or 58 percent, were college graduates compared to the nearly 70 percent for the legal profession as a whole for the pre–1840 period. But in urban Boston, 63 percent of the lawyers admitted between 1870 and 1890 were college graduates. Many more lawyers were professional school graduates in the post–Civil War period than before 1840, and urban areas such as Boston and neighboring Norfolk County attracted more law school graduates than rural areas such as Berkshire County.[23] In fact, very few lawyers admitted to practice in Massachusetts between 1870 and 1890 did not take at least one term of study at one of the law schools.

The decline in college education also extended to professional school graduates. A study of the graduates of twelve New England professional schools for the period 1870 to 1890 indicates that professional school graduates had less formal education than during the pre–Civil War period. (See Table 12.) For the legal profession, this translates to slightly more than 50 percent of the graduates of law schools (Harvard, Boston University, Yale) being college graduates, compared to Harvard Law's 73.5 percent for the period 1820 to 1840.[24] The decline also extended to theology school graduates who dropped to slightly more than 65 percent college graduates from 83.4 percent during the pre–1840 period. Only medical school graduates increased from 26.4 percent college graduates to 27.7 percent for the years 1870 to 1890. This decline in collegiate education cannot be attributed to a decline in college enrollment. With the exception of Harvard Law (beginning in 1875), no professional school made any serious effort to encourage prior undergraduate training. Moreover, and perhaps more important, college graduates were increasingly attracted to commerce and industry rather than to the professions. Whereas before 1840, college graduates overwhelmingly entered the fields of law, medicine, and theology, during the post–Civil War period, this was not the case—at Harvard College, for example, law had been the leading occupational choice before 1840, but by 1881, it was second to commerce, whereas at Williams College, located in rural western Massachusetts, law and education were the leading choices.[25]

A correlative development to the decline in collegiate education was the growth in Massachusetts law school graduates. For many prospective lawyers, law school replaced college as their stint of formal education—professional respectability did not require an undergraduate degree. Excluding temporary students, law school graduates grew from 158 for Harvard Law, 1820–1840, to 1,453 for Harvard Law and Boston University Law in a corresponding twenty-year period, 1870–1890. Many other Massachusetts men were among Yale Law's 539 graduates, and still others attended more distant schools, such as Columbia or Michigan.[26]

No evidence was found to substantiate the claims of some scholars, such as Lawrence M. Friedman and Gary B. Nash, that "the rise of the law schools was linked to a social change in the character of the bar—from strongly aristocratic to middle class in family background."[27] On the contrary, there is no apparent significant difference in the paternal occupations or marriage patterns of law school graduates and the profession as a whole. (See Tables 8–11.) In a study of Harvard Law School graduates admitted to practice between 1870 and 1890, 40 percent were found to be the sons of professional men, and 40.1 percent were found to be the offspring of businessmen. Boston University Law graduates showed comparative figures of 35.1 percent and 31 percent. (See Table 9.) There were some basic differences between the two law schools. Most lawyers of Irish ancestry, who went to law school, attended Boston University—thirty-six of fifty-three Irish law school graduates practicing in Boston in 1889 had attended Boston University Law. Moreover, women were excluded from Harvard, but seventy-seven women graduated from Boston University Law between 1874 and 1920. On the other hand, most of the black law school graduates went to Harvard.[28]

There were similarities in other areas. Harvard Law School graduates married daughters of professionals in 39.8 percent of the cases and children of businessmen in 30.3 percent of the instances counted; for Boston University Law School, these figures were 24.8 percent and 44.8 percent, respectively. (See Table 10.) Law school graduates were also only slightly more mobile than all of the lawyers admitted between 1870 and 1890. Less than 5 percent were foreign-born, but approximately 20 percent of the 701 lawyers in the study were born outside of Massachusetts. More than 90 percent of the lawyers practiced in one town.[29] (See Tables 8 and 11.) An analysis of Harvard Law School graduates in the 1870 census reinforces the view that at that point, law school graduates were not substantially statistically different from apprenticed lawyers. (See Tables 5–8.) In urban Suffolk County, however, they were younger as a group in 1870 and probably, as a consequence, had lower average wealth and a lower percentage of property-holders than the overall profession. In counties such as Worcester, Middlesex, and Norfolk, despite being younger, law school graduates were more likely to be property-holders and their average property was worth more than that of the average lawyer.[30] If anything, law schools reinforced the trends in the profession toward a broadening of its recruitment and marriage patterns into the business community, but this can hardly be defined as vertical mobility. It does reflect both the legal profession's intensifying connection with the commercial and industrial elements in society and the simultaneous decline of the inbred professional class so evident before 1840.

The evolving education of lawyers was closely tied to the rise of industrialism and its concurrent organizational impulse. The triumph of professional schools was undoubtedly due, in part, to the entrepreneurial efforts of educators. But the emphasis of the theme of law as a science caught the dominant pragmatism of industrial society. This idea was nurtured by the national law schools, such as Harvard, Michigan, Yale, and so forth, that emphasized a common law education for lawyers. While they became antivocational in approach, the national law schools fit in better with the national scope of modern America and with the national vision of large corporate law firms whose clients and cases were regional and national in character rather than local. As a result, large corporate law firms found graduates of law schools who were trained in the broad perspective of scientific law rather than the narrow, local vocational aspects of legal practice to be better suited to their clients and their legal problems. Moreover, there were practical aspects of this symbiotic relationship between law schools and large law firms. As one recent student of the legal profession has stated so well: "It was obviously much simpler" for law firms "to discriminate among recruits in terms of the law school they had attended than the type of law office in which they had apprenticed. In addition, the law school provided a convenient measure of competence in their ratings of students by academic achievement."[31] Conversely, the reliance of large law firms on law schools enhanced the prestige of national law schools and increased demands for their services by prospective, elite practitioners.

Harvard Law School and its new instructional orientation were major beneficiaries as well as causal factors in this change. Langdell's case method, an emphasis on legal theory and common law, the imposition of stricter admission and graduation standards, and the use of legal education specialists composed a program that was a rational response to the demands on the profession. Its most important clients, industrial and commercial firms, wanted lawyers whose legal knowledge would guide them on a national level and keep them out of court, while using the growing corpus of corporate law to their advantage. The judiciary's emphasis on appellate courts required lawyers who were well trained in brief preparation (a strength of the Langdell method) rather than in oral argument (the forte of the Socratic method). Intellectually oriented lawyers wanted a legal education that stressed science—the leading intellectual as well as industrial theme of the time. As Oliver Wendell Holmes and Arthur G. Sedgwick, two young spokesmen for the cultural and legal elite of Boston society, wrote in 1870 on the eve of Langdell's remodelling of the law school: "The object of a law department is not precisely and only to educate young men to be practicing lawyers, though it will be largely used for that purpose. It is to furnish all students who desire it the same facilities to investigate the science of human law, theoretically, historically, and thoroughly, as they have to investigate mathematics, natural sciences, or any other branch of thought."[32] The rise of science and the emergence of modern America went hand in hand.

The close ties between rising industrialism with its drive for scientific research and scientifically trained personnel were most evident in the research orientation of university science and engineering departments, such as those at the Massachusetts Institute of Technology, Clark University, the University of Chicago, and Johns Hopkins University.[33] But the emphasis on scientific research and the need to provide trained personnel for business and industry was not absent from the nation's medical and law schools. In fact, both seized on the scientific emphasis in promoting the need for professional school training where law or medicine could best be studied as a science.

Just as industry urged the universities to center their research on pure science and leave the practical training of scientists to industry schools, national law school proponents concentrated on the law as a science and left the practical aspects of legal training to the law firms. Ephraim W. Gurney, Dean of the Harvard faculty, argued against a faculty of young legal scholars rather than older practitioners. He claimed that it would "build up a great school of law as an exact science, and divorce it more and more from its actual administration." He decried the refusal of the school to provide anything "except the pure science of the law," because the school would then commit itself to "breeding within itself its Corps of instructors and thus sever itself from the great current of legal life."[34]

While the national law schools that emphasized the study of law as a science and legal theory proved most attractive to large corporate law firms, large businesses and the federal government, vocationally oriented law schools and night schools such as Boston University Law School and the Y.M.C.A. Law School (Northeastern University Law School) catered to those who, for various reasons (including family background and monetary problems), aimed at neighborhood or community practices, as shown in the differences between Harvard and Boston University students. The case was clearly stated by George R. Swasey, a law professor at Boston University. He argued that the Boston University Law School did not owe its existence to a "prevailing desire to add new departments to the University" or to "any one man devoted to the theory of the law." The school resulted from "conditions" in the profession. According to Swasey, there was "a feeling that the best system" of legal education "embraced lectures in connection with the practical work of an office.... It was further felt that the instruction at the nearest law school, namely, at Cambridge, was particularly technical and historical, and when completed necessitated an apprenticeship in some good attorney's office."[35] Langdell's approach to legal studies was based on his insight that in order to best serve their corporate and nationally oriented clients, lawyers had to be more skilled in the process of legal thinking and in brief preparation than in the technical vocational skills that were invaluable to the solo practitioner. Ultimately, the vocational schools would offer more theoretical courses to bolster their educational images and meet the standards of the Association of American Law Schools, and the national law schools would offer access to vocational training through course work and neighborhood legal clinics. But no compromise had been arrived at by 1900.

Law schools not only stressed the scientific theme of industrial America, but also adopted the techniques of industrial mass-production employed in the factory system that limited individuality of student preparation in favor of uniformity. Too much can easily be made of a direct analogy between professional schools and factories. Nevertheless, the new professional school did seem to emphasize large-scale production through group instruction and systematic studies of interlocking courses to be followed by all students in a standard sequential pattern with periodic inspections (i.e., examinations) to determine quality control that would produce a uniform product whose consistency was to be guaranteed by the educational trademark of a professional degree that had been scientifically produced. Law school proponents sought a standardized product that would be readily accepted by its label rather than by its demonstrated vocational ability. It was not mere coincidence that many of the men (such as Dana, Parker, Story, James B. Thayer, Washburn, Metcalf, John Davis, Asahel Stearns, Charles Jackson, Theophilus Parsons, Jr., Oliver Wendell Holmes, Roscoe Pound, and Louis Brandeis) who helped forge the law into instruments for commercial and industrial growth, were also the exponents of systematic instruction in law schools and standardized law through legal writing and judicial interpretation. Despite the 1871 protest of Prof. Henry Bigelow of Harvard that "you cannot turn out medical men with the uniform perfection of Ames shovels or Springfield muskets," the standardization movement of educational reformers was irresistible.[36]

The formation of the Association of American Law Schools in 1900, largely through the efforts of Harvard Law School professor James B. Thayer, symbolized the profession's recognition that control of the education of lawyers and their subsequent admission to practice was shifting from individual lawyers (masters and apprenticeships) to institutions—law schools (managers and factories)—and was thus beyond the control of voluntary societies, such as the resurging bar associations, that were still organized around individuals rather than institutions.[37]

Although in this brief paper much of the supporting evidence had to remain in the background, enough evidence has been presented to show that the legal profession adapted readily to industrial society, and, in fact, that it and the other traditional professions eagerly sought the techniques of business and industry and, in some cases, pioneered their development. There is little evidence that a conservative, nostalgic legal profession hoped that the new bar associations would lead the elite bar back to their pre–Civil War "golden era" except in the minds of a few legal scholars. From this perspective, the learned professions were not conservative strongholds wedded to a less complicated and more idealistic, individualistic, or humanistic past.[38] Rather, the learned professions were full participants and often leaders in the headlong drive toward a modern heterogeneous, industrial, institutional society in nineteenth-century Massachusetts, even if it meant the erosion of the independent professional and the autonomous profession.

**TABLE 1**
**Geographic Mobility of Massachusetts Lawyers, 1870–1890**

| Geographic Location | College Graduates Massachusetts | | Boston | | Non-College Graduates Massachusetts | | Boston | | Total State | |
|---|---|---|---|---|---|---|---|---|---|---|
| | A | B | A | B | A | B | A | B | A | B |
| Practiced in Native Town | 30.9% (66) | 42.3% (63) | 21.1% (73) | 19.6% (67) | 26% (50) | 34.7% (49) | 16.3% (29) | 14.9% (32) | 23.4% (218) | 25.2% (221) |
| Practiced in One Town | 82.6% (176) | 83.2% (124) | 87.9% (305) | 89.7% (306) | 89.1% (171) | 92.9% (158) | 95.5% (170) | 94.4% (204) | 88.4% (822) | 90.4% (792) |
| Practiced in Two Towns | 16.4% (35) | 14.1% (21) | 11% (38) | 8.8% (30) | 8.9% (17) | 7.1% (12) | 3.9% (7) | 5.5% (12) | 10.4% (97) | 8.6% (75) |
| Practiced in Three or More Towns | .9% (2) | 2.7% (4) | 1.1% (4) | 1.5% (5) | 2% (4) | 0 0 | .6% (1) | 0 0 | 1.2% (11) | 1% (9) |
| Moved into State | 23% (49) | 20.1% (30) | 27.1% (94) | 28.7% (98) | 12.5% (24) | 15.9% (27) | 21.9% (39) | 15.3% (33) | 22.2% (206) | 21.5% (188) |
| Moved out of State | 6.1% (13) | 5.4% (8) | 9.5% (33) | 3.8% (13) | 3.1% (6) | .6% (1) | 1.1% (2) | 1.4% (3) | 5.8% (54) | 2.8% (25) |
| Foreign Born | 2.8% (6) | 2.7% (4) | 1.7% (6) | 2.3% (8) | 8.9% (17) | 4.1% (7) | 3.4% (6) | 2.3% (5) | 3.8% (35) | 2.7% (24) |
| Number of Lawyers Admitted | 213 | 149 | 347 | 341 | 192 | 170 | 178 | 216 | 930 | 876 |

A stands for 1871-1880; B stands for 1881-1890

Massachusetts includes all lawyers who began practice in the state outside of Boston.

Boston includes all lawyers who began practice in the city of Boston.

## TABLE 2
## Massachusetts Lawyers: Recruiting Patterns (Paternal Occupation), 1870–1890

| | Massachusetts College Grads | | Boston College Grads | | All College Graduates | |
|---|---|---|---|---|---|---|
| | A | B | A | B | A | B |
| Lawyers | 24.6% | 34.8% | 25.1% | 28.3% | 25.6% | 30.2% |
| Doctors | 3.8% | 4.5% | 7.9% | 5.5% | 6.4% | 5.2% |
| Minister | 8.5% | 3.4% | 8.4% | 3.7% | 8.4% | 3.8% |
| Manufacturer | 10.4% | 10.1% | 7.9% | 5.5% | 8.7% | 6.8% |
| Retail-Wholesale | 11.4% | 12.4% | 11.0% | 17.8% | 11.1% | 16.2% |
| Mechanic-Laborer | 5.6% | 4.5% | 2.1% | .9% | 3.3% | 1.9% |
| Artisan-Machinist | 12.3% | 12.4% | 5.8% | 6.4% | 8.0% | 8.1% |
| Farmer | 6.6% | 4.5% | 4.2% | 4.1% | 5.1% | 4.2% |
| Merchant | 6.6% | 1.1% | 15.2% | 8.2% | 12.1% | 6.2% |
| Clerk Salesman | .9% | 1.1% | 4.7% | 4.1% | 3.3% | 3.2% |
| Administrator | 3.8% | 2.2% | 3.1% | 2.7% | 3.0% | 2.6% |
| Other Business | 1.8% | 4.5% | 3.1% | 8.2% | 2.7% | 7.1% |
| Other Professional | 2.8% | 1.1% | .5% | 3.7% | 1.3% | 2.9% |
| Other | .9% | 3.4% | 1.0% | .9% | 1.0% | 1.6% |
| All Business | 34.0% | 30.3% | 40.3% | 42.4% | 38.5% | 38.9% |
| All Professional | 39.7% | 43.8% | 41.9% | 41.2% | 41.7% | 42.1% |

A stands for 1871-1880; B stands for 1881-1890.

Massachusetts includes all areas of the state except the city of Boston.

## TABLE 3
## Massachusetts Non-College Lawyers: Recruiting Patterns (Paternal Occupation), 1870–1890

| | Massachusetts | | Boston | | Combined | |
|---|---|---|---|---|---|---|
| | A | B | A | B | A | B |
| Lawyers | 14.8% | 15.9% | 23.1% | 34.6% | 18.7% | 23.4% |
| Doctors | 6.8% | 2.4% | 6.2% | 1.8% | 6.5% | 2.2% |
| Ministers | 6.8% | 3.7% | 4.6% | 1.8% | 5.8% | 2.9% |
| Manufacturers | 10.8% | 9.8% | 3.1% | 3.6% | 7.2% | 7.3% |
| Retail-Wholesale | 5.4% | 8.5% | 13.8% | 18.2% | 9.3% | 12.4% |
| Mechanic-Laborer | 4.1% | 7.3% | 6.2% | 7.3% | 4.3% | 7.3% |
| Artisan-Machinist | 16.2% | 23.2% | 12.3% | 12.8% | 14.4% | 19.0% |
| Farmer | 14.8% | 13.4% | 4.6% | 1.8% | 10.1% | 8.8% |
| Merchant | 2.7% | 2.4% | 7.7% | 0 | 5.0% | 1.5% |
| Clerk-Salesman | 1.4% | 3.7% | 4.6% | 7.3% | 2.8% | 5.8% |
| Administrator | 1.4% | 1.2% | 3.1% | 3.6% | 2.2% | 2.2% |
| Other Business | 12.2% | 6.1% | 7.7% | 3.6% | 10.1% | 5.0% |
| Other Professional | 2.7% | 1.2% | 1.5% | 3.6% | 2.9% | 1.5% |
| Other | 0 | 1.2% | 1.5% | 0 | .7% | .7% |
| All Business | 32.5% | 28.0% | 35.4% | 29.0% | 33.8% | 28.4% |
| All Professional | 31.1% | 23.2% | 35.4% | 41.8% | 33.9% | 30.0% |

A stands for 1871-1880; B stands for 1881-1890.

Massachusetts includes all areas of the state except the city of Boston.

## TABLE 4
**Massachusetts Lawyers: Marriage Patterns (Father-in-law's Occupation), 1870–1890**

| | Massachusetts College Grads | | Boston College Grads | | All College Graduates | |
|---|---|---|---|---|---|---|
| | A | B | A | B | A | B |
| Lawyers | 10.1% | 8.8% | 19.7% | 11.5% | 14.8% | 10.5% |
| Doctors | 5.8% | 8.8% | 10.6% | 9.9% | 8.1% | 9.5% |
| Ministers | 4.4% | 2.9% | 4.5% | 13.1% | 4.4% | 9.5% |
| Manufacturer | 11.6% | 17.7% | 10.6% | 18.0% | 11.1% | 17.8% |
| Retail-Wholesaler | 15.9% | 20.6% | 12.1% | 13.1% | 14.1% | 15.7% |
| Mechanic-Laborer | 0 | 2.9% | 1.5% | 9 | .8% | 1.1% |
| Artisan-Machinist | 18.8% | 8.8% | 4.5% | 1.6% | 11.9% | 4.2% |
| Farmer | 4.4% | 2.9% | 3.1% | 0 | 3.7% | 1.1% |
| Merchant | 4.4% | 2.9% | 7.6% | 8.2% | 5.9% | 6.3% |
| Clerk-Salesman | 8.7% | 0 | 4.5% | 6.6% | 6.6% | 4.2% |
| Administrator | 0 | 5.9% | 9.1% | 4.9% | 4.4% | 5.3% |
| Other Business | 13.1% | 11.8% | 3.1% | 6.6% | 8.2% | 8.4% |
| Other Professional | 1.4% | 0 | 7.6% | 4.9% | 4.4% | 3.2% |
| Other | 1.4% | 5.9% | 1.5% | 1.6% | 1.5% | 3.2% |
| All Business | 45.0% | 58.9% | 42.5% | 50.8% | 43.7% | 53.5% |
| All Professional | 21.7% | 20.5% | 42.4% | 39.4% | 31.8% | 32.7% |

A stands for 1871-1880; B stands for 1881-1890.

## TABLE 5
## Massachusetts Lawyers: Geographic Factors, 1870

| County | Total | Born in Mass. | Born in U.S., Not Mass. | Foreign Born | Mass. Born Property Holders | U.S. Born Property Holders | Foreign Born Property Holders |
|---|---|---|---|---|---|---|---|
| Middlesex | 312 | 185(59.3%) | 114(36.5%) | 13(4.2%) | 120(64.9%) | 196(65.5%) | 9(69.2%) |
| Worcester | 86 | 66(76.7%) | 18(20.9%) | 2(2.4%) | 58(87.9%) | 72(85.7%) | 2(100%) |
| Norfolk | 128 | 105(82%) | 21(16.4%) | 2(1.6%) | 89(84.8%) | 103(81.7%) | 2(100%) |
| Suffolk | 301 | 187(62.1%) | 100(33.2%) | 14(4.7%) | 81(43.3%) | 126(43.9%) | 7(50%) |
| Berkshire | 49 | 35(71.4%) | 13(26.5%) | 1(2.1%) | 1(2.1%) | 33(94.3%) | 1(100%) |
| Hampshire | 24 | 16(66.6%) | 7(29.2%) | 1(4.2%) | 14(87.5%) | 20(87%) | 1(100%) |
| Plymouth | 35 | 35(100%) | 0 | 0 | 31(88.5%) | 0 | 0 |
| Barnstable | 15 | 12(80%) | 3(20%) | 0 | 10(83.3%) | 13(86.6%) | 0 |
| Essex | 144 | 108(75%) | 31(21.5%) | 5(3.5%) | 83(76.8%) | 108(77.7%) | 2(40%) |
| Bristol | 56 | 44(78.6%) | 11(19.6%) | 1(1.8%) | 36(81.8%) | 44(80%) | 1(100%) |
| Dukes | 4 | 4(100%) | 0 | 0 | 4(100%) | 4(100%) | 0 |
| Franklin | 22 | 12(54.5%) | 10(45.4%) | 0 | 10(83.3%) | 18(81.8%) | 0 |
| Hampden | 51 | 37(72.5%) | 13(25.5%) | 1(2%) | 30(81.1%) | 42(84%) | 0 |
| Nantucket | 3 | 3(100%) | 0 | 0 | 3(100%) | 3(100%) | 0 |
| Totals | 1230[A] | 849(69%) | 341(27.7%) | 40(3.3%) | 602(70.9%) | 793(66.6%) | 25(62.5%) |

A. The United States Census for 1870, pp. 674-75, reports 1,270 lawyers in Massachusetts. Assuming the printed census figure is correct, the author found 97 percent of the lawyers on Schedule 1, NARS microfilm. Thus these tables are based on a nearly complete record of all lawyers in Massachusetts in 1870.

**TABLE 6**
**Massachusetts Lawyers: Factors of Wealth, 1870**

| County | Property Holders | Non-Property Holders | Average Wealth of All | Average Wealth of Property Holders | Average Wealth of Ten Wealthiest | Median Wealth of Property Holders |
|---|---|---|---|---|---|---|
| Middlesex | 205(65.7%) | 107(34.3%) | $16,572 | $25,222 | $161,000 | $13,000 |
| Worcester | 74(86%) | 12(14%) | $24,457 | $28,424 | $111,050 | $12,600 |
| Norfolk | 105(82%) | 23(18%) | $30,211 | $36,829 | $205,300 | $13,000 |
| Suffolk | 133(44.2%) | 168(55.8%) | $22,858 | $51,731 | $329,800 | $17,500 |
| Berkshire | 45(91.8%) | 4(8.2%) | $20,042 | $21,824 | $70,460 | $13,000 |
| Hampshire | 21(87.5%) | 3(12.5%) | $37,995 | $43,423 | $89,300 | $18,000 |
| Plymouth | 31(88.5%) | 4(11.5%) | $21,952 | $24,785 | $63,150 | $9,000 |
| Barnstable | 13(86.6%) | 2(13.4%) | $37,445 | $43,205 | $56,000 | $7,500 |
| Essex | 110(76.4%) | 34(23.6%) | $16,777 | $21,963 | $132,400 | $10,000 |
| Bristol | 45(80.4%) | 11(19.6) | $12,005 | $14,940 | $41,350 | $11,000 |
| Dukes | 4(100%) | 0 | $5,225 | $5,225 | N/A | $3,600 |
| Franklin | 18(81.8%) | 4(18.2%) | $19,810 | $24,212 | $43,530 | $5,400 |
| Hampden | 42(82.4%) | 9(16.6%) | $27,726 | $33,667 | $109,300 | $11,500 |
| Nantucket | 3(100%) | 0 | $5,100 | $5,100 | N/A | $6,000 |
| Totals | 848(69%) | 381(31%) | $21,316<br>($26,219,754) | $32,053 | $82,997<br>($9,959,710) | |

## TABLE 7
## Massachusetts Lawyers: Age, Race, and Sex Factors, 1870

| County | Ave. Age | Ave. Age of Property Holders | Ave. Age of Non-Property Holders | Ave. Age of Ten Wealthiest Property Holders | Male | White |
|---|---|---|---|---|---|---|
| Middlesex | 42.8 | 44.5 | 39.5 | 51.2 | 100% | 100% |
| Worcester | 44.7 | 46.8 | 32 | 53.7 | 100% | 100% |
| Norfolk | 41 | 43.2 | 30.8 | 53.5 | 100% | 100% |
| Suffolk | 40.5 | 46.5 | 37.5 | 61.4 | 100% | 99.3% |
| Berkshire | 40.1 | 39.7 | 44 | 48.3 | 100% | 100% |
| Hampshire | 46.6 | 49.6 | 26 | 58 | 100% | 100% |
| Plymouth | 48.4 | 50.8 | 29.7 | 64.5 | 100% | 100% |
| Barnstable | 52.1 | 52.9 | 46.5 | 53.9 | 100% | 100% |
| Essex | 44.8 | 48.9 | 31.4 | 50.3 | 100% | 100% |
| Bristol | 45.5 | 47.9 | 35.2 | 52.4 | 100% | 98.2% |
| Dukes | 53.5 | 53.5 | N/A | N/A | 100% | 100% |
| Franklin | 44.3 | 44.7 | 42.7 | 47.9 | 100% | 100% |
| Hampden | 42.95 | 45 | 33.3 | 51.6 | 100% | 100% |
| Nantucket | 68.6 | 68.6 | 0 | N/A | 100% | 100% |
| Totals | 43.7 | 45.9 | 38.8 | 53.9 | 100% | 99.8% |

## TABLE 8
**Analysis of Harvard Law School Graduates in Select Counties, 1870**

| County | Total | Born in Mass. | Foreign Born | Property Holders | Average Wealth of All | Average Wealth of Property Holders | Average Age of All |
|---|---|---|---|---|---|---|---|
| Norfolk | 33(25.8%) | 30(90.9%) | 1(3%) | 29(87.9%) | $41,378 | $47,086 | 36.8 |
| Middlesex | 44(14.1%) | 32(72.7%) | 1(2.3%) | 24(54.5%) | $15,320 | $28,087 | 36.4 |
| Worcester | 13(15.1%) | 12(92.3%) | 0 | 12(92.3%) | $40,329 | $43,690 | 44.8 |
| Suffolk | 61(20.3%) | 47(77%) | 1(1.6%) | 18(29.5%) | $5,672 | $19,222 | 33.6 |
| Berkshire | 1(2%) | 1(100%) | 0 | 1(100%) | $15,000 | $15,000 | 52 |
| Essex | 19(13.2%) | 18(94.7%) | 0 | 17(89.5%) | $21,684 | $24,235 | 39.8 |
| Totals | 171(16.8%) | 140(82.5%) | 3(1.8%) | 101(59.5%) | $19,513 | $33,038 | 36.02 |

## Massachusetts Law School Graduates: (Paternal Occupation) Recruiting Patterns, 1870–1890

| | Boston University | Harvard Law School |
|---|---|---|
| Lawyer | 22.4% | 27.1% |
| Doctor | 4.6% | 6.8% |
| Minister | 5.7% | 3.1% |
| Manufacturer | 4.6% | 7.8% |
| Retail-Wholesale | 16.6% | 18.2% |
| Mechanic-Laborer | 6.9% | 2.1% |
| Artisan-Machinist | 14.9% | 3.7% |
| Farmer | 6.9% | 4.7% |
| Merchant | 5.7% | 10.4% |
| Clerk-Salesman | 4.6% | 5.2% |
| Administrator | 0 | 3.7% |
| Other Business | 4.0% | 4.2% |
| Other Professional | 2.3% | 3.0% |
| Other | .6% | 0 |
| All Business | 31.0% | 40.1% |
| All Professional | 35.1% | 40.0% |

## TABLE 10
## Massachusetts Law School Graduates: (Father-in-law's Occupation) Marriage Patterns, 1870–1890

| | Boston Univ. Law School | Harvard Law School |
|---|---|---|
| Lawyer | 8.9% | 26.3% |
| Doctor | 9.0% | 3.9% |
| Minister | 3.9% | 3.0% |
| Manufacturer | 14.9% | 9.2% |
| Retail-Wholesale | 22.4% | 5.3% |
| Mechanic-Laborer | 4.5% | 2.6% |
| Artisan-Machinist | 11.8% | 7.9% |
| Farmer | 3.0% | 0 |
| Merchant | 3.0% | 10.5% |
| Clerk-Salesman | 6.0% | 7.9% |
| Administrator | 4.5% | 5.3% |
| Other Business | 6.0% | 6.6% |
| Other Professional | 3.0% | 6.6% |
| Other | 0 | 0 |
| All Business | 44.8% | 30.3% |
| All Professional | 24.8% | 39.8% |

**Geographical Mobility of Massachusetts Law School Graduates, 1870–1890**

| Geographic Location | Boston University | Harvard Law School |
|---|---|---|
| Practiced in Native Town | 107(28.8%) | 93(28.2%) |
| Practiced in One Town | 351(94.6%) | 300(90.9%) |
| Practiced in Two Towns | 15(4.1%) | 25(7.6%) |
| Practiced in Three or More Towns | 5(1.3%) | 5(1.5%) |
| Moved into State | 87(23.5%) | 59(17.9%) |
| Moved out of State | 11(2.9%) | 26(7.9%) |
| Foreign Born | 16(4.3%) | 12(3.6%) |
| Number of Graduates | 371 | 330 |

## TABLE 12
## Institutional Distribution of College Graduates (Lawyers), 1870–1890

| | Harvard Law Grads | Boston U. Law Grads | Boston Lawyers | Non-Boston Lawyers | All Mass. Lawyers |
|---|---|---|---|---|---|
| Harvard | 217 | 61 | 431 | 99 | 530 |
| Amherst | 10 | 24 | 31 | 52 | 83 |
| Boston U. | 0 | 12 | 14 | 12 | 26 |
| Dartmouth | 5 | 15 | 34 | 29 | 63 |
| Brown | 4 | 19 | 30 | 26 | 56 |
| Bowdoin | 2 | 8 | 29 | 11 | 40 |
| Yale | 5 | 9 | 23 | 20 | 43 |
| Boston C. | 0 | 10 | 9 | 3 | 12 |
| Holy Cross | 3 | 10 | 6 | 24 | 30 |
| Others | 12 | 42 | 82 | 86 | 168 |
| Total | 258[a] | 210[b] | 688[c] | 362[d] | 1050[e] |

a. 78.2 percent of HLS graduates were college graduates.

b. 56.6 percent of BULS graduates were college graduates; 66.8 percent of BULS and HLS graduates were college graduates.

c. 63.6 percent of the lawyers practicing in Boston were college graduates.

d. 50 percent of the lawyers practicing in Massachusetts outside of Boston were college graduates.

e. 58.1 percent of all the lawyers admitted to practice in Massachusetts between 1870 and 1890 were college graduates. 25.9 percent of all the college graduate lawyers admitted to practice in Massachusetts between 1870 and 1890 were graduates of Boston University Law School or Harvard Law School. 38.8 percent of all the lawyers admitted to practice in Massachusetts between 1870 and 1890 were graduates of Boston University Law School or Harvard Law School.

## NOTES

1. United States Census, 1870 and 1900, National Archives; Gerard W. Gawalt, *The Promise of Power: The Emergence of the Legal Profession in Massachusetts, 1760–1840* (Westport, Conn., 1978), Tables 1 and 7.
2. U.S. Census, 1870; Worcester, Mass., Assessors Records, 1890 and 1900.
3. U.S. Census, 1870; Gawalt, *Promise*, 108–15, 176–79; John T. Cumbler, *Working-Class Community in Industrial America: Work, Service, and Struggle in Two Industrial Cities, 1880–1930* (Westport, Conn., 1979), 25–27.
4. Massachusetts Supreme Judicial Court, *Cases Argued and Determined in the Supreme Judicial Court of Massachusetts* (Boston, 1872–1891), vols. 103–52. For the emergence of the commuter, see Samuel B. Warner, *Street Car Suburbs: The Process of Growth in Boston, 1870–1900* (Cambridge, 1962).
5. Wright, Brown, & Quimby Papers, Baker Library, Harvard University; Dun & Bradstreet Records, Attorneys Book, Baker Library, Harvard University; Walcott-Pickman Papers, Massachusetts Historical Society.
6. George A. Torrey, *A Lawyer's Recollection in and out of Court* (Boston, 1910), 82–83; John R. Thayer, Autobiographical Letter in *Record of the Class of Sixty-Nine, Yale College, 1894–1909* (New Haven, 1910), 118; Worcester, Mass., Assessors Records, 1900; Dun & Bradstreet Records, Attorneys Book, Baker Library, Harvard University; Peter C. Bacon Papers, American Antiquarian Society; John H. Clifford Papers, Massachusetts Historical Society.
7. Joseph H. Choate to his mother, March 21, 1859, quoted in Edward Martin, *Life of Joseph Choate*, 2 vols. (New York, 1920), 1:212.
8. Louis Brandeis to William H. Dunbar, August 19, 1896, quoted in Alpheus T. Mason, *Brandeis: A Free Man's Life* (New York, 1946), 83–87, 691; "What Great Lawyers Receive for Their Work," *American Legal News* 27 (September 1916):21–26.
9. Oakey Hall, "A Noted Law Firm," *Green Bag* 11 (October 1899):460–65, quote on 460; Richard Henry Dana III to Richard Henry Dana, Jr., July 22, 1881, Dana Papers, Massachusetts Historical Society; Harvard Class of 1879, *Report* (Cambridge, Mass., 1929), 266; Harvard Class of 1886, *Report* (Cambridge, Mass., 1936), 401; Jerold S. Auerbach, *Unequal Justice: Lawyers and Social Change in Modern America* (New York, 1976), 21.
10. Gawalt, *Promise*, Table 5; and Table 1.
11. Tables 2 and 3; Gawalt, *Promise*, Table 20, and 171–74. Particularly precipitous was the decline in the sons of ministers entering the legal profession—perhaps a reflection of ministers' reduced status and income.
12. Table 4; Gawalt, *Promise*, Table 21, and 174–76.
13. *Rules of Admission to the Bar in the Several States and Territories of the United States* (St. Paul, Minn., 1902).
14. See Marcia G. Synnott, *The Half-Opened Door: Discrimination and Admissions at Harvard, Yale, and Princeton, 1900–1970* (Westport, Conn., 1979); and Harold S. Wechsler, *The Qualified Student: A History of Selective College Admissions in America* (New York, 1977).
15. James B. Cullen, *The Story of the Irish in Boston* (Boston, 1889), 285–300; Geoffrey Blodgett, *The Gentle Reformers: Massachusetts Democrats in the Cleveland Era* (Cambridge, Mass., 1966), 149.
16. U.S. Census, 1870 and 1890.

17. U.S. Census, 1870; Cullen, *Irish in Boston*, 285–300.

18. G. S. Hilliard to J. Henry Hill, August 7 and 15, 1862, and Matthew McCafferty to Hilliard, August 14, 1862, Hill Papers, American Antiquarian Society; Torrey, *Recollection*, 95.

19. U.S. Census, 1870, and Tables 5–7.

20. U.S. Census, 1870; William I. Davis, *Bench and Bar of the Commonwealth of Massachusetts*, 2 vols. (Boston, 1895), 1:527; Walter J. Leonard, *Black Lawyers Training and Results: Then and Now* (Boston, 1977), 103–4, 108–15.

21. U.S. Census, 1870 and 1890; *Green Bag* 3 (September 1891):441; *Fitchburg Sentinel*, January 1, 4, 6, and 7, 1898; Charles F. Thwing, "What Becomes of College Women," *North American Review* 161 (November 1895):546–53; Beatrice Doerschuch, *Women in the Law: An Analysis of Training, Practice, and Salaries* (New York, 1920), 19, 24–25, 57, 118, 122; Boston University, *Yearbook*, 1874–1900; Barbara J. Harris, *Beyond Her Sphere: Women and the Professions in American History* (Westport, Conn., 1978), 116–17; Duncan Crow, *The Edwardian Woman* (New York, 1978), 140–41.

22. David F. Noble, *America by Design: Science, Technology, and the Rise of Corporate Capitalism* (New York, 1977), 39, 40–51; Stephen Thernstrom, *The Other Bostonians: Poverty and Progress in the American Metropolis, 1880–1970* (Cambridge, 1973), 52–57; Joseph Kett, *The Rites of Passage* (New York, 1977), 151–52.

23. See Tables 1, 8, and 11.

24. See Table 12; Gawalt, *Promise*, Table 19.

25. Bailey B. Burritt, "Professional Distribution of College and University Graduates," *U.S. Bureau of Education Bulletin* 19 (1912):79–114; Gawalt, *Promise*, Tables 14–17. These figures were compiled from the 1870–1890 catalogs of Harvard College, Boston University, Bowdoin College, Yale University, Dartmouth College, Bangor Theological Seminary, and Newton Theological Seminary.

26. Ibid.

27. Lawrence M. Friedman, *A History of American Law* (New York, 1973), 526; Gary B. Nash, "The Philadelphia Bench and Bar, 1800–1861," *Comparative Studies in Society and History* 3 (1965), 203, 207–8.

28. See Tables 8 and 9; and Cullen, *Irish in Boston*, 285–300.

29. See Tables 10 and 11.

30. See Table 8.

31. Jerome E. Carlin, *Lawyers on Their Own: A Study of Individual Practitioners in Chicago* (New Brunswick, 1962), 20–21. See also Charles Warren, *History of Harvard Law School*, 2 vols. (New York, 1908), 2:407; William J. Johnson, *Schooled Lawyers: A Study in the Clash of Professional Cultures* (New York, 1978), 42, 140–41; Joel Seligman, *The High Citadel: The Influence of Harvard Law School* (Boston, 1978), passim.

32. *American Law Review* 5 (October 1870):177.

33. See Noble, *America by Design*.

34. Ephraim W. Gurney to Charles Eliot, 1883, quoted in Arthur G. Sutherland, *The Law at Harvard* (Cambridge, 1967), 187–90.

35. George R. Swasey, "The Boston University Law School," *Green Bag* 1 (January 1889):54–65, quote on 54–55.

36. Henry J. Bigelow, *Medical Education in America* (Cambridge, 1871), 13.

37. Correspondence of James B. Thayer, James B. Thayer Papers, Harvard Law Library.

38. This traditional view was first established by Roscoe Pound and has been continued by many legal scholars—most recently, for example, by Jerold Auerbach, Jerome E. Carlin, Lawrence Friedman, Gary Nash, Joel Seligman, and David Wigdor.

*GORDON MORRIS BAKKEN*

# *Industrialization and the Nineteenth-Century California Bar*

The industrialization of California in the late nineteenth century had substantial impact upon the urban bar. The coming of both the railroad and manufacturing to such cities as San Francisco created new business for resident attorneys and gave the emigrant bar incentives to specialize their practices. Land title and debt collection business accounted for the bulk of fees for most of the rest of the California bar, especially in urban areas. The growth of regulation in the late nineteenth century, however, changed the nature of practice for specialists and general practitioners alike.

This study is based upon two basic types of sources. First, in order to discuss the California bar, we must identify the members of the bar and analyze their characteristics. City, county, and bar histories provide biographical information on the nineteenth century and produce a sample of 1,168 persons admitted to the bar through 1900.[1] Although city and county "mug books" and bar directories contain the biases of the editors at the time of the collection of the data, the biographical facts do provide information sufficiently useful for computer analysis. The second source of information on the nineteenth-century bar is manuscript materials on what the lawyers did. The first type of source provides context and the second type of source provides evidence of behavior. In addition, of course, the secondary works on California's social and economic development provide additional context for the analysis of the behavior of the nineteenth-century California bar.

One-half of the attorneys in the sample practiced law in San Francisco or Los Angeles. The fact is certainly not surprising since the two cities accounted for most of the business of the state and, in the late nineteenth century, dominated the financial, manufacturing, and distribution sectors of the state's economy. Furthermore, as an indication of the impact of industrialization and financial concentration, 51.9 percent of the San Francisco bar entered practice in that city during the period from 1889 to 1900 and 66.2 percent of their counterparts did so in Los Angeles during the same period.

Lawyers as well as miners and merchants flocked to San Francisco in the 1850s. The *San Francisco Herald* reported sixty-four attorneys practicing in the city in 1855.[2] Heading the list were Henry W. Halleck, Frederick Billings, and Archibald C. Peachy, members of the city's first large law firm. In fact, Halleck, Peachy, Billings, and Park had erected a "large new building" on the corner of Washington and Montgomery Streets in 1853 and had taken in Kilduff and Company as tenants to operate a saloon.[3] Los Angeles developed in the last quarter of the century, and the boom of the 1880s drew attorneys as well as developers. A second factor was the depression of the 1870s, which turned attorneys vistas away from the Bay Area. A San Francisco attorney, J. M. Kennedy, wrote to John D. Bicknell in Los Angeles in 1874 explaining the problem:

> I have been unable as yet to get into any Law Office, although I have been introduced to many of the best firms here. The trouble is that I being a stranger and not acquainted with the general vocation of the practice in a large city, would not be of sufficient assistance to justify them in paying me enough to live upon. They can get plenty of office boys living with their parents for $10 per month and here again there are hundreds of young fellows just standing in the profession and living at home who are glad to accept positions in Law Offices for the purpose of studying, so that I have concluded to give up the practice of Law and try something else.[4]

But San Francisco was not the only area having economic trouble. C. W. Treasher, a Neosho, Missouri, attorney, asked Bicknell about Los Angeles in 1874 because "law business here has fallen off more than one-half since you left [1872] and there is very little money in the country except what come from lead and Zinc."[5] Treasher's reaping of chaff story was followed by another attorney's inquiry. J. M. Richardson's 1875 letter asked whether "a lawyer [could] make a living there [Los Angeles]."[6] Things were no better in Springfield, Missouri, than Neosho. Another Springfield attorney, P. H. Ward, "formerly from South Carolina," wrote Bicknell in 1875 that he was "contemplating settling in California to practice my profession—law." He had noticed that "Los Angeles [was] a town offering as good inducements to Attys as any place of its size in the State."[7] Los Angeles appeared to have promise.

The birthplaces of these lawyers were concentrated in California, the midwest, and the northeast. Twenty-seven and one tenth percent of the nineteenth-century bar were born in California. These men were born in the 1870s and entered the practice of law in the last decade of the century. The emigrant bar came predominantly from the midwest; 26.7 percent of the bar came from the states of Illinois, Indiana, Iowa, Michigan, Minnesota, Ohio, and Wisconsin. Illinois with 8 percent and Ohio with 5.8 percent of the state bar lead the region. Seventeen and six tenths percent of the bar hailed from the northeastern states of Connecticut, Maine, Massachusetts, New Hampshire, New Jersey, New York, Pennsylvania, and Vermont; of these states, New York produced 8 percent and Pennsylvania produced 4.1 percent of the California bar in the nineteenth century. The old South did not contribute as many attorneys as did the states of Kentucky, Tennessee, and Missouri. Alabama was home for .5 percent of the bar, Georgia .8 percent, North Carolina .3 percent, South Carolina .8 percent, Mississippi .9 percent, Louisiana .5 percent, and Maryland .6 percent compared with 1.7 percent from Kentucky, 1.7 percent from Tennessee, and 3.5 percent from Missouri. The foreign-born even outnumbered the southerners, numbering 7.9 percent of the bar, the bulk (2.7 percent) from Canada. The large numbers born in California were, of course, second generation Californians going off to law study and returning home to practice. The emigrant bar came to California lured by the prospects of opportunity.

The speculation in land and the uncertainty of land titles in California were factors in making money dealing in both land and land titles. In the latter, attorneys were expert. H. F. Felland of Springfield, Missouri, expressed the sentiment well to John D. Bicknell in 1872: "I am of the opinion [that] there is money to be made by engaging in the. . . business [of] investigating titles and getting up an abstract in connection with some reliable person living in Washington."[8] The land title business was profitable for the Washington attorney as well, as John B. Clark reported to Bicknell in 1876: "My prospects are most flattering. I am getting business far beyond my most sanguine expectations."[9] The rampant land speculation in San Francisco and Los Angeles created a burgeoning business for lawyers. John Center purchased a downtown San Francisco lot for $1,000 down, a six-week note at 3 percent per month, and a long-term note of five months for $2,500 at the same interest.[10] Los Angeles was little different. Benjamin D. Wilson purchased numerous city lots in the 1850s for $300 to $4,500 each on terms of 2 to 5 percent interest per month for eighteen days to six months.[11] Cave Johnson Couts accurately observed in 1852 that "speculations in land is rife."[12] In the basin, the boom of the 1880s was of the same character. As William Warner reported to his family, "the people are getting the Los Angeles fever. Billy Miner was down 3 or 4 weeks and in that short time he made $5,000 speculating in property."[13] The speculation and its accompanying frenzied transactions often created errors that required the services of an attorney.

Haste in transactions occasionally created problems of title that in turn created opportunity for the members of the California bar. John D. Goodwin, a Plumas County attorney, wrote to his "Friend Smith" in 1884 concerning a note and mortgage, "the former [was] all right but the later [was] all wrong" because the clerk had "failed to copy either of the notes into the mortgage correctly. . . nor did he copy your names to the notes."[14] John Markey, the Monterey County undersheriff and former county clerk, lamented to his client, David Jacks, a substantial landowner and entrepreneur, that "it is hard to tell what is included in your descriptions [in deeds], if anything."[15] On occasion, property boundary lines such as "an oak standing on the east and in contact with rocks forming the first rocky point on the south side of the Meadow Valley" and "the Rocky Wall at the San Jose Indian Village" were not as clear with time as they were when the seller's eye set them to paper.[16] Such was the stuff of lawsuits and lawyers' fees. The uncertainty of titles was only a single element in the perception of lawyers about opportunity in California; the combination of law practice and speculation in lands gave opportunity its essence. O. H. Picher, a Joplin, Missouri, attorney ably saw the connection in 1885 when he wrote to John D. Bicknell that his father desired that he "join him in investing to some extent in your country." But moving to California was no simple decision in 1885; rather, "it [was] a very serious matter to make such a change." It would be difficult "making a new acquaintance and building up a new practice." However, there was money to be "made there in law and land." So concluding, Picher inquired about buying part of Bicknell's practice or forming an association "for the purpose of dealing in land."[17] The alternative to law practice in California was dealing in real estate and it was equally attractive and lucrative.

The lawyers of the California bar of the nineteenth century were well educated persons. Seventy-six and eight-tenths percent of the members of the bar had attended college. More important, 40.8 percent had attended a law school, and 35 percent had graduated. Jesse W. Lilienthal, for example, graduated from the University of Cincinnati in 1872 and then went to the Harvard Law School, graduating in 1876. Lilienthal entered practice in New York in 1876 and continued in the profession until 1893 when he hung out his shingle in San Francisco.[18] John T. Harrington followed a similar educational path, but to a rural practice in California. Harrington was born in Shelby County, Kentucky, in 1843, attended college, served in the Confederate army, returned from the war, and entered the University of Louisville Law School. He graduated in 1866 and set up a practice in Louisville. In 1870, Harrington settled in Colusa, California, and by 1880 he had "accumulated a considerable property by his profession and through speculations." Harrington owned "over two thousand acres of land situated in different parts of the county [which comprised] three or four desirable ranches."[19]

Second generation Californians similarly went to college and law school. For example, Arthur Wellsley Hill was born in Eureka in 1864, attended the University of California, and graduated from the Hastings Law School in San Francisco in 1893. Hill passed the bar prior to graduation and entered practice in the City by the Bay, but returned to his home town to practice his profession. In 1897, he won election to the California assembly and later served as deputy district attorney and county district attorney.[20] Thomas E. Haven was another San Francisco attorney who was a California native. He was born in Downieville and educated at the Hopkins Academy in Oakland, graduating in 1883. Haven then went east to attend Williams College. After graduation in 1887, he returned to California and graduated in Hastings' class of 1890.[21]

The alternative form of legal education during the century was "reading law."

This form of education consisted of either self-study or study in the law office of a practitioner. Even with a college education and law study, reading law in California also was a felt need for some desirous of practicing in California. David Murray of Delphi, New York, wrote to John D. Bicknell in 1877 that he was a college graduate (1876) and had read law in the office of the county judge and with his father, "one of the Justices of the Supreme Court of the State." He had read "thoroughly most of the leading elementary works," but wanted to read law in California. Murray thought that he "could pass any examination for admission to practice after a few months of study." That study would give him "time to become familiar with the practice of the Court."[22] On July 16, 1877, Murray accepted the position of clerk in Bicknell's law office.

T. K. McDowell of Grand Ronde, Oregon, was not so fortunate. McDowell wrote to Bicknell in 1872, confiding that "my education I fear is deficient as I have never studied Latin nor had that drilling of the mind which is consequent to a collegiate course. At the same time, however, I cannot say that my education is much more limited than many of the lawyers that succeed in the business." McDowell hit a covering law thesis here, as others would observe, that education was not always a guarantee of success in law practice. He continued, "I should have prepared myself by study—at least on Contracts and Evidence as Blackstone and Kent are about as far as I got when the question would come up whether I should attend law school or not. In studying law again I should prefer your plan explained to me several times in Greenfield [Missouri], to wit, search all the authors on questions of law, instead of reading by rote a volume at a time." With education behind him sometime in the future, McDowell saw the pot of gold: "I may be wrong but it does seem to me that the practice of law and the chances connected with that profession is the best plan for me to make money." McDowell saw the elephant and came to California in 1873, but turned to farming and herding sheep near Santa Ana.[23] John James Cairns was a cattle rancher who read law at home when convenient and later in a San Jose law office. He was admitted to the bar in 1900 and opened a practice in San Jose. Cairns, without benefit of "that drilling of the mind," nonetheless practiced in San Jose for seven years before moving to Eureka where he became a referee in bankruptcy for both Humboldt and Del Norte counties and city attorney for both Blue Lake and Eureka.[24]

Other members of the California bar were fortunate to have fathers in the practice of law. George Flournoy's father, also named George, was a University of Georgia graduate who had practiced in Austin, Texas, had been elected attorney general of that state, and had been a colonel in the Sixteenth Texas Infantry during the Civil War. In 1867, he returned to practice in Galveston. His son George was born in Austin in 1863 and, after receiving "a classical education" at Jesuit College in Washington, D.C., went on to graduate from the University of Georgia. Colonel Flournoy moved his practice to San Francisco in 1879, and his son joined him to read law. George then attended Hastings Law School for two years, gaining admission to the bar in 1884. He entered practice in Bakersfield in that year and returned to San Francisco in 1885. Seven years later, Flournoy returned to Bakersfield and set up practice.[25] William N. Goodwin's father, John D., was one of Plumas County's first attorneys and became one of its most substantial landowners. William attended the public schools of Plumas County, Wright's Classical School in Oakland, Hopkins Grammar School in New Haven, Connecticut, and Yale University. Then he returned to his home town of Quincy to read law with his father and entered practice with him. In 1892, William Goodwin moved to San Francisco where he remained until 1903.[26]

Jesse William Curtis had a family of lawyers to draw to in California. His father, Israel Coleman Curtis, had attended Miami Universtiy of Ohio and had read law in Indiana before moving to Iowa. He was district attorney of Marion County, Iowa, 1857–1860 and moved to California in 1864, settling in San Bernardino. His brother, W. J. Curtis, was educated at Central College of Iowa, a college his father had helped to found, and in his father's law office. When the family moved to California, W. J. Curtis was a partner in his father's firm. Jesse was born in California and graduated from the University of Southern California and the University of Michigan Law School in 1891. He then joined the firm of Curtis, Oster, and Curtis in San Bernardino. In 1914, Jesse Curtis won election to the Superior Court bench and reelection in 1920.[27]

Although the advantages of having a family to study law with were apparent, few California attorneys had the luxury. Only 20 percent of the members of the nineteenth-century bar arrived with their parents, and fewer were fortunate enough to have local relatives in the profession. Interestingly, the fact of having a practicing relative did not limit education. As evident from the Flournoy, Goodwin, and Curtis family experiences, education—including legal education—was highly valued.

More than one-third of California's attorneys had been admitted to the bar of another state prior to admission in California; 35.6 percent of the lawyers in the sample had been admitted in the United States and abroad prior to hanging out a shingle in California. Midwestern lawyers made up the most significant portion of the emigrant bar. The states of Illinois, Indiana, Iowa, Michigan, Minnesota, Missouri, Ohio, and Wisconsin contributed 17 percent of the sample to the nineteenth-century California bar. Like John Dustin Bicknell, a Greenfield, Missouri, attorney, they sold or left their practices to try their profession in a new state. New York attorneys made up 4.1 percent of the California bar. Of the foreign attorneys, Canadian lawyers were the largest group, but only 1 percent of the bar. These experienced lawyers located predominantly within Los Angeles or in one of the smaller growing communities of the late 1880s or 1890s like Bakersfield; 32 percent located in Los Angeles and 32 percent in the smaller communities during the period. Only 21 percent moved to San Francisco, 10 percent to Sacramento, and 9 percent to San Diego.

The fact that the major period of emigration and admission to the California bar was 1889 to 1900 correlated, in part, with the attraction of the boom of the

1880s in Los Angeles and the rise of industrialization. The speculation in Los Angeles land was, of course, an attraction. The profits were well known. William H. Avery of Lamar, Missouri, read about them in his home-town newspaper, the *Weekly Miner*. The story chronicled transactions involving a single tract on Spring Street in 1881. It was sold to J. F. Ponder for $5,600, then to a Mr. Hubbell for $6,000, Hubbel to Spence for $11,000, Spence to Ponder and Jones for $20,000, and finally, after being held for six months, to John Bryson for $18,500.[28]

But the boom did not last; in 1888, it was over. John Mohler Studebaker summed it up very well in an 1888 letter to Bicknell: "I think the California real estate craze gave me my belly full, and it will last me some time. Mr. Monroe. . .he was like many others—a great enthusiast on the future of California, and did not realize that lightning would strike as soon as it did."[29] Monroe was Studebaker's real estate agent in California and left him with a great pile of paper and few profits.

Although the profits and fees from real estate were gone, the railroad was by then a significant part of California business and legal fees. The Southern Pacific Company law department headed by Creed Haymond parcelled out substantial business and fees to attorneys, including Bicknell. Finally, there was that other tangible attraction for lawyers to move to California, the weather. As Milton Smith of Ithaca, New York, told Bicknell in 1888, "I like a milder climate than we have here and expect to locate at Los Angeles after Nov." Smith was an 1887 graduate of Cornell and had one year of clerkship under his belt when he inquired of Bicknell for a position in his Los Angeles office. John D. Bryan, a Las Cruces, New Mexico Territory, attorney, saw another tangible advantage in moving his practice to California—its schools and churches. As he told John D. Bicknell in a letter, he was thinking of moving to Los Angeles "where I can have the benefit of good schools and churches. I have two boys to educate and my family are Catholics. I understood that in your city, there are good schools and that the Catholics are well represented."[30] California was truly a state of opportunity.

Just as California's lawyers had come from many states, they came from many previous employment experiences; 13.9 percent of the sample had employment experiences prior to becoming lawyers. The occupations were many. School teacher-administrator was the leading prior occupation constituting 4.6 percent of the total bar; 2.1 percent had experiences in journalism, and 1.4 percent as miners. Three members of the bar were bankers, two were railroad executives, one was a corporate executive, eight were merchants, one was a pharmacist, one was a physician, five were civil engineers, one was an insurance executive, and one was a minister. Nine members of the bar had been professional military men prior to taking up the practice of law. Other attorneys, however, had more humble beginnings; one was a hotel clerk, another was a tanner, six were ranchers, seven were farmers, eight were clerks, one was a livery stable worker, another was a salesman, one was in construction, and another was a farm laborer.

John S. Beard tried his hand at many professions and tasks. Beard was admitted to the Pennsylvania bar on April 7, 1857 and practiced in the Keystone state until 1859. Then he moved to Oregon and engaged in mining until 1862 when he moved to the mines of Siskiyou County, California. In 1864 and 1865, Beard exchanged his miner's tools for those of the butchering trade. Then, in 1865, he started another career as a grammar school teacher and continued in the classroom until 1872 when he was admitted to practice. The people of Siskiyou County made him their district attorney in 1876 and their Superior Court Judge in 1884. Beard brought a wealth of experience to the bench.[31]

One hundred sixty-four attorneys in the sample listed concurrent employment. Banking dominated the concurrent occupation categories; thirty-one (2.7 percent) of the members of the bar held positions with banking concerns in California. Harry L. Titus, a San Diego attorney, while in private practice with John D. Works and James A. Gibson, was vice president of the Coronado Bank.[32] Jackson Alpheus Graves, a pioneer Los Angeles attorney and partner of Henry O'Melveny, had extensive dealings with Isaias W. Hellman, Sr., president of the Farmers and Merchants Bank of Los Angeles and became its vice-president in 1903 and its president from 1920 to 1933. Attorneys also pursued concurrent careers in journalism (24), as corporate executives (16), law professors (15), ranchers (10), teachers (9), and fruit and vegetable company executives (7). Six lawyers in the sample became railroad executives and an equal number pursued mining and real estate occupations. The distribution of these concurrently employed attorneys was not surprising. Seventy-seven lawyers (47 percent) in the sample of the concurrently employed resided outside Los Angeles, San Francisco, Sacramento, or San Diego. Eleven of the twenty-four journalists worked for or owned newspapers outside the metropolitan areas. Eight were ranchers, five of the nine were teachers, four were farmers, and all three general store owners resided in the smaller towns. L. Gill, a Leon, California, attorney, also concerned himself with procuring grass for his ranching operation by soliciting a lease agreement from another attorney, John D. Bicknell, in 1890 at $25 per acre for "this year's grass. . .cash down."[33] Sixty-one percent of the bankers/attorneys did business in the smaller towns. Given the fact that the practice of law in rural California could be less financially rewarding than in the larger cities, the frequency distributions are about as expected.

In the fifty-year period under study, the practice of law changed. The first decade found lawyers encountering major problems just in finding the law. Law books were in short supply; legal forms were even scarcer. This support problem only complicated the difficulties of determining title to land and collecting debt, the two major sources of fees for attorneys during the century. Finally, the rise of industrialization created the opportunity for employment as well as ingenuity in practice.

The decade of the 1850s found California lawyers without the aid of substantial law libraries, but they worked diligently to ameliorate the situation. John Currey, a San Francisco attorney, wrote to Amos Catlin, a Sacramento lawyer, regarding an 1850 case as follows: "The action against the Dana is as we would say *Case* for *negligently* running over the plaintiff's boat. You had better get hold of Cowen's Treatise (Mr. Winans has a copy at Sacramento City) and see what is said under 'Trespass on the case' on this subject. See also the question of Damages in same book, and in Greenleaf on Evidence (Tarr has my copy)." Obviously, Currey had loaned out some books and was very cognizant of the location of others. He continued: "You can find quite a variety of lawbooks at Col Zubriskie's office." But Currey had needs too: "I shall want a few of my books again, to wit: Abbott of Shipping and such Laws of California as you can spare." Currey borrowed as well: "I did not mention that I would like to have Greenleaf's Evidence. It belongs to D. R. Wright and he spoke to me about returning it."[34] W. L. Dudley arrived in California with the rush of 1849. In April 1851, he saw that prospecting with the law could yield more than the pick, so he returned to New Hampshire to get his law library. Dudley landed in California again in May 1852, and set up his practice in Mokelumne Hill.[35] But getting the law books to California was only half the battle. Joseph W. Winans, who had Cowen's Treatise, as Currey had noted, was another forty-niner who practiced in Sacramento. In 1852, the building in which he practiced and kept his law library burned down. Winans went to San Francisco and scoured the city for books to constitute another law library. Having assembled his precious cargo, Winans returned to Sacramento and there guarded his library night and day from fire and theft. One night when Winans was sleeping with his treatises, however, a rain storm destroyed the building's roof and his library.[36] While heaven was a place to store up treasure, heaven's earthly fruits could do greater and swifter damage to law practices than the worms of time.

But lawyers organized to overcome the ravages of nature and to fulfill the needs of the profession. The San Francisco Law Library opened on August 1, 1853, with over 2,500 books on the shelves.[37] The Los Angeles Bar Association formed to fund a law library, and in 1886, the Law Library of Los Angeles was incorporated issuing 300 shares of stock offered at $100 each to any attorney wishing to use the library. In 1891, the Board of Law Library Trustees purchased the library of 4,649 volumes and opened the stacks to the public.[38] One problem the corporation had was the failure of members to pay their $100 yearly assessment in a timely manner.[39]

The search for California law was often as demanding as finding law books in general. John D. Bicknell worked with L. W. Mason of Newark, New Jersey, to acquire a set of the California *Reports*. Mason went to New York to look for a set and, "after considerable hunting," found "a set (44 vols.) for $300."[40] Even with the *Reports* in hand, specialized questions required special treatises or digests. For example, in seeking the answer to a federal mining law question, the firm of R. W. Scott and V. Montgomery of Anaheim asked John D. Bicknell in 1879: "Has there been a decision either in this state, Nevada, or Colorado, giving a construction to the latter clause of 'Sec. 2324 regulations made by miners' United States Statutes, Act May 10, A.D. [1882?] particularly as to work by copartners, notice by publication, to parties failing to perform labor required, their forfeiture of interest in mines, etc., etc., etc." The case they were handling was in Arizona Territory, and they wrote Bicknell "not having the authorities at hand."[41]

By the 1880's the transportation network enabled the purchase of law books and the Bancroft-Whitney Company of San Francisco provided a local publisher and distributor for the profession. During the 1880s, Bancroft-Whitney stationery proudly proclaimed: "The Survival of the Fittest—A Trinity of Reports Selected and Annotated." This was the marketing slogan for the *American Decisions and Digests*, 1760-1869 (103 vols.); the *American Reports, Digests and Index*, 1869-1888 (63 vols.); and the *American State Reports* (6 vols. per annum).[42] But even as late as 1889, M. B. Beattie, an attorney in the office of Stephen M. White of Los Angeles, would have to send a letter of introduction to John D. Bicknell for a law clerk in the office to borrow a copy of Kent's *Commentaries*.[43]

The fittest lawyer did not survive by law books alone; he thrived on information. To obtain information, lawyers often had to rely upon other members of the profession. The information system was rudimentary with lawyers exchanging letters of inquiry. When John D. Bicknell wanted information on the contents of a judgment, for example, he wrote to Robert Leslie. Leslie replied from Julian City: "Gold coin is not mentioned in the judgment nor in the complaint of Thomas Carlisle vs. J. T. Gower. The Docket is in such a bungled state that is hardly possible to read it as Murphy is a most miserable scribe. The note I cannot find among his papers and suppose it must be lost as his children have free access to his desk."[44] Other records were in better condition. The firm of Luce, McDonald, and Torrance of San Diego "examined the judgment roll and record of proceedings in [the] action," examined the abstract of title, and interviewed the attorney that had appeared for one of the defendants before giving Bicknell needed information on his case.[45] Lawyers also learned about legal developments through the popular press. T. H. Laine, a San Jose attorney, wrote to Bicknell in 1889 that he was "engaged in the investigation of the rights of Southern Pacific RR Co. to lands in our part of the State and observed that there is a suit pending in the Circuit court of your district by the U.S. questioning [the] Co.'s right to any land under their grant and to set their patents aside."[46] Gathering information pursuant to litigation was a continuing problem, and missives of inquiry dominate the manuscript record of nineteenth-century practitioners.

Another information mechanism in use was the referral system. Lawyers wrote one another to promote business. They advertised themselves by letter, letterhead, and bold-letter print in the local press. An attorney named Sexton of Burt and Sexton of Oroville wrote to John D. Goodwin in Quincy soliciting referrals. He told Goodwin that they had formed a partnership

> for the purpose of assisting any poor devil to swindle any other poor devil, provided one first aforesaid has costs—or to assist any poor devil to get swindled provided he is willing

to pay for such a luxury. In fact we might indulge in something of a swindle ourselves, provided we could see spoundilic[k]s gleaming in silvery & golden sheen in sufficient quantities to cast a respectable rainbow here over the dark cloud of the swindle—Eh? In short we are going to work and if assiduous & attentive, labor will command success. . . .[47]

John B. Clark, Jr., asked John D. Bicknell to "give [him] a list of attorneys, with their P.O. addresses in Southern & other parts of California and Territories" so that he could send them his "cards and circulars."[48] Other attorneys went to the top to obtain referrals. H. W. Latham, a Los Angeles attorney, had Collis P. Huntington on his side. Huntington wrote to John D. Bicknell from New York telling him to "let him attend to any Southern Pacific Company business that you may have to place outside of your own office."[49] Lawyers knew that one had to get the client in order to grasp the spoundulicks.

Once the client was in hand, nineteenth-century California attorneys most often handled land title litigation. But lawyers were also active in land promotion, brokerage, and investment counseling. T. K. McDowell of Anaheim perceived the value of having an experienced attorney promote land sales. He wrote John D. Bicknell in 1887: "What we need is some live energetic capitalist like you. . . to take hold of this matter and push things. As it is the Kraemer boys hold back & do nothing and nobody else seems moving at present."[50] Bicknell's prowess as a land broker and agent for William S. Rosecrans and Michael J. O'Connor was well established. But he also handled smaller tracts of land. William Hickman of Banning authorized him to sell 320 acres to raise "some money."[51]

In the boom of the 1880s in Los Angeles, lawyers made numerous land deals, but there were pitfalls. Jackson A. Graves wrote in 1883 that "there has already been much inquiring for small lots but the parties invariably want immediate possession and there are plenty of lands selling here. When possession cannot be given, they soon get located in other quarters. Freman will hold us to the strict letter of our contract. If we don't sell enough land to pay him $5,000 by April 5th up goes our whistle."[52] Lawyers also provided services as mortgage brokers. Graves worked heavily in the business and eventually became president of the Farmer and Merchants Bank of Los Angeles. Bicknell similarly developed financing for ventures in land. From as far away as Salinas City, Henry Gleason requested that Bicknell structure a loan, pay a preceding obligation, and provide for his fee. Gleason concluded: "In raising that money don't forget to raise the amount of your fee also as I don't think it right that I should give you so much trouble without some recompense."[53] Lawyers readily agreed with Gleason's sentiment.

Lawyers also functioned as rental agents and rent collectors. John D. Bicknell performed such duties for William S. Rosecrans and in so doing made it easier on the general than Chickamauga had been a decade before.[54] Bicknell also negotiated settlements of disputes arising from the acquisition of land. One such case was the dispute between Henry C. Austin of Los Angeles and William

Warnack of San Diego. Austin had agreed to obtain title to two plots of land, had received $150, and had produced nothing but promises. George N. Hitchcock, a San Diego attorney, wrote Bicknell in 1880 hoping for a settlement. Austin, Hitchcock alleged, had "broken the terms of the contract and [was], of course, liable to return the amount paid. But [was] he responsible, and [could] we get it? Law [was] too expensive a luxury for a poor man like Warnack to indulge in."[55] Settlement rather than litigation was preferable to avoid the costs of courts and attorneys.

Another major source of legal business was debt collection. Throughout the nineteenth century, lawyers pursued debtors for clients. Some of the debts were incurred prior to arrival in California, others had been incurred in the bustle of the frontier economy. With a boom psychology at work, creditors loaned money with many of the same expectations that debtors brought to transactions—namely, quick profits. As William Higby told his father in 1851, San Francisco was "busy and bustling and like a sprightly, healthy, fat infant, with a kind and capable mother to nourish it, [was] growing lusty and increasing in size rapidly."[56] In this context, dealers used promissory notes to structure transactions as well as chattel and real estate mortgages. These notes frequently passed as currency in a frontier economy often critically short on specie.[57]

When the excitement disappeared, debtors often evaporated as well. Five years later, Higby wrote to his father from Mokelumne Hill that "it is all the bustle of business and strife for money. It is all taxing the integrity of the man until he finds himself not only selfish but too often knavish. I have lost confidence in men since witnessing what I have here and am growing more cautious in business transactions."[58] Even with cautious procedure, debtors did drift away. J. M. Richards of Donner Lake wrote the sheriff of Plumas County in 1865 soliciting his aid in collecting on a promissory note. Richards held the note of W. and J. Dickenson and "John Dickenson was with McDougle's pack train the last I know of him. John said last winter when I seen [*sic*] him he wood [*sic*] pay me all he could. If you can get anything by complimise [*sic*] or any other way, pleas [*sic*] do it and pay your selfe [*sic*] well for your trouble. . . ." Richards also expressed a degree of moral indignation concluding, "if you can make anything off John any way on Earth pleas [*sic*] do it for they are trying to Swindle Me out of that Money."[59] The sheriff turned the note over to John D. Goodwin, a prominent Quincy attorney.

But even in the hands of an attorney, a creditor had to risk the system of debt collection as well as the mobility of debtors in the west. In that system, lawyers sometimes made fatal errors on behalf of their clients. For example, Creed Hammond, a Sacramento attorney and later general counsel for the Southern Pacific Company, chided his short-time partner, John Goodwin, in 1869 as follows:

When I received the papers in Madden v. Reynolds I felt like murdering you—how did you expect the sheriff of this county to make an arrest on an order directed to the Shff of Plumas County. You must be more careful my boy when you proceed under "the statute." See sec 77, Pr(actice) Act for form of order [1851 statute provided a civil remedy of arrest and bail of debtors]. We of course could do nothing in the premises. You may tell your client that we raised heaven and earth, pursued the defendant with a vigilance worthy of the cause, charged you 100$ for expenses, but could not capture him.[60]

Although the lawyer might misfire on the fleet-footed debtor, more often, the debtor, when found, received a standard demand letter. Jackson A. Graves sent such a letter in 1879 to J. M. Soto simply stating that he had certain promissory notes in hand for collection in the amount of $651 and asking whether Soto could "pay them now." Immediate settlement was requested because Graves did "not want to sue."[61] John D. Bicknell similarly informed Rafael Machado and Manuel F. Cornell in 1874 that he held a note to "H. A. DuBois for $420 date March 30, 1874 due six months after date. . . ." The note was then one month overdue and Bicknell had been "directed to collect the note at once." To avoid court and attorney costs, Bicknell directed them to "call and settle the same." Nineteen days later, Bicknell reported to DuBois that "I am promised the money this week. If it is not paid I will take steps to collect the same."[62]

This was a demand-litigation mode for attorneys, but with the stabilization of the banking system and with the rise of credit bureaus and collection agencies, lawyers turned to advice as well as litigation in the practice of law. The Los Angeles firm Graves, O'Melveny, and Shankland, for example, advised the Farmers and Merchants Bank of Los Angeles in 1890:

As a matter of strict business, justified by the decisions on the subject—and also as a matter of policy, to prevent hardship to debtors, which you would not like to see occur, we would advise you in all cases when you take promissory notes, whether secured by mortgage or not, as collateral security, to notify the makers of said notes in writing that you hold them as security, and that you look to them for payment. You will by such means put an end to all dealing between the maker and payee of such paper; or at least put the maker in such a position, that any dealings had by him with the original payee will be with full notice of your rights, and at his, the maker's, risk and peril; and he cannot, if seeking clemency at your hands, say that he did not have knowledge of your rights.[63]

The lawyer's debt collection practice by the turn of the century matured from the demand-and-sue mode to the office practice of advice and policy-making.

With the rise of industrialization, attorneys turned their attention to the developing field of tort law. This was particularly evident in the practice of John D. Bicknell who turned from acquiring land and litigating titles for William S. Rosecrans and others to representing the Southern Pacific Company. Occasionally, the iron horse literally belched fire into the dry grass that kindled litigation. Bicknell prepared for trial with the zeal evidenced in previous decades when ejecting squatters from his client's land. In one fire case, he told George C.

Fabens, the Southern Pacific Company's claims adjuster that "we must certainly have one Henry Fox, who was brakeman on the train; also Conductor C. R. Cotter, who saw the tramps cooking over a fire near the track as the train passed...." Three months later Bicknell, tried the case without a jury on the theory of causation being other than the railroad's locomotive and lost to the tune of $1,256.45 plus $98.15 in costs. He told Creed Haymond (Creed found a new spelling of his surname, which had been Hammond, with the title of general counsel) that "there [was] some evidence sustaining each and all of the findings of the Court, and I consider an appeal on motion for a new trial hopeless; I, therefore, recommend the payment of this judgment." The new trial would be hopeless because "they had the evidence of one witness positive that the fire started something near three hundred feet from the camp fires, that it started immediately after the locomotive passed, and while I proved that our locomotives were in good condition and equipped with the best possible appliances to prevent sparks escaping, they proved that dry grass was left within three feet of the track at the point where the fire started. The amount of damage awarded is low enough admitting that we started the fire."[64]

With fires, the best policy, more often than not, was to settle claims. Bicknell made this judgment clear to Fabens in 1889. "M. G. Watson has turned up again claiming that he has been damaged by fire started by a locomotive," Bicknell relayed, and Watson was "willing to settle for ten dollars or...two wagon loads of old posts or ties...." Bicknell advised settlement and proposed a remedy for the recurring liability exposure. "It is fair to presume from our experience that the grasses growing upon the land of Watson in the neighborhood of Cerritos are about as inflammable as gun-powder and it would be well for our section men to put the right of way in the very best condition through his premises to prevent fires."[65] In addition to business management and litigation management, Bicknell's role was also becoming one of risk management with the rise of liability exposures due to industrialization.

Another common liability exposure was the locomotive's proclivity for grinding up beef and other livestock as it coursed down the tracks. Here again, the lawyer's role was in litigation and policy advice. For example, Bicknell's advice to Creed Haymond on a case involving cattle killed on the Southern Pacific track was to settle after trial and not appeal:

> Taking the whole case together it is evident that it was an unavoidable accident and that we are not liable and that we ought not to pay, but there is just enough in it to make it difficult about setting aside the verdict. That is to say, there is proof going to show that a large amount of dust was raised by the travelling cattle; that the cattle were strung out on both sides of the track and in a position to be easily seen by the engineer upon the approaching train. If we are liable for this beef, it is cheap beef on the verdict [$300 plus $100 costs]. I think I have a fighting chance on appeal, but like all cases of this class it is doubtful about our ever getting a verdict. Upon the whole I consider it the best business policy to pay the judgement....[66]

The reason that Bicknell advised against trying for a new trial was significant: another jury would more likely than not give the verdict to the plaintiff. On most tort claims, the best policy was to settle, and so Bicknell told W. T. Rankin, assistant general counsel of the Pullman Palace Car Company of Chicago: ''I have been an attorney for the Southern Pacific Railroad for some years and tried too many damage cases not to be alarmed at the case where there is a controversy between the person injured and the employees of the road as to the facts of the case. My advice in this case is if we can get a reasonable settlement to adjust them.''[67] There was the additional risk with Los Angeles juries in that ''there [was] not doubt but what the plaintiffs in these cases would obtain a judgment, and while the actual damages sustained by both would not be that much ($1,200) yet we take the chances of a jury running away in their verdict and the judgment would probably be affirmed by the Supreme Court to that amount.'' Because Bicknell had ''had too much experience in this class of cases to expect much favor at the hands of a jury,''[68] and the risks of a runaway jury were even more costly, Bicknell recommended settlement. Pullman agreed and Bicknell settled the claim for $500.

The railroad injured more than dry grass and livestock. Tragically, people suffered the pain of industrialization. Again, Bicknell litigated and advised. One such case was that of *Barrett v. The Southern Pacific Company* (1889) as told to Creed Haymond:

> I tried the case of Barrett v. The Southern Pacific Company last week. This was an action brought by the mother to recover damages sufferred [*sic*] by her by reason of the injury of her child sufferred [*sic*] while playing on our turntable at Santa Ana. The jury awarded a verdict in favor of the plaintiff for three hundred dollars, added to this there is one hundred and thirteen dollars costs. This case was tried before a jury and I recommend the payment of the judgment. The plaintiff in this action would be very glad to have a new trial.
>
> In view of the decisions of the Courts of several of the states as to the liability of railroad companies in keeping their turntables unlocked where children are in the habit of playing on them, I would suggest for your consideration the propriety of locking turntables when they are located out in the country towns and places like this turntable at Santa Ana where children are in the habit of playing. It seems to me that if turntables could be locked with the same lock as used upon switches, so that the keys in the hands of the trainmen who attend to the switches would serve as well upon the turntables, we might without much inconvenience save a great deal of vexatious difficulty in this matter.[69]

Although this suggestion was not heeded in San Francisco, Bicknell persisted and, seventeen months later, prevailed. Haymond wrote back in August 1890: ''I concur with you in the suggestion which you make as to fastening turntables in towns like Santa Ana &c.''[70] Again, Bicknell saw a liability exposure and a means to avoid injury as well as expense. The lawyer's office practice was as significant as his courtroom practice in representing the interests of his industrial client.

Industrialization also brought regulatory law to the practice of California attorneys. The O'Connor Act of 1876 created a California Railroad Commission, required railroads to submit annual reports and empowered the Commission to issue administrative orders.[71] Abolished two years later, but resurrected by the 1879 constitution, the Railroad Commission held extensive hearings and investigation prior to the issuance of administrative rulings. These procedures intimately involved legal staff. Rate orders also involved litigation in the U.S. Circuit Court for Northern California.[72] While legislative committee, administrative agency, and federal court practice was the stuff of regulatory law practice, lawyers had to concern themselves with many of the local ordinances as well. John M. Crawley, the Assistant General Passenger and Freight Agent for the Southern Pacific Company gave John D. Bicknell such a question in 1890:

> Now comes the County Board of Horticultural Commissioners of San Bernardino, who have resolved to quarantine Los Angeles county, and ask us to receive trees at San Fernando if destined to that county. I wrote to them and explained that a common carrier was bound to receive whatever was offered to them which was not offensive and that the carrier could not be the judge as to whether plants or trees were infected or not, and we certainly could not afford to have an expert at each station to pass on the health of trees.
>
> I will frankly state to you that at the start we refused to receive plants and trees destined to San Bernardino county points until a permit accompanied the same. But this action on our part lost us some business so I immediately considered the affair a dead letter and since then we have been receiving and forwarding trees to destination, without troubling ourselves about inspection.
>
> The question arises with me—can a county interfere with shipments from another county, and if they can is it not their duty to be on hand at destination, on the look out for trees and not expect any assistance from us, because if we render assistance to them we antagonize shippers and they seek some other outlet.[73]

Although business necessity dictated rejection of the law's provisions, Bicknell recommended cooperation with local authorities. The interests of the agricultural community were closely identified with the interests of shippers due to their close business relationship.

Municipal regulations cost the railroad money while, at the same time, they provided for the interests of the city's residents. Los Angeles required the railroad to place flagmen at street crossings, and the immediate question came to Bicknell whether the ordinance was enforceable. Bicknell answered in 1889 finding a New Jersey case holding such an ordinance valid and an Illinois case finding it invalid. However, "the general current of decisions is that such regulations must be reasonable, and when the ordinance imposes an unreasonable burden upon the railroad the courts have held it to be invalid." To sum it up, Bicknell noted that "the courts seem to concede the power to the municipality to make the regulations but reserve the right to determine whether the services required are reasonable or not.''[74] The ordinance, Bicknell thought, could be enforced and the railroad should comply. Again, Bicknell's office practice was important to the ability of the enterprise to deal with the growing complexity of doing business amid regulatory schemes.

In dealing with the legal problems of industrialization, lawyers came into contact with the prominent businessmen of the day, and some became businessmen through their efforts in the developing areas of law and enterprise. The attitude toward the capitalist was ably summed up by Bicknell in an 1889 letter to J. M. Griffith:

> The longer I live the more profound respect I have for a successful business man. Men may command armies and be honored as great generals; they may be prominent in politics and be applauded by admiring citizens, but for a man to start out in life poor and make an even-handed fight in a busy world and pay his honest debts, support for his family and save enough to build a block possesses more of the qualities that go to make up a man than any of the other classes mentioned above. It is something, in my opinion, in this busy, rattling and wicked world for a man to accumulate and keep a fortune.[75]

While admiring the capitalist, Bicknell became one investing in and operating mining interests as well as irrigation ventures. Henry W. O'Melveny began work with the electric power industry in Los Angeles in 1891 and became intimately involved with its operations for the next thirty-four years.[76] Jackson A. Graves and four others incorporated the Oil Storage and Transportation Company in 1899 with Graves as its president.[77] Graves also developed extensive holdings in orange growing with Erskine M. Ross.[78] Moses L. Wicks ''gave up law for real estate and in the 1880s was an active subdivider.''[79] The lure of enterprise was often as strong as that of practice for some.

The expansion of agriculture, urbanization, and industrialization from the 1880s to the close of the century also created demand for lawyers conversant with water law. Water litigation in Los Angeles County during the twenty year period distinguished many lawyers and identified them as specialists in the field.[80] Many of the issues, such as condemnation and contracts, were familiar to the bar. G. L. Russel of Santa Ana wrote to Bicknell in 1873 citing a number of problems:

> We have the right of way guaranteed by nearly all the parties on the line of our now proposed line. Our main opposition will come from Chapman and Glassell. They have said to us that they would law us to the last inch, in fact we expect no other opposition only in crossing his lands. We wish to pursue a different course this time. Our idea is this [time] to go before the district court & ask the court to grant us the right of way by condemning the lands to the use of the ditch and paying the damage if any something similar to obtaining a right of way for a road.
>
> Now we have had so much law and been so badly imposed upon that most of our members are shakey about trusting any lawyers. . . .[81]

The problem of landowners using the legal process to delay the construction of ways of necessity was not new.

Delay has always been a part of the legal system. Industrialization merely added new subject matter to the age-old procedural skirmishes that surrounded legal battlefields. When "the Motor line" was negotiating with the Los Angeles city council "for a privilege to land freight and passengers in the center of the city," A. N. Towne, Third Vice-President and General Manager of the Southern Pacific Company, told Bicknell to "keep this matter a little in mind with a view to obstructing in the city council any movement in his direction if it can be done with any hope of success and without too much exposure. . . .[82] In 1889, W. G. Curtis, Assistant to the General Manager of the Southern Pacific company, told Bicknell that "in case Ainsworth persists in his attempt to cross our line without proper arrangement for the construction of safety appliances, will you please take the necessary action on behalf of our Company, instructing Messrs. Hewitt and Hawgood to carry out whatever you may require them to do and proceed, if necessary, until every obstacle known to the law has been interposed to defeat Captain Ainsworth's design."[83]

But lawyers also used the law against Bicknell and the railroad to a frustrating degree at times. On the advice of their attorney, E. E. Keech, the Ferris family of Tustin had taken up the company's track claiming trespass and making the section useless. Bicknell thought that "to arrest them criminally with the showing of their acting under legal advice" would have "little chance" of success and could "leave us in a worse position than if we proceed with an action at law to obtain an order restraining them from molesting the road." So observing to Haymond, Bicknell commented with greater relish that "it would have been a source of great satisfaction if I could have got evidence sufficient to justify the arrest of the lawyer, as he is evidently one of those anti-railroad cranks that it would be a source of great satisfaction to punish if we could."[84] The procedural delays inherent in the legal process were part of doing business in California and a two-edged sword in the hands of the profession.

Although the traditional procedural frustrations of the system caused delay, the uncertainty of law, particularly in the latter part of the century, created a degree of professional anxiety in the state bar. In 1883, David Jacks's attorney wrote that:

> the Supreme Court has often held that a defendant in ejectment cannot defeat a recovery by conveying the land or transferring the possession pending the suit, but the statute requires a Lis Pendens to be filed in all actions affecting the title to real estate and with our Supreme Court as erratic as the present we should not be surprised at its holding at any time that the title was tried in such an action, and a Lis Pendens therefore necessary and for safety we had perhaps best file one.[85]

Charles H. Lorrobee, a San Francisco attorney, wrote to John D. Bicknell in 1874 about another procedural quirk telling him that "notice to take depositions must be sent on [the attorney] also—so the Supreme Court says—this is the *decision*—if even *not law*. See Griffiths. v. Gruner, Jan. term 1874.''[86] The law to Larrobee was distinguishable from the decisions of the California Supreme Court. Similarly, Graves, O'Melveny, and Shankland (Los Angeles) wrote to Jarboe, Harrison, and Goodfellow (San Francisco) in 1890:

As to the necessity of including the description of the mortgaged premises in the foreclosure summons, we refer you to People v. Greene, 52 Ca., p. 577. This was an action to foreclose the interest of the purchaser of lands from the State of California, holding under a certificate of purchase, and, while the point was not directly decided, still we think there is enough in the case to justify a Court as eccentric as the present Supreme Court of this State is in holding it to be conclusive of the proposition. However, as we agree that it is well to avoid all possible chances, we will insert description in the summons, irrespective of the law of the case.[87]

S. F. Lieb, a San Jose attorney, found another decision on summons law of interest and wrote to John D. Bicknell in 1890:

I notice in the Pacific Reporter just come to hand in the case of Reinhardt vs. Lugo, the court uses the expression that jurisdiction of the court is acquired not from the *fact* of service of the summons, but from the proper *proof* thereof. I notice that you are for the appellant in the case, and it seems to me that that view is not only contrary to what I always supposed the law to be, but also to section 416 of the C[alifornia code of] C[ivil] P[rocedure]. The point was also expressly decided in the Estate of Newman, 75 Cal.220. I send you this memorandum that you may suggest to the court, if you think advisable, that we may have our decisions, at least, consistent with themselves, although it is probable that you have already done so.[88]

Bicknell found a shocking result in one case and sent it to Haymond in 1889:

As a matter of light reading and a chapter in the legal romances of Southern California that will be particularly interesting to Mr. Brown I send you a copy of the decision of the court in the case of Brock v. Pearson. It would be well to have at hand some restoratives to use on Mr. Brown, an electric battery or something of that sort at the time you submit it to him.[89]

The complexity of the developing law in the context of industrialization as well as the perceived inconsistencies of the California judiciary led lawyers to specialization, to consulting specialists, and to expanding the size of counsel staff. The Southern Pacific Company created a legal department for California with Haymond as general counsel. It also established a network of counsel around the state on retainer.

Regardless of the size or expertise of counsel, statute as well as case law led attorneys to anxious research. Bicknell's interpretation of a San Bernardino county ordinance was tempered by the observation that ''while we lawyers guess at the meaning of a law or ordinance, unfortunately the court has the last guess and may possibly guess the other way. I deem it much safer for the company to comply with federal law and discuss the possible conflict with the county officials.''[90] As with dealing with decisions of the California Supreme Court, legal advice was conservative to protect the interests of the client. Occasionally, the advice had to be based on legislation that was less clear than the missives from the Supreme Court. The firm of Jarboe, Harrison, and Goodfellow of San Francisco wrote to Bicknell in 1888 regarding the incorporation of the Los Angeles City Water Company. The firm required additional documentation for the filing of the incorporation papers evidencing the election of the corporation to continue in existence under the Civil Code. The documentation was important because

> unless a proper certificate of such proceedings has been filed as well in the Clerk's office as in the office of the Secretary of State, the election made by the Board of Directors has not resulted in bringing the Corporation under the Civil Code. The Act of March, 1885, under which it is proposed to issue bonds being merely an amendment of the Civil Code, could not be invoked to support any action by a Corporation that has not elected to be governed by those provisions.
>
> The Statute above referred to is very meagre and almost blind in its language. There is nothing in the body of the section after providing that a ''Corporation may increase its bonded indebtedness at a meeting called by Directors as follows'': providing for such bonded indebtedness at the mode in which the increase thereof shall be had until the last clause of the section is reached, in which there seems to have been injected as an after thought by some legislator the words, ''Or the Bonded indebtedness may be increased accordingly.'' We think, however, that by a fair reading of the entire section the legislature intended to provide that the bonded indebtedness of a corporation may be increased in accordance with the procedure prescribed for increasing its capital stock.[91]

Even the specialists did not always have more than a fair reading. At times, the developing law even left the specialists divided. In 1890, Bicknell turned to the specialists to get an answer on the question of cutting timber on government land and wrote to S. Slusher at Gorman's Station that

> the whole question seems to be very much confused but by a recent decision rendered by Judge Sawyer it seems that he construes the law to mean that a person owning a mining location can cut timber on the location for the purposes of the mine. Some of the attorneys here who make the land laws a specialty say that the owner of one location can not sell wood from his location to be used on another mining location. Upon this question other attorneys think to the contrary.[92]

The challenge of law practice was clear—more so, at times, than the law.

Not surprisingly, the lawyers who held themselves out to be specialists in a particular field of law practiced in San Francisco or Los Angeles. Of the 1,168 lawyers in the sample, only 18.5 percent listed specializations or had specializations noted by compilers or editors. Forty-seven attorneys focused upon corporation law; seventeen practiced in San Francisco, and fourteen practiced in

Los Angeles. Thirty-one concentrated on railroad law; ten had offices in San Francisco, four had offices in Los Angeles, five in Sacramento, three had offices in San Diego, and nine practiced railroad law in other communities. By 1890, the Southern Pacific Company had lawyers on retainer in Oakland, Fairfield, Stockton, and Santa Barbara in addition to Los Angeles. Fifteen lawyers specialized in commercial law; of these, ten practiced in San Francisco. Fourteen attorneys listed water law as their forte; two practiced in Los Angeles, and one Sacramento attorney was a water law specialist. Many of the water law specialists practiced in the inland empire of Riverside County or the central valley (ten in number). Banking law became the specialty of thirteen attorneys in the sample; five practiced in Los Angeles; one each were San Francisco and San Diego bar members, and six practiced in the smaller towns. Other specialties included oil and gas law, which gushed from the Bakersfield area; insurance and patent law, which was concentrated in San Francisco; admiralty law, which was afloat in the Golden Gate harbours; and mining law, which was stamped out mainly in Los Angeles.

Importantly, the legal profession concentrated specialties where the work existed. The lawyer followed the practice dollar and some specialized to meet the needs of a rapidly urbanizing and industrializing population. As noted above, the numbers of lawyers increased dramatically during the final decade of the period. These lawyers flocked to the urban areas where they established practices and specializations suited to the needs of the economy and developed law of a state emerging from a hectic frontier period.

Despite the impact of industrialization, California attorneys prospered as did their ante-bellum counterparts. They acquired wealth, as had their predecessors in the generations before them, in land speculation, occupational diversification, and litigation. Although industrialization was an emerging phenomena in the century, California remained largely an agricultural-mercantile-service economy with its attendant legal opportunities. The economic diversification arising from industrialization presented new opportunities for a bar accustomed to the challenge.

## NOTES

1. Thomas H. Thompson and Albert A. West, *History of Sacramento County*, (1880; reprint, Berkeley, 1960); *San Francisco: Its Builders, Past and Present*, 2 vols. (Chicago, 1913); *Past and Present of Alameda County, California*, 2 vols. (Chicago, 1914); George C. Mansfield, *History of Butte County* (Los Angeles, 1918); *San Joaquin County, California* (Chicago, 1890); *History of San Mateo County, California* (Chicago, 1928); Bailey Millard, *History of the San Francisco Bay Region* (San Francisco, 1924); *San Diego County, California* (Chicago, 1913); William L. Willis, *History of Sacramento County, California* (Los Angeles, 1913); Eugene T. Sawyer, *History of Santa Clara County, California* (Los Angeles, 1922); John Brown, Jr., and James Boyd, *History of San Bernardino and Riverside Counties* (Chicago, 1922); W. B. Lardner and M. J. Brock, *History of Placer and Nevada Counties, California* (Los Angeles, 1924); Paul E. Vandor,

*History of Fresno County, California* (Los Angeles, 1919); *A History of California, Los Angeles and Environs* (Los Angeles, 1915); *A History of Monterey and Santa Cruz Counties, California* (Chicago, 1925); Tom Gregory, *History of Solano and Napa Counties, California* (Los Angeles, 1912); idem, *History of Sonoma County, California* (Los Angeles, 1911); *History of Tulare and Kings Counties, California* (Chicago, 1926); *History of Long Beach and Vicinity* (Chicago, 1927); John Outcalt, *History of Merced County, California* (Los Angeles, 1925); J. P. O'Brien, ed., *History of the Bench and Bar of Nevada, Included in This Volume Is the Bench and Bar of California* (San Francisco, 1913); Annie L. Morrison and John H. Haydon, *History of San Luis Obispo County and Environs* (Los Angeles, 1917); Will S. Green, *The History of Colusa County, California* (Sacramento, 1950); Frederick J. Hulaniski, ed., *The History of Contra Costa County, California* (Berkeley, 1917); Leigh H. Irvine, *History of Humboldt County, California* (Los Angeles, 1915); Finis C. Farr, ed., *The History of Imperial County* (Berkeley, 1918); Wallace M. Moran, *History of Kern County, California* (Los Angeles, 1921); Samuel Armor, *History of Orange County, California* (Los Angeles, 1921); Willoughby Rodman, *History of the Bench and Bar of Southern California* (Los Angeles, 1909).

2. *San Francisco Herald*, December 25, 1855, in Adams and Co. Collections, Scrapbook, Huntington Library, MSS, vol. 6, p. 49.

3. Ibid., vol. 1, p. 12, *San Francisco Herald*, July 28, 1853, and December 19, 1853.

4. J. M. Kennedy to John D. Bicknell, September 12, 1874, Bicknell Collection, Huntington Library, MSS, Box 1.

5. Treasher to Bicknell, December 20, 1874, Bicknell Collection, Huntington Library, MSS, Box 1.

6. Richardson to Bicknell, February 24, 1875, Bicknell Collection, Huntington Library, MSS, Box 1.

7. Ward to Bicknell, April 14, 1875, Bicknell Collection, Huntington Library, MSS, Box 1.

8. H. F. Felland to Bicknell, October 10, 1872, Bicknell Collection, Huntington Library, MSS, Box 1.

9. John B. Clark (Washington, D.C.) to Bicknell, January 16, 1876, Bicknell Collection, Huntington Library, MSS, Box 2.

10. John Center Collection, March 18, 1851, deed and notes, Huntington Library, MSS, Box 1.

11. Benjamin Davis Wilson Collection, Huntington Library, MSS, Boxes 2 and 3.

12. Couts to Stearns, July 12, 1852, Cave Johnson Couts Colleçtion, Huntington Library, MSS, Box 18.

13. Warner to Geo, Allice, and Elsie Warner, October 23, 1887, Warner Collection, California State Library, California Section, Box 327.

14. Goodwin to Smith, November 2, 1884, Goodwin Collection, California State Library, California Section, Box 730.

15. Markey to Jacks, April 13, 1881, Jacks Collection, Huntington Library, MSS Box C(4).

16. *Gage v. Downey* (1889), 79 Cal. 140.

17. O. H. Picher to Bicknell, May 20, 1885, Bicknell Collection, Huntington Library, MSS, Box 4.

18. Millard, *San Francisco Bay Region*, 47.

19. Green, *History of Colusa County*, 79.

20. Irvine, *History of Humbolt County*, 207.
21. O'Brien, *History of the Bench and Bar of Nevada*, 346.
22. Murray to Bicknell, July 9, 1877, Bicknell Collection, Huntington Library, MSS, Box 2.
23. McDowell to Bicknell, October 27, 1872, January 17, 1873, March 22, 1873, Bicknell Collection, Huntington Library, MSS, Box 1.
24. Irvine, *History of Humbolt County*, 1093.
25. Morgan, *History of Kern County*, 581.
26. Rodman, *History of the Bench and Bar of Southern California*, 164.
27. Brown and Boyd, *History of San Bernardino and Riverside Counties*, 701–6.
28. Avery to Bicknell, March 29, 1883, Bicknell Collection, Huntington Library, MSS, Box 4.
29. Studebaker to Bicknell, July 21, 1888, Bicknell Collection, Huntington Library, MSS, Box 5.
30. Smith to Bicknell, August 21, 1888; John D. Bryan to Bicknell, January 29, 1890, Bicknell Collection, Huntington Library, MSS, Boxes 5–6.
31. O'Brien, *History of Bench and Bar of Nevada*, 204.
32. Clarence A. McGrew, *City of San Diego and San Diego County* (Chicago, 1922), 28–29.
33. On Graves, see Robert Glass Cleland and Frank B. Putnam, *Isaias W. Hellman and the Farmers and Merchants Bank* (San Marino, 1965); Gill to Bicknell, February 10, 1890, Bicknell Collection, Huntington Library, MSS, Box 6.
34. Currey to Catlin, July 2, 1850, Amos Parmalee Catlin Collection, Huntington Library, MSS, Box 1.
35. Mansfield, *San Joaquin County*, 379.
36. Noel C. Stevenson, "The Glorious Uncertainty of the Law, 1846–1851," *The Journal of the State Bar of California* 28 (1953): 374, 380.
37. *San Francisco Daily Herald*, August 2, 1853, in Adams and Co. Collection, Scrapbook, Huntington Library, MSS, vol. 1, p. 34.
38. W. W. Robinson, *Lawyers of Los Angeles* (Los Angeles, 1951), 5–8.
39. For example, Lucien Shaw, the treasurer of the Los Angeles Law Library sent John D. Bicknell his overdue notice on September 1, 1887, when the $100 was nine months overdue; Shaw to Bicknell, Bicknell Collection, Huntington Library, MSS, Box 5.
40. Mason to Bicknell, April 2, 1874, Bicknell Collection, Huntington Library, MSS, Box 1.
41. Scott and Montgomery to Bicknell, February 24, 1879, Bicknell Collection, Huntington Library, MSS, Box 3.
42. See stationery, F. G. Sanborn to Bicknell, January 16, 1889, Bicknell Collection, Huntington Library, MSS, Box 6.
43. Beattie to Bicknell, June 12, 1889, Bicknell Collection, Huntington Library, MSS, Box 6.
44. Leslie to Bicknell, August 30, 1873, Bicknell Collection, Huntington Library, MSS, Box 1.
45. Luce, McDonald, and Torrance to Bicknell, November 16, 1889, Bicknell Collection, Huntington Library, MSS, Box 6.
46. Laine to Bicknell, November 25, 1889, Bicknell Collection, Huntington Library, MSS, Box 6.

47. Sexton to Goodwin, n.d., Goodwin Collection, California State Library, California Collection, Box 735.

48. Clark, Jr., to Bicknell, January 16, 1876, Bicknell Collection, Huntington Library, MSS, Box 2.

49. Huntington to Bicknell, December 12, 1889, Bicknell Collection, Huntington Library, MSS, Box 6.

50. McDowell to Bicknell, May 2, 1887, Bicknell Collection, Huntington Library, MSS, Box 5.

51. Hickman to Bicknell, June 30, 1878, Bicknell Collection, Huntington Library, MSS, Box 2.

52. Graves to Easton, December 15, 1883, Jackson A. Graves Collection, Huntington Library, MSS, 1883–1885 Letterbook.

53. Gleason to Bicknell, October 18, 1876, Bicknell Collection, Huntington Library, MSS, Box 2.

54. Rosecrans to Sergt. Jos. Schneider, August 29, 1873; and Annie E. Rosecrans to Bicknell, November 18, 1874, Bicknell Collection, Huntington Library, MSS, Box 1.

55. Hitchcock to Bicknell, March 8, 1880, Bicknell Collection, Huntington Library, MSS, Box 3.

56. Higby to father, January 23, 1851, William Higby Collection, California State Library, California Section, MSS, Box 218.

57. Gordon M. Bakken, "Law and Legal Tender in California and the West," *Southern California Quarterly* 57 (Fall 1980):239–59.

58. William Higby to father, February 3, 1856, William Higby Collection, California State Library, California Section, MSS, Box 218.

59. J. M. Richards to sheriff, August 16, 1865, John D. Goodwin Collection, California State Library, California Section, MSS, Box 735.

60. Hammond to Goodwin, February 28, 1869, John D. Goodwin Collection, California State Library, California Section, MSS, Box 731.

61. Graves to Soto, July 21, 1879, Jackson A. Graves collection, Huntington Library, MSS, 1879-1880 Letterbook.

62. Bicknell to Machado and Cornell, October 15, 1874; Bicknell to H. A. DuBois, November 3, 1874, Bicknell Collection, Huntington Library, MSS, Letterbook no. 1.

63. Graves to Merchants Bank, July 31, 1890, Jackson A. Graves Collection, Huntington Library, MSS, 1890–1891 Letterbook.

64. Bicknell to Fabens, January 9, 1889; and Bicknell to Creed Haymond, March 18, 1889, Bicknell Collection, Huntington Library, MSS, Letterbook no. 4.

65. Bicknell to Fabens, August 2, 1889, Bicknell Collection, Huntington Library, MSS, Letterbook no. 5.

66. Bicknell to Haymond, March 27, 1890, Bicknell Collection, Huntington Library, MSS, Letterbook no. 6.

67. Bicknell to Rankin, April 9, 1889, Bicknell Collection, Huntington Library, MSS, Letterbook no. 4.

68. Bicknell to Rankin, June 10, 1889, Bicknell Collection, Huntington Library, MSS, Letterbook no. 4.

69. Bicknell to Haymond, March 18, 1889, Bicknell Collection, Huntington Library, MSS, Letterbook no. 4.

70. Haymond to Bicknell, August 27, 1890, Bicknell Collection, Huntington Library, MSS, Box 7.

71. Gerald D. Nash, *State Government and Economic Development: A History of Administrative Policies in California, 1849-1933* (Berkeley, 1964), 161-62.

72. Ibid., 162-75; Mansel G. Blackford, *The Politics of Business in California, 1890-1920* (Columbus, 1977), 81-86.

73. John M. Crawley to Bicknell, July 10, 1890, Bicknell Collection, Huntington Library, MSS, Box 7.

74. Bicknell to J. A. Muir, September 6, 1889, Bicknell Collection, Huntington Library, MSS, Letterbook no. 5.

75. Bicknell to J. M. Griffith, July 20, 1889, Bicknell Collection, Huntington Library, MSS, Letterbook no. 5.

76. William W. Clary, *History of the Law Firm of O'Melveny and Myers, 1885–1965* (Los Angeles, 1966), 82–91.

77. Ibid., 110–12.

78. Robinson, *Lawyers of Los Angeles*, 236.

79. Ibid., 236.

80. Ibid., 91.

81. Russell to Bicknell, December 9, 1873, Bicknell Collection, Huntington Library, MSS, Box 1.

82. Towne to Bicknell, July 17, 1889, Bicknell Collection, Huntington Library, MSS, Box 6.

83. Curtis to Bicknell, August 22, 1889, Bicknell Collection, Huntington Library, MSS, Box 6.

84. Bicknell to Haymond, April 30, 1889, Bicknell Collection, Huntington Library, MSS, Letterbook no. 4.

85. S. O. Houghton to David Jacks, May 28, 1883, Jacks Collection, Huntington Library, MSS, Box C(4).

86. Larrobee to Bicknell, February 21, 1874, Bicknell Collection, Huntington Library, MSS, Box 1.

87. Graves et al., to Jarboe et al., March 19, 1890, Jackson A. Graves Collection, Huntington Library, MSS, 1890–91 Letterbook.

88. Lieb to Bicknell, December 12, 1890, Bicknell Collection, Huntington Library, MSS, Box 7.

89. Bicknell to Haymond, May 8, 1889, Bicknell Collection, Huntington Library, MSS, Letterbook no. 4.

90. Bicknell to J. M. Crawley, April 4, 1890, Bicknell Collection, Huntington Library, MSS, Letterbook no. 6.

91. Jarboe et al., to Bicknell, March 10, 1888, Bicknell Collection, Huntington Library, MSS, Box 5.

92. Bicknell to Slusher, April 25, 1890, Bicknell Collection, Huntington Library, MSS, Letterbook no. 6.

*MAXWELL BLOOMFIELD*

# *From Deference to Confrontation: The Early Black Lawyers of Galveston, Texas, 1895–1920*

The history of minority professionals in the formative decades from the Civil War to the New Deal remains largely unexplored. Instead of analyzing court records, census data, and other "hard" evidence, scholars have preferred to rely upon facile generalizations and negative stereotypes. The first important survey of black attorneys in the United States—Carter G. Woodson's *The Negro Professional Man and the Community* (1934)—set the tone for subsequent interpretations of the black professional experience. Based upon information supplied by 503 of the nation's 1,230 black lawyers, the Woodson study classified practitioners along generational lines and drew an unflattering portrait of the "old Negro lawyer of the early days." According to Woodson, the black practitioner at the turn of the century tended to be poorly trained, self-serving, indifferent to movements for racial betterment, and unable to attract the legal business of middle-class blacks. The "new Negro lawyer" of the 1920s, in contrast, reflected the modernizing trends that were transforming the legal profession as a whole. He was more likely to be educated in a law school, to support the formation of black law firms and bar associations, to develop a commercial and corporate practice, and to participate actively in community projects of all kinds.[1]

In addition to the general disadvantages enumerated in the Woodson survey, pioneer black attorneys in the South confronted a legalized caste system that developed gradually in the quarter century preceding World War I. Forced to practice in a repressive racial environment, they have been pictured as submissive and demoralized. One recent historian charges that black professionals in Texas adopted an accommodationist stance out of self-interest: to protect their privileged position in a segregated society.[2] Other commentators point to the hopelessness of fighting a white-dominated political and legal establishment. After *Plessy v. Ferguson*, observed Kenneth S. Tollett in 1972, "The law had completely, for all practical purposes, turned its back upon Blacks and the legal profession declined in status and only those professions or callings which had some economic promise were pursued with any vigor or earnestness almost until just yesterday."[3] Either assessment leads to the same conclusion: Black attorneys were the passive victims of Jim Crow legislation in the South. They either would not, or could not, resist an unjust legal system.

How accurate is this appraisal of early black professionalism? An examination of the careers of minority practitioners in a representative southern city demonstrates that they served their community and the law far more effectively than conventional mythology suggests. As spokesmen for racial justice, they sometimes used their legal skills in creative ways to attack the institutionalized racism of the New South.

## BEGINNINGS OF THE BLACK BAR IN TEXAS

Black attorneys did not appear in Texas until the period of Radical Reconstruction (1867-1874) had ended. The earliest practitioners established themselves in the black belt counties that stretched along the Trinity, Brazos, and Colorado rivers in east Texas. Blacks made up a majority of the population in these rich farming areas, and elected other blacks to various county offices until a new era of white repression began in the 1890s. W. A. Price, the first black lawyer to be admitted to the Texas bar, served as county attorney of Fort Bend County in 1876. Although little is known about his background, contemporary newspapers described him as a competent practitioner.[4] Information concerning other pioneer black country lawyers is impossible to verify. It seems clear, however, that developments in Texas paralleled those in Mississippi, where black lawyers first settled in the predominantly black delta region and handled cases involving labor contracts, debts, family disputes, and crimes.[5]

A black urban bar, in any meaningful sense, did not emerge until the mid-1880s. S. H. Scott may have practiced briefly in Dallas in 1881, and George W. Fremont studied law under the direction of several white attorneys in San Antonio around the same time.[6] But the first successful urban practitioner was Joseph E. Wiley, who opened an office in Dallas in 1886. Wiley, a graduate of the Union College of Law of Chicago, maintained an active legal practice until the turn of the century. He also trained John L. Turner of Dallas, who became his partner.[7]

By 1890, there were only twelve black lawyers in Texas, most of whom lived in rural areas or small towns. During the next decade, however, this professional population more than doubled. In contrast, the Texas bar as a whole grew by only one-third, from 3,555 lawyers in 1890 to 4,617 in 1900. Behind the surprising upsurge of minority professionals lay a decisive shift from rural to urban lawyering. Cities such as Galveston and Houston, which had no black attorneys in 1890, saw an influx of five or six during the course of the decade. Indeed, Houston, Dallas, and Galveston together accounted for almost half of the twenty-eight black lawyers reported in 1900. Several of the remaining ones could be found in urban areas as well.[8]

To evaluate the capabilities of these early practitioners, I chose to study the conditions of professional life as they existed in a single representative city. Galveston, Texas, a major seaport on the Gulf of Mexico, promised several advantages to a prospective researcher. As one of the oldest cities in the state, its turn-of-the-century population of 37,789 persons included a large, well established, and litigious black community. Blacks owned a variety of small businesses: three grocery stores, a laundry, a drug store, one hotel, several furniture stores and barber shops, a restaurant, a blacksmith shop, and an ice cream parlor. Although none of these enterprises employed more than ten persons, the overall value of black property in Galveston—including homes, churches, and fraternal lodges—approached a quarter of a million dollars. The black community of 8,291 persons supported a professional class of four doctors, five lawyers, twenty-three teachers, sixteen ministers, and two newspaper editors. The ratio of black attorneys to potential clients was 1 to 1,658, and practitioners might hope to attract some white patronage as well.[9]

The black press provided indispensable insights into the community activities and reputation of professionals. Each of Galveston's weekly "race papers" has survived to some extent. The Rosenberg Library Archives contain a generous run of the accommodationist *City Times* from 1900 to 1925, and scattered issues of the more militant *New Idea* are also available, chiefly for the period 1905 to 1908. A full set of case files and other lower court records, including Justice of the Peace Court dockets, enables one to track individual lawyers through the court system. And the papers of local white attorneys offer an occasional glimpse of personal, as well as professional, contacts across the color line.[10]

## BIOGRAPHICAL PATTERNS

Eleven black lawyers practiced in Galveston between 1895 and 1920.[11] Two had been born into slavery; one was a free man of color in the ante-bellum years; and one was the son of a white plantation owner. The rest were the offspring of former slaves. In age they ranged from 58 to 26 at the turn of the century, with most of them born during the decade following the Civil War: two were born in the 1840s, one in the 1850s, five in the 1860s, and three in the 1870s.[12]

The oldest became a lawyer at 53; the youngest began to practice at 21. The median age for entering the legal profession was 35 for the group as a whole. Most of Galveston's white attorneys, in contrast, established a practice by the time they reached their mid-twenties. The age differential reflected the formidable obstacles that confronted blacks from working-class backgrounds who wished to enter a "gentleman's" profession.[13]

Six of the eleven black lawyers were born and reared in Texas. The rest, with the exception of one who came from Afghanistan, migrated from other Southern states: two from Georgia and one each from Mississippi and Louisiana. Galveston itself claimed four of these men as native sons. Allen G. Perkins, the son of a drayman, was valedictorian of the first graduating class at the local black high school in 1891. Perkin's grandfather, Alfred, had settled with his family in Galveston shortly after the Civil War and had helped to establish the Barnes Institute, the first school for freedmen in the city.[14] The other Galveston-born attorneys had similarly strong ties to the black community. Cornelius Williams, Jr., had the unique experience of representing the Eighth Ward as a city alderman for two years (1893–1895) before embarking on a legal career. Of the seven black lawyers who came to Galveston from other places, four established a local reputation by working at various occupations for at least a decade before taking up the law.[15]

With one exception, all of these men for whom family data is available came from humble backgrounds. Only Joseph Cuney, the son of a white slaveholder, enjoyed social and educational advantages that placed him in the ranks of the black elite. Born at "Sunnyside," his father's plantation on the Brazos River, Cuney completed his early education at the Wyle Street School in Pittsburgh and would have gone on to Oberlin College had the Civil War not intervened. He saw military service with the Sixty-third Pennsylvania Volunteers and settled in Galveston after the war. Through the influence of his brother Norris, a black politician of national stature in the late nineteenth century, Cuney became clerk at the U.S. Customhouse in Galveston during the administration of Benjamin Harrison. In 1897 he began to practice law at the age of fifty-two.[16]

Cuney's contemporaries at the bar were more typically the sons of urban or rural laborers: three were sons of draymen, two were sons of farmhands, one was the son of a white plantation owner, and one was the son of a carpenter; occupations of the fathers of four, however, are unknown. Despite the limited educational opportunities available to working-class blacks, five members of the group managed to attend college and/or law school. Allen G. Perkins studied at Bishop College in Marshall, Texas; J. Vance Lewis received some training at Leland University in New Orleans and at Lincoln University in Lancaster, Pennsylvania; and D. Webster Wilson graduated from Prairie View State Normal and Industrial College in Prairie View, Texas. These institutions were black schools founded after the Civil War to train teachers and ministers. The choice of law schools was more varied: Joseph Cuney studied for a time at Howard Law School; D. Webster Wilson graduated from Howard in 1902; Wilford H. Smith obtained his LL.B. degree from Boston University Law School in 1883; and J. Vance Lewis received degrees from both Michigan Law School (1894) and the Chicago College of Law (1897).[17]

How did the seven men with no law school training prepare for the bar? While hard evidence on this point is lacking, several possibilities deserve some consideration. A prospective black lawyer at the turn of the century might, for example, have chosen to take a correspondence course in law. The Galveston *New Idea*, which claimed to have the "largest circulation among colored people" of any local newspaper, ran frequent advertisements for the Sprague Correspondence School of Law in Detroit, Michigan:

STUDY LAW AT HOME

Prepare for success at the bar, in business or public life, by mail, in the ORIGINAL SCHOOL. Founded in 1890. Successful graduates everywhere. Approved by bar and law colleges. Regular College Law Course and Business Law Course. Liberal Terms, Special Offer now.

Catalogue Free[18]

George O. Burgess, a black attorney in the neighboring city of Houston, Texas, learned enough law from the Sprague course to pass the state bar examination in 1906.[19] One or two Galveston lawyers may well have studied law in the same fashion.

Others may have received some training in the offices of black practitioners. Wilford H. Smith had practiced successfully in the courts of Greenville, Mississippi, for ten years before he moved to Galveston in 1894.[20] Smith may have assisted another pioneer lawyer, Cornelius Williams, to establish a practice the following year. In turn, Williams probably encouraged his friend Alexander Green to enter the legal profession. Green and Williams formed a short-lived partnership in 1897, the first black law firm to appear in Galveston. Black attorneys often collaborated on individual cases, and their minority status may have prodded them to help other ambitious blacks to gain at least a working knowledge of the law.

Certainly, no black student could expect to clerk for a white attorney in Galveston by the 1890s. As the color line was more sharply drawn in local society, even well-intentioned whites hesitated to flout the racial sensibilities of the majority in any flagrant way. Still, some sympathetic white practitioners—especially Republican officeseekers who cultivated good relations with the black community—may have made their law libraries available to black students and offered an occasional word of advice.[21] White patrons also vouched for the character and competence of those black applicants who obtained their law licenses prior to the introduction of standardized bar examinations in July 1903. All but one of Galveston's black lawyers fell into this category; they were admitted to the bar after passing a perfunctory oral quiz before the judge of a district court.[22]

Lax admission procedures did not imply inadequate preparation or lack of ability on the part of minority professionals, however. Each of the Galveston group practiced law with some success. Seven appeared regularly before the local trial courts, and four argued cases before appellate tribunals as well. Like the ethnic lawyers of New York City and Philadelphia, they represented the victims in personal injury suits, defended the accused in criminal cases, and litigated claims arising out of insurance policies issued by fraternal orders.[23] In the absence of local banks or large business establishments owned by blacks, the colored lodges provided the best fee-generating opportunities for black practitioners. Walter R. Hill, an officer in the Colored Knights of Pythias and attorney for the group, reported that the Knights had paid nearly $20,000 in benefits during the first quarter of 1905.[24] Other black lawyers represented clients with substantial claims against such organizations as the Ancient Order of Pilgrims, the Grand United Order of Odd Fellows, the Knights and Daughters of Tabor, the Rising Sons and Daughters of Progress, and the United Brothers of Friendship and Sisters of the Mysterious Ten. Allen G. Perkins summarized the range of services offered by minority practitioners in a 1915 advertisement:

> LAW—Bonds, Deeds, Bills of Sale, Releases, Deeds of Trust, Chattel Mortgages, Collections of all Debts (new and old), Wills, Contracts, Articles of Co-partnership, Permits and Applications for Charters of Corporations, Guardianships, Administration of Estates, both Civil and Criminal Cases in all Courts, etc., given prompt and satisfactory attention.[25]

Perkins combined a successful law practice with an equally thriving real estate business ("A. G. Perkins & Co., LAW—LAND—LOANS"). In March 1914, he opened a branch office in Houston, which also prospered. Similarly, J. Vance Lewis, a Houston-based attorney, responded to the demands of an expanding practice by opening a Galveston office in 1914, to which he commuted several times a week. Less successful was Charles D. McBeth, whose frequent moves from one Texas city to another signaled a lack of strong client support.

As members of a professional class, lawyers shared leadership of the black community with other minority elites: ministers, doctors, dentists, teachers, and newspaper editors. They achieved a high level of visibility by participating in community affairs of all kinds, from political rallies and church socials to high school commencements and lodge meetings. While the oratorical tradition was dying out in the profession at large, black practitioners spent much of their time making public speeches. Through their frequent appearances before black audiences they exerted an influence on popular opinion second only to that of ministers. (The ubiquitous Allen G. Perkins may have gained a slight edge over his competitors by embracing the ministry as well as the law. Ordained a minister of the Macedonia Baptist Church in 1905, lawyer Perkins thereafter added church services to his schedule of speaking engagements.)[26]

On the whole, Galveston's black attorneys discharged their responsibilities to clients and community in exemplary fashion. Only twice did issues of professional misconduct arise. The facts concerning Alex Green were uncontested: he took money from a client after promising to institute divorce proceedings on her behalf. Instead, he did nothing; and when the client later complained of excessive delay in the handling of her case, he gave her two handwritten documents which he claimed were her divorce papers. She noted that her name was nowhere mentioned in the papers and "thought there was something funny about the seal." (She was right. It looked like a bunch of red ostrich feathers, and was apparently a magazine illustration that Green had cut out and pasted on the lower left corner of his "divorce decree.") After the disgruntled client brought these matters to the attention of the district court clerk, Green became the subject of a disbarment suit. Judge Robert G. Street, finding him guilty of "fraudulent and dishonorable conduct as an attorney," ordered him "forever disbarred" from practicing law in the state courts and sentenced him to serve one day in the county jail for contempt of court.[27]

The case of J. Vance Lewis was less clear-cut. Before he began to plead regularly in the Galveston courts, Lewis was twice suspended from practice by Houston judges because of alleged misconduct. In 1903, he defended himself against charges that he had forged the signatures on citations in a number of divorce suits. Angrily denying these accusations, Lewis contended that they sprang from a "conspiracy" against him by jealous competitors:

> There was a little two-by-four colored lawyer, and one or two low class white ones in Houston, who made a living out of the little cases, especially the divorce cases which were now coming to us. When not drunk they watched our success with ever-increasing envy and finally reported to Judge Chas. E. Ashe and also to Judge W. P. Hamblen that there was some irregularity in the citation of every case that I had on file.[28]

Although Judge Hamblen concluded that the evidence was insufficient to warrant disbarment, he reprimanded Lewis for "indiscretion" and suspended him from practice for six months.

When Lewis attempted to resume lawyering after a lengthy trip abroad, he found himself the target of a renewed attack by his enemies: "Colored lawyers and white lawyers, too, got together as soon as they knew I was in town, and I saw them as busy as ants, carrying news to the grand jury."[29] This time, the charge was swindling an elderly black couple—Lewis's clients—out of real estate worth $1,500. After being indicted by a grand jury, Lewis was released on bail but forbidden to practice in the criminal district court of Harris County until he had been cleared of the criminal charges pending against him. At the request of the district attorney's office, the case was continued from term to term for several years. When a trial at last took place, a jury found Lewis innocent. In the meantime, he managed to carry on a profitable civil practice: "[A]fter thinking the matter over I made up my mind to make a specialty of divorce cases in the district courts of Harris county, and during my seven years suspension I filed 3820 divorce cases, all of which netted me a neat little fee of $25.00 in each case."[30]

The repeated efforts by some Houston lawyers to force Lewis out of the profession raise some troublesome interpretive problems. Admittedly, he could be careless and amateurish in his work habits on occasion. Although his briefs were generally well researched and articulate, an appellate judge rightly characterized his original petition in one case as "crudely drawn and barely intelligible."[31] Still, similar deficiencies could be found in the work of other attorneys, black and white. Why was Lewis singled out for disciplinary action? His own belief in a vindictive biracial "conspiracy," though far-fetched, perhaps contains a germ of truth. Lewis was an outspoken and abrasive individual who would not accept the deferential role assigned to him within an evolving caste system. As an early civil rights lawyer, he angered conservative Texans by his frequent attacks upon Jim Crowism. Perceiving him to be an irresponsible troublemaker, some Houston attorneys may well have seized upon minor irregularities in his practice to harass and discredit him.

The most instructive lesson to be drawn from Lewis's experience, however, is that few of his clients deserted him. Despite his narrow escapes from disbarment, he managed to maintain, and even expand, his legal practice. A supportive clientele played a similarly important role in the careers of other black attorneys who practiced in Galveston at the turn of the century.

## IN THE COURTS: THE WILFORD SMITH YEARS, 1895–1901

Members of Galveston's black bar represented clients before local trial courts of four kinds. At the lowest level were two Justice of the Peace Courts, whose jurisdiction extended to minor criminal and civil cases involving sums no greater than $200. The Galveston County Court tried civil cases for larger amounts, up to $500, and handled probate matters. A Criminal District Court had jurisdiction over more serious misdemeanor cases and all felonies. Appeals from Justice of the Peace Courts resulted in trials de novo before the County or Criminal District Court. Finally, the Tenth Judicial District Court and the Fifty-sixth Judicial District Court heard civil cases involving $500 or more, as well as divorce cases.[32]

During the six years that he resided in Galveston, Wilford H. Smith practiced before each of these courts and also pleaded successfully before the appellate courts of the state and the United States Supreme Court. Smith's prior experience as a lawyer in Mississippi gave him a decided advantage over other black attorneys. He represented white as well as black clients, and the volume of his business equaled, or surpassed, that of some white solo practitioners. A glance at some aggregate figures reveals both the extent of Smith's predominance and the types of cases he and other black lawyers handled.

In one Justice of the Peace Court, Smith represented clients in thirty-two civil actions from July 26, 1898 to June 8, 1900. Of the other black attorneys who practiced in this court, Alex Green appeared in three cases, and Henry H. Swanston and Joseph Cuney each represented one client. Of the thirty-four cases argued, most involved either wage claims or attempts to recover specific property (from "one gray pony mare. . . named Fannie" to items of household furniture) through sequestration proceedings: account for services rendered, nine; damages, four; garnishment, two; claim for insurance benefits, one; sequestration, eighteen.[33] In the same court, Smith represented defendants in six criminal cases between 1897 and 1900. Swanston had two such clients during that period, and

Green had one. Five cases involved prosecutions for aggravated assault, two for vagrancy, and one each for unlawfully carrying a pistol and "malicious mischief."[34]

At the county court level, the pattern of unequal client distribution persisted. Four black attorneys engaged in probate work: Between 1898 and 1901 Smith handled seventeen probate cases; Green handled two; and Cuney and Swanston each had one. During that same period, Stubbs & Stubbs, a leading white firm, appeared on the probate docket thirty-seven times.[35] Smith also argued thirty nonprobate cases before the county court; these were primarily personal injury suits and sequestration and debt actions. No other black lawyers maintained a general practice in the county court.[36]

Divorces provided the major source of business for black and white practitioners in the district court. Between 1899 and 1902, black attorneys participated in a total of 122 cases, of which 103 were divorce suits, eleven damages, two garnishment, two removal of cloud from title, and one each trespass to try title, note and foreclosure, mandamus, and probate (appealed from county court).[37] Smith alone handled eighty of these cases. The rest were divided among six other black attorneys: Alex Green (twenty-seven), C. J. Williams (six), Allen Perkins (six), Joseph Cuney (two), H. H. Swanston (one), and Walter R. Hill (one).

Even when compared to the practice of many white lawyers, Smith's record was impressive. A tabulation of the cases argued in the district court during the year 1901 by five white solo practitioners reveals the following breakdown: Florence T. Atkins (three cases); A. B. Buetell (two cases); John L. Darrouzet (two cases); John Grothgar (seventeen cases); and Matthew Mulcahy (one case).[38] But an extensive practice did not mean a very lucrative one, since most of Smith's cases involved small sums of money. Representing plaintiffs in personal injury suits offered the best possibility for sharing in a large financial settlement, and Smith—like other black attorneys—advertised "DAMAGE SUITS A SPECIALTY."[39] The average contingent fee seldom measured up to its potential, however.

In *Arthur Mack v. Galveston, Houston & Henderson R.R. Co.* (1900), for example, Smith as co-counsel represented a young black dockworker whose leg had been permanently injured in an accident caused by the negligence of a railroad engineer. The complaint demanded $10,000 in damages, and the plaintiff assigned a one-half interest in his claim to his attorneys. Within weeks, an out-of-court settlement was made with the railroad company for $500. Acceptance of this modest sum pointed to a hidden limitation in personal injury suits: All-white juries would not award substantial damages to black plaintiffs.[40]

As the size of Smith's practice demonstrates, Galveston blacks relied extensively upon the courts to settle both individual disputes and contests for power within black institutions. Two cases that Smith argued before the Texas Court of Civil Appeals arose out of factional quarrels that threatened to destroy prominent community organizations. In *A. Hubbs v. George Perkins et al.* (1899),

Smith represented a group of trustees from the Avenue L Baptist Church, the city's oldest black congregation. His clients sought to enjoin their pastor from continuing to occupy the pulpit after his resignation had been accepted by a majority vote of the congregation. The church's property, Smith pointed out, was held under the terms of a charitable trust, whose purposes were being thwarted by the arbitrary practices and scandalous personal life of Reverend Alfred Hubbs:

The plaintiffs say that such church is an independent religious society, where the majority rules, sovereign in itself, with no right of appeal to any other higher body, except the courts of the country, that said society is governed and controlled by the Holy Bible and Hiscocks Baptist Church Directory whose principles act in the place of by-laws in the government of said church and the members are entitled as a matter of right to not be deprived of any of their privileges in said church except in accordance with said directory; and that without relief from this Hon. Court, they are utterly remediless at law or equity.[41]

Smith and the trustees won in both the trial and appellate courts, and the controversial Hubbs was forced to vacate his office. A less successful outcome resulted from Smith's efforts to assist members of the Nineteenth of June Committee to obtain control of funds in the hands of the Committee's treasurer. Formed in the 1880s to commemorate the anniversary of black emancipation in Texas, the committee was an informal association whose sole function was to stage an appropriate celebration of that event each year in Galveston. After 1896 two rival groups, each with some justification, claimed to represent the committee. Confronted with a mass of conflicting evidence, the courts, in effect, threw up their hands and refused to order the treasurer to turn over the funds to either faction.[42]

Although Smith did not appear in many criminal cases, he did carry several to the Texas Court of Criminal Appeals. Of some local importance were two companion cases in which the editor and business manager of the *Galveston Times* were charged with libel for publishing an intemperate attack upon an unnamed Irish streetcar conductor:

It is really disgusting, to say the least, for one to take notice and see how the *irish snides* employed by the street car company as conductors on the various lines of this city discriminate. . . . Some few nights ago a colored lady while dismounting from an East L car was thrown to the ground by the mangy ape, that poses as conductor ringing the bell before she was off the step. And the lousy little puppy that scarcely speaks English, said to a white gentleman, that spoke of the danger of such proceedings, that she was "a she coon." Has it come to this? Such pimps as this; men so low that they would willingly sell the virtue of their sister for a drink; the descendants of Oscar Wilde; greasy curs, foul smelling scavengers are imported to this country to insult and humiliate the people that help to make these enterprises; that build up and support these public affairs. . . . It's time that the car company should right these wrongs and employ only respectable, intelligent men that will do justice to all alike. We pay a nickel and we *demand* a nickel's worth. . . .[43]

In his brief for the defense, Smith argued that his clients' statements were not libelous, since they did not falsely accuse anyone of a crime or other notoriously bad conduct, as required by state law. The court disagreed, holding that the case was one of group libel and that the reputation of every conductor employed by the Galveston City Railroad Company had been damaged by the article in question. W. L. Jones, editor of the paper, was sentenced to one year's imprisonment in the county jail; W. H. Noble, his business manager and the reputed author of the piece, had to pay a fine of $100.[44] (A few years later, Noble became a newspaper editor himself. His early acquaintance with libel law may account for the tone of resolute civility that characterized the *City Times* under his direction.)

Smith displayed his talents as a criminal lawyer to better advantage in *Carter v. Texas* (1900), his most celebrated case and the capstone of his career at the Galveston bar. Seth Carter, the defendant, was a black man who had been indicted by a white grand jury for the murder of his girl friend. At the opening of the trial, Smith moved to quash the indictment. His client, he argued, had been denied the equal protection of the laws through the discriminatory action of the jury commissioners in excluding all blacks from jury service. The trial judge overruled Smith's motion, and the defendant was eventually convicted of first degree murder and sentenced to death. After an unsuccessful appeal to the Texas Court of Criminal Appeals, Smith carried the case on writ of error to the United States Supreme Court. In a unanimous opinion written by Justice Horace Gray, the Court held that Smith had properly raised an issue of constitutional right and should have been permitted to offer proof of racial discrimination in the selection of grand jurors. Gray accordingly ordered the judgment reversed and the case remanded to state authorities for further proceedings.[45]

The *Carter* case gave Smith a national reputation among black professionals, and encouraged him to seek new career opportunities by moving to New York City in 1901. Soon after his arrival, he reported on his prospects to Galvestonian James B. Stubbs, a prominent white practitioner who had agreed to take charge of several pending insurance claims for Smith:

> I am very much pleased at the cordial spirit of the people about the courts and in fact everywhere. I have every reason to believe that I shall succeed here, after I am known. . . .
>
> I find much pleasure however in reflecting upon the very cordial way I was treated at Galveston, and especially by yourself, and the remark you made the last day I was at the office I will remember and cherish to my grave: "If the Yankees don't treat you right, come back to us, and we will show them who you are."[46]

Soft-spoken and deferential, Smith combined technical proficiency with a shrewd sense of public relations. Unlike J. Vance Lewis, he projected an image of modest craftsmanship that did not appear to threaten the institutional bases of southern white hegemony. As Jim Crow laws multiplied in the early twentieth century, however, Smith's successors abandoned a deferential style of lawyering in favor of more assertive and confrontational tactics.

## CONFRONTING A CASTE SYSTEM, 1902–1919

Smith's departure created a leadership gap in Galveston's black bar that no single practitioner was able to fill. Between 1902 and 1919, the volume of cases handled by black attorneys remained relatively constant, but they were now distributed more equitably among three or four leading practitioners. In the district court, black lawyers appeared in 102 cases from 1905 to 1908. Allen G. Perkins represented the largest number of clients (thirty-four), followed by Joseph Cuney (twenty-three), Walter R. Hill (eighteen), Webster Wilson (eleven), C. J. Williams (seven), Alex Green (five), and Allen D. Bridge (four).[47]

A similar breakdown occurred in connection with the 118 cases argued by black attorneys before the district court between 1914 and 1917. Joseph Cuney handled forty-one of these cases, followed by J. Vance Lewis (thirty-four), A. G. Perkins (twenty-seven), C. J. Williams (nine), Webster Wilson (five), M. G. Lewis (one), and M. H. Broyles (one).[48] The lower trial courts witnessed a comparable division of labor.

Little overall change was discernable in the types of cases that came to black attorneys after 1900. Divorces, personal injury suits, debt collections, wage claims, and suits on insurance policies continued to form the staples of their practice, as in the 1890s. For the first time, however, they became actively involved in civil rights activities, as they sought to develop new strategies for combating racial discrimination in three areas: transportation, criminal justice, and voting rights.

Although the Texas legislature had required intrastate railroads to provide separate coaches for blacks as early as 1891, municipal streetcar lines remained desegregated until the twentieth century. Galveston's City Commissioners began to consider segregating the local streetcars only after 500 citizens signed a petition requesting such action in the spring of 1906. The proposal drew an immediate letter of protest from lawyer Joseph Cuney, whose remarks were published in the leading white newspaper as well as the black press. "When the street railway system was first introduced into Galveston this same thing was attempted by a few people," Cuney recalled, "but Julius Runge, C. W. Hurley, the agent for Morgan's steamship company, and others, refused to tax the city with such an uncalled for regulation. It was an impulse then and is a mere impulse now. The passing years have vindicated the wisdom of those men, for things have gone well with us since. . . ."[49] Despite the objections of Cuney and other black spokesmen, the Commissioners passed the proposed ordinance, albeit with little enthusiasm, on June 28, 1906.[50]

Several younger practitioners, instead of confining themselves to dignified protests, attacked Jim Crowism more dramatically through the courts. Cornelius

J. Williams joined Allen G. Perkins in bringing dual damage suits against the Galveston, Harrisburg & San Antonio Railway Company in 1905. The railroad had advertised the introduction of a special train, called the Motor Car, for carrying passengers more quickly between Galveston and Houston, and indicated that seats would be available only for white travelers. Williams and Perkins went together to the depot and attempted to purchase tickets on the Motor Car. When they were refused, each represented the other in suing the railroad for $10,000 in actual and punitive damages. In their complaints, they charged that the railroad had violated the separate accommodations law of the state by failing to partition off a portion of the Motor Car for use by black patrons. The cases remained on the docket of the Tenth Judicial District Court for several years, without ever reaching a jury. After the court had granted numerous continuances (presumably at the request of the railroad's attorneys), the plaintiffs were required to give security for the costs of further prosecution. When they failed to do so, the cases were dismissed.[51] Perkins and Williams did attract much public attention through their defiant actions, however. "Many white dailys and every negro paper in the country had an account of that suit in their news columns," reported the editor of the *New Idea*.[52]

Attorney Walter R. Hill likewise attempted to assert the rights of black travelers against a railroad that did not strictly comply with the "separate but equal" provisions of state law. In *C. J. Walker v. International & Great Northern Railway Company* (1908), the plaintiff and his wife were sitting in a coach reserved for blacks when several white passengers entered and began to curse and threaten them. A brakeman witnessed the disturbance, but did nothing to stop it. Hill argued that the railroad was negligent in failing to ensure the safety of its passengers and that it had violated the state law by allowing whites to enter and remain in the black coach. The railroad's lawyers responded that the brakeman had no authority to eject a passenger, but that he had immediately summoned assistance and effected the removal of the offending whites within a few minutes. Trial juries twice found for the defendant railroad, and the Court of Civil Appeals affirmed the verdict.[53]

To better protect the rights of black defendants in criminal cases, Galveston's black lawyers helped to organize the Anti-Lynching and Protective Association of Texas in July 1914. The lynching problem was especially severe in the state during the early twentieth century. Between 1904 and 1919, Texans reportedly lynched 130 blacks, a record exceeded only in Mississippi and Georgia. The Galveston protest group, which claimed to be the first of its kind in the South, aimed at influencing the state legislature to pass antilynch laws and other measures designed to force peace officers "to follow their sworn duty in giving the same protection to their Negro prisoners as is given to white prisoners."[54]

Individually, several practitioners took steps to remedy injustices committed against blacks in the Justice of the Peace Courts. Webster Wilson initiated habeas corpus proceedings on several occasions to effect the release of low-income clients who, he charged, were being illegally confined under excessive bail requirements.[55] More dramatic was the frontal assault launched by a trio of black lawyers against Justice of the Peace Sydney T. Fontaine for allegedly violating the constitutional rights of their client.

Fontaine was an elderly attorney who had practiced for decades at the Galveston bar. Elected Justice of the Peace for Precinct One in 1904, he heard a case on April 18, 1906, involving one Payton Glover, who was charged with uttering threats to do serious bodily harm to a Mrs. Talbert. According to Glover's sworn complaint, he brought his attorney with him to court and requested a trial. Fontaine, however,

> absolutely refused him the privilege of pleading to the said charge and denied him the constitutional right to be tried or present any defense whatever, but found him guilty and assessed his punishment by requiring him to give a bond to keep the peace for one year towards all persons, in the sum of One Hundred Dollars and ordered him incarcerated in the body of the jail until said bond was given and approved. . . .[56]

Glover spent three and one-half hours in confinement, subjected to "hardships, privations, humiliations, and disgrace," before yielding to necessity and giving bond. His lawyer was less fortunate; Fontaine ordered him jailed for twenty-four hours.

On the basis of these allegations, Glover's counsel (Allen G. Perkins, Alexander Green, and Cornelius J. Williams) brought two actions against Fontaine: a damage suit for wrongful imprisonment, and a petition to the district court to have him removed from office for official misconduct. Neither effort succeeded. A jury acquitted Fontaine of misconduct, and the damage suit was eventually dropped.[57] The whole episode nonetheless demonstrates that Galveston's black attorneys—especially those with little formal training—welcomed abrasive confrontations with white officials in some civil rights situations.

Their sporadic activism seems all the more impressive in light of the limited encouragement they received from a badly divided black community. There were all too many "Jim-Crow Niggers" in Galveston, complained the editor of the *New Idea* in 1906: "They are the first to ride on separate cars and shame the race, the ones who feed in the kitchens of white chop-houses, and for a few dimes will betray every man, woman and child of their race."[58] Even the local Republican party—to which almost all Galveston blacks belonged—was split into contending factions by the turn of the century, as the "lily whites" fought the "black-and-tans" for control of patronage and policy-making within the organization. The black bar itself reflected these divisions: Williams, Green, and Hill adhered to the regular Republican organization, while Cuney and Perkins supported the maverick "black-and-tans" in their demand for greater black participation in leadership posts.[59]

Whatever their intraparty differences, however, the lawyers united in efforts to organize black voters against the threat of disfranchisement posed by successive Democratic measures. Chief among these was a poll tax requirement adopted as an amendment to the state constitution in December 1902. The new law required all citizens between the ages of twenty-one and sixty to pay an annual poll tax in order to vote in any election. Since blacks made up almost one-fourth of Galveston's population, their votes were potentially decisive in many city elections. Webster Wilson accordingly helped to organize a Poll Tax Club in 1908 and served as its president. The announced purpose of the group was to stir up "an interest among the colored citizens to qualify for the necessary political standing in the city as there is an election here next May for commissioners." Although no other formal organizations of this sort were created prior to World War I, Cuney, Williams, and Perkins regularly addressed poll tax rallies and other public meetings designed to mobilize black voting strength.[60]

## CODA: ENTER A NEW GENERATION

By 1920, the pioneer black bar of Galveston was fast disappearing. Death had claimed Henry Swanston, Webster Wilson, and Charles McBeth; Alex Green had been disbarred; and Wilford Smith, Walter Hill, Allen Bridge, and J. Vance Lewis had relocated elsewhere. Cornelius Williams, Joseph Cuney, and Allen Perkins remained, but only Perkins carried on a very active law practice. The brief outburst of professional militancy that had occurred in the prewar years had no sequel thereafter. Even the NAACP, whose work Perkins supported, could not gain a firm foothold in postwar Galveston.[61]

During the 1920s, the first new minority recruits in more than a decade joined the local bar. John H. Barbour, the son of a minister, practiced only a few years. Thomas H. Dent, who came from a working-class background, established a practice in 1926 that he still maintains, more than fifty years later. Dent's extraordinary career recalls that of Wilford Smith, whom he knew personally. The two men shared not only superior professional skills, but also a common philosophical attitude toward lawyering in the South.

"All you have to do is know the law," Smith once advised his young acquaintance. "The Judge don't care whether you're white or black. Just have the law for him." Dent received similar counsel from his law professors at Howard Law School, from which he graduated in 1925. They also pointed out the practical advantages of a deferential demeanor when pleading before southern courts. "They told those of us who were planning to practice in the South that we should always make our objections to the judge in high-toned and flowery language, and avoid trouble that way," Dent recalls. He seems to have followed these precepts in his own practice, with beneficial results. He can not remember ever being abused or mistreated by white judges or lawyers; on the contrary, one district court judge befriended and helped him in his early years, and a white attorney let him use his law library. As the only black law school graduate then practicing, he enjoyed strong client support and earned a good income from the inception of his career. He did not associate with the older black lawyers, however, since he had been warned by white practitioners that their reputation was bad. Nor did he see any need for a local NAACP.[62]

Yet Dent was by no means either a toady or a detached clinician. The contrast between himself and some earlier black attorneys was more a matter of style than of substance. He, too, represented black defendants in many controversial criminal cases and handled other civil rights litigation. For him, as for Smith, deference did not imply servility; it represented a tactical concession to southern racial mores. Although custom, like law, changed with glacial slowness in the area of race relations, Dent and his predecessors did much to keep the promise of equal justice alive during a period of often brutal repression.

## NOTES

I am most grateful to the following archivists for their generous assistance and encouragement: Jane Kenamore and Michael Wilson, Rosenberg Library Archives, Galveston, Texas; Robert L. Schaadt, Regional Historical Resource Depository and Local Records Division of the Texas State Library, Houston Metropolitan Records Center, Houston, Texas; and Ramonda Jo Seeber and her staff assistant, Stephenie Mattes, Galveston District Court Archives, Galveston County Courthouse.

1. Carter Godwin Woodson, *The Negro Professional Man and the Community, With Special Emphasis on the Physician and the Lawyer* (1934; reprint, New York, 1970), 184–97, 221–39.

2. Bruce Alden Glasrud, "Black Texans, 1900–1930: A History" (Ph.D. diss., Texas Technological College, 1969), 300–301.

3. Kenneth S. Tollett, "Black Lawyers, Their Education, and the Black Community," *Howard Law Journal* 17 (1972): 326, 346.

4. Lawrence D. Rice, *The Negro in Texas, 1874–1900* (Baton Rouge, 1971), 86–94.

5. Irvin C. Mollison, "Negro Lawyers in Mississippi," *Journal of Negro History* 38 (January 1930): 38–71.

6. Scott is listed as a "col'd atty" in Gillespie & Work's *Dallas Texas City and County Directory* (1881–1882); on Fremont, see Rice, *Negro in Texas*, 194.

7. Biographical information on Wiley and Turner appears in James B. Bradwell, "The Colored Bar of Chicago," *Michigan Law Review* 5 (1896): 385, 397–98. Morrison & Fourmy's *General Directory of the City of Dallas* (1886–1887) contains the first reference to Wiley, who is designated as "(c) attorney." The compilers of some city directories in Texas continued to identify black residents by race down to World War II.

8. Aggregate bar figures are taken from [U.S. Bureau of the Census] *Eleventh Census: 1890—Report on Population of the United States*, vol. 1, pt. 2 (Washington, D.C., 1897), Table 79, 306; *Twelfth Census: 1900—Population*, vol. 2, pt. 2 (Washington, D.C., 1902), Table 93, 541; and *Negroes in the United States* (Washington, D.C., 1904), Table 26, 185. The appearance of black lawyers in specific cities was determined by consulting all available city directories for the years 1865 to 1900 at the Library of Congress.

9. For statistical information on Galveston's black community, see *Galveston City Times*, May 1, 1909, 4; and March 25, 1916, 2.

10. Galveston's turn-of-the-century court records are presently housed in two separate

locations: the dockets of the Justice of the Peace Courts (First and Second Precincts), the County Court, and the Probate Court, together with case files from the County Court and the Texas Court of Civil Appeals, are in the Regional Historical Resource Depository (RHRD) at the Houston Metropolitan Records Center (hereafter cited as HMRC), Houston Public Library, Houston, Texas; the dockets and case files of the Criminal District Court, the Tenth Judicial District Court, and the Fifty-sixth Judicial District Court are in the District Court Archives, Galveston County Courthouse (hereafter cited as GCC), Galveston, Texas. The James B. and Charles J. Stubbs Papers (Rosenberg Library Archives, Galveston, Texas) contain some interesting letters from two black attorneys, D. Webster Wilson and Wilford H. Smith.

11. A complete list of these practitioners appears in the concluding section of this essay. I have included in this study only those lawyers who practiced regularly in the Galveston courts and who advertised themselves as attorneys in the annual city directories. Other lawyers whose names turn up occasionally in the records, such as O. C. Millard, M. G. Lewis, and M. H. Broyles, were Houston-based practitioners. James D. Moore represents a special case. For part of the period in question, he practiced law in Houston; when he lived in Galveston, he made only rare appearances in the courts. He was also a practicing physician and always classified himself as such in the Galveston City Directories. On the basis of those facts, I chose to exclude him from consideration.

12. For data on age, geographical origins, and paternal occupations, I relied largely on the manuscript census records at the National Archives, especially: U.S. Bureau of the Census, *Population Schedules of the Twelfth Census of the United States: 1900*, RG 29, T623, Microfilm Roll 1637, vols. 44, 45 (Galveston County, Texas); and *Population Schedules of the Thirteenth Census. . . : 1910*, RG 29, T624, Microfilm Roll 1554, vols. 55, 56 (Galveston County, Texas).

13. City directories disclosed the year in which native Galvestonians began their practice. For the others, I consulted biographical and autobiographical sketches, including obituaries in the *Galveston City Times*. The data on Galveston's white lawyers come from research I did for a previous essay, "The Texas Bar in the Nineteenth Century," *Vanderbilt Law Review* 32 (1979): 261.

14. For a brief biography of Perkins written around 1916, see *The Red Book of Houston* (Houston, n.d.), 142–44; included is a photograph of Perkins and his office staff.

15. According to the city directories, Henry H. Swanston was a barber and saloon-keeper; Walter R. Hill advanced from laborer to proprietor of a barber shop and bathhouse; Webster Wilson taught school, clerked at the post office and customhouse, and became Deputy Collector of Customs in 1898; and Joseph Cuney, in addition to the customhouse job mentioned in the text, worked as a teacher and a building contractor.

16. For Cuney's family background and early years, see Maud Cuney Hare, *Norris Wright Cuney: A Tribune of the Black People* (New York, 1913).

17. Perkins's education is discussed in *The Red Book of Houston*, 143. On Smith, see Mollison, "Negro Lawyers in Mississippi," 63; and W. J. Maxwell, comp., *General Alumni Catalogue of Boston University* (Boston, 1918), 164. D. Webster Wilson's obituary in the *Galveston City Times*, July 15, 1916, 2, provides details concerning his education; see also *Howard University Alumni Directory, 1870–1919* (Washington, D.C., n.d.). J. Vance Lewis published a valuable autobiography, *Out of the Ditch: A True Story of an Ex-Slave* (Houston, 1910), in which he discussed his education (pp. 28–31). Cuney's attendance at Howard Law School is mentioned in an article on his son, Washington Attorney Charles S. Cuney, in the *Galveston City Times*, Feb. 5, 1916, 1.

18. *Galveston New Idea*, March 4, 1905, 4.

19. See the sketch of Burgess in *The Red Book of Houston*, 107.

20. Mollison, "Negro Lawyers in Mississippi," 40.

21. Thomas H. Dent, a black attorney still in active practice in Galveston, recalls that several white lawyers allowed him to use their law libraries in the 1920s. Similar courtesies were probably extended to some earlier black practitioners. Interview with Thomas H. Dent, Galveston, Texas, July 23, 1981.

22. On state bar admission requirements in the late nineteenth century, see Oran M. Roberts, "Legal Education and Admission to the Bar," in Texas Bar Association, *Proceedings of the Third Annual Session* (1884): 43–48; and see, in general, Ralph W. Yarborough, "A History of Law Licensing in Texas," in Committee on History and Tradition of the State Bar of Texas, *Centennial History of the Texas Bar, 1882–1982* (Burnet, Texas, 1981), 181–93.

23. For a good account of the problems faced by ethnic practitioners in major metropolitan centers at the turn of the century, see Jerold S. Auerbach, *Unequal Justice: Lawyers and Social Change in Modern America* (New York, 1976), 40-73.

24. *Galveston New Idea*, April 12, 1905, 4.

25. *Galveston City Times*, August 28, 1915, 1.

26. *The Red Book of Houston*, 143.

27. *State v. Alex Green, Atty.*, case file 25975, Fifty-sixth Judicial District Court, District Court Archives, GCC.

28. Lewis, *Out of the Ditch*, 84.

29. Ibid., 92.

30. Ibid., 99.

31. *Samuel Turner and Martha Willis v. Effie Turner et al.*, case file 7364, Texas First Court of Civil Appeals, RHRD at HMRC.

32. On the evolution of the Texas Court System, see Spurgeon E. Bell, "A History of the Texas Courts," in *Centennial History of the Texas Bar*, 194–215. Galveston had only one district court (Tenth Judicial District Court) to handle civil cases prior to 1900, when the Fifty-sixth Judicial District Court was established.

33. Civil Docket No. 13, Galveston County Justice of the Peace Court, Pct. 1, RHRD at HMRC. The slight discrepancy between the appearance and case figures arises from the fact that two black attorneys were involved in the same case on three occasions.

34. Criminal Dockets (1897–1900), Galveston County Justice of the Peace Court, Pct. 1, RHRD at HMRC.

35. General Probate Docket, County Clerk of Galveston County, RHRD at HMRC.

36. The county court figures were compiled from County Court Dockets 45 to 56 covering individual terms of court and General Dockets 5 and 6, County Clerk of Galveston County, RHRD at HMRC.

37. General Docket No. 10 (July 29, 1898–December 8, 1908), District Court Archives, GCC.

38. Ibid.

39. Smith, Cuney, and Green each made mention of damage suits in the advertisements they published in the *Galveston City Times*, September 29, 1900, 4.

40. *Arthur Mack v. Galveston, Houston & Henderson R.R. Co.*, case file 22197, Fifty-sixth Judicial District Court, District Court Archives, GCC.

41. *A. Hubbs v. George Perkins et al.*, case file 2151, Texas First Court of Civil

Appeals, RHRD at HMRC. The quoted statement comes from Smith's application to the county court for a writ of injunction in March 1898.

42. *Nineteenth of June Committee v. F. Z. Miller et al.*, case file 1904, Texas First Court of Civil Appeals, RHRD at HMRC. For the result of the case, which was decided without a written opinion, see Minutes of the Court of Civil Appeals (April 11, 1895–April 20, 1898), HMRC.

43. *State v. W. L. Jones*, case file 11334, Criminal District Court, District Court Archives, GCC. The text of the newspaper article is included in the summary of evidence prepared by counsel for submission to the Texas Court of Criminal Appeals.

44. *Jones v. State*, 38 *Tex. Crim. Rep*. 364 (1897); *Noble v. State*, 38 *Tex. Crim. Rep*. 368 (1897).

45. *Carter v. Texas*, 177 *U.S.* 442 (1900).

46. Wilford H. Smith to James B. Stubbs, July 9, 1901, in James B. and Charles J. Stubbs Papers, Box 19, Rosenberg Library Archives, Galveston, Texas. Smith did succeed in New York. Apart from his regular practice, he served as a pioneer legal counsel for the New York office of the NAACP. He also became Booker T. Washington's personal attorney, and later represented Marcus Garvey's ill-fated steamship company, the Black Star Line.

47. General Docket No. 10 (July 29, 1898–December 8, 1908), District Court Archives, GCC.

48. General Docket No. 12 (May 20, 1913–August 15, 1916), District Court Archives, GCC.

49. Cuney's letter, which appeared in the *Galveston Daily News* on May 15, 1906, was republished in the *Galveston City Times*, May 19, 1906, 1. On the evolution of Jim Crow transportation laws in Texas, see Glasrud, "Black Texans," 177–181.

50. The text of the ordinance was published in the *Galveston Daily News*, June 29, 1906, 5. The commissioners split 2 to 2 over the adoption of the measure, and the mayor cast the deciding vote.

51. *Allen G. Perkins v. Galveston, Harrisburg & San Antonio Ry. Co.*, case file 25469, Fifty-sixth Judicial District Court; *Cornelius J. Williams v. Galveston, Harrisburg & San Antonio Ry. Co.*, case file 25470, Tenth Judicial District Court, District Court Archives, GCC. The final outcome of each case was noted on the respective court docket: Fifty-sixth Judicial District Court (February Term 1908); Tenth Judicial District Court (October Term 1907).

52. *Galveston New Idea*, December 23, 1905, 1.

53. *C. J. Walker v. International & Great Northern R.R. Co.*, case file 26152, Tenth Judicial District Court, District Court Archives, GCC.

54. On the organization and early activities of the association, see *Galveston City Times*, August 8, 1914, 4; August 22, 1914, 4; and October 24, 1914, 4. The statistics on lynchings were taken from Walter White, *Rope and Faggot: A Biography of Judge Lynch* (reprint ed., New York, 1969), 254–59.

55. See, for example: *State ex rel. Willie Fance v. Henry Thomas, Sheriff* (1907), case file 26017; *State ex rel. William Marshall v. Henry Thomas, Sheriff* (1908), case file 26647, Fifty-sixth Judicial District Court, District Court Archives, GCC.

56. *State ex rel. Payton Glover v. Sydney T. Fontaine*, case file 25660, Tenth Judicial District Court, District Court Archives, GCC.

57. The damage suit was *Payton Glover v. S. T. Fontaine et al.*, case file 25627, Fifty-sixth Judicial District Court, District Court Archives, GCC.

58. *Galveston New Idea*, March 31, 1906, 1.

59. On Republican party politics in Texas during the early twentieth century, see Glasrud, "Black Texans," 40 ff.

60. The formation of the Poll Tax Club was reported in the *Galveston City Times*, December 26, 1908, 1. Glasrud traces the progress of disfranchisement in "Black Texans," 55–57.

61. Galveston blacks formed a potentially strong branch of the NAACP in December 1918, with 140 charter members. By 1921, however, it was moribund; all further attempts during the 1920s to create an active local organization failed. NAACP Records, Branch Files, G–202, Manuscript Division, Library of Congress.

62. Interview with Thomas H. Dent, Galveston, Texas, July 23, 1981.

*W. HAMILTON BRYSON AND E. LEE SHEPARD*

# *The Virginia Bar, 1870–1900*

An essay on the Virginia bar from 1870 to 1900 must begin with a definition of a Virginia attorney-at-law. In 1870 and for the next twenty-five years, a Virginia lawyer was "any person" over the age of twenty-one of "honest demeanor" who had been examined for fitness and licensed to practice law by any two judges of Virginia courts of record. Having been licensed, each attorney must have then "qualified" to practice in each court in which he wished to appear. This was done by swearing in that court to demean himself honestly in the practice of law and to support the Commonwealth.[1]

No one could quarrel with the theory of licensing lawyers in nineteenth-century Virginia. In practice, however, there was a seriously weak link in the chain that was to ensure competent and moral legal advice to the general public. This weak link was the examination by the judges of the applicant for the license to practice law. Sometimes there was a serious questioning and probing of the applicant's knowledge of legal theory and doctrine, but as often as not the examination was less than superficial. There can not possibly have been any uniformity of procedures or standards from county to county. Some judges were easier than others. Some were reluctant to be strict with their neighbors' sons. Some believed that anyone who could get clients should have the right to practice law and would therefore sign licenses without any examination at all.[2] Moreover, judicial courtesy required the second judge to sign the license without any further examination. One attorney, B. B. Munford, recalled being examined by two judges, but the examination was not difficult.[3] H. R. Pollard, who presented himself for examination in 1867, was not questioned at all when he produced his law school diploma.[4]

One of the original stated goals of the Virginia State Bar Association, which was founded in 1888, was to require higher qualifications for the admission to practice law in Virginia. The standing Committee on Legal Education and Admission to the Bar was erected at the first meeting of the association. It was noted that "the tests prescribed for determining fitness for admission to the bar in Virginia are a mocking farce." The committee was therefore directed to draft an act making the examination for admission to the bar a meaningful experience.[5]

The draft act, which required a bar examination to be conducted by three attorneys who were to be appointed by the local circuit judge, was presented to the General Assembly, but it was defeated. The reason for the failure of the bill seems to have been a feeling that anyone who could get clients should have the right to practice law.[6] This philosophy was directly counter to that of the association, which was trying to raise the level of professional excellence by excluding those who lacked knowledge or intelligence or integrity.

In 1895, the Committee on Legal Education and Admission to the Bar presented to the Virginia State Bar Association two proposed bills: The first would set up boards of bar examiners; the second would transfer the examination of applicants from the circuit judges to the justices of the Supreme Court of Appeals. Although the committee favored the first, the association voted to recommend the second.[7] In 1896, the General Assembly finally acted and passed a bill requiring the Supreme Court of Appeals to license future members of the Virginia bar after an examination pursuant to regulations to be promulgated.[8] Rules for a written bar examination were promptly published,[9] and the first bar exam was given on January 8, 1897.[10] In 1910, the Virginia Board of Bar Examiners was created to relieve the court of this time-consuming administrative responsibility.[11]

This is enough on the subject of who could practice law. Let us now turn to the subject of who did practice in Virginia. In 1870, Virginia was restored to democratic and constitutional government when the new state constitution came into force and the military government was withdrawn. The subsequent moderation in Virginia politics can be explained by the fact that Virginia was relieved of radical misrule sooner than most of the southern states.

The bar of Virginia in 1870 was dominated by former Confederate officers.[12] These men used their military titles for the rest of their lives, which must have seemed strange to the northerners who considered themselves the victors in the struggle for national unity. It might seem strange also to mention this here, but it helps to explain the character of both the South in general and of the Virginia bar in particular. The Virginia bar in the 1870s, certainly its leaders, were men trained in leadership, taught courage on the battlefield, and matured by adversity. Defeat one day did not deter them from renewed battle the next, whether on the battlefield or in the courtroom. They had been reared before the war in a tradition of personal honesty and strict integrity. During the last third of the nineteenth century, Virginians were generally excluded from the national legal scene,[13] but within the Commonwealth reputations were to be made.

That Virginia had suffered economic disaster by the defeat of the Confederacy has never been contested. The value of real and personal estates as reported in the 1870 United States Census had declined a significant 48.3 percent from 1860, and was down from that of 1850 as well, indicating the magnitude of Virginia's depression. The number of improved acres of land in farms dropped by more than 3 million. Although the number of manufacturing establishments had increased by about 600 from 1860 (5,385 to 5,933), the amount of capital available for improvement and production had plummeted and the dollar value of products had likewise declined. The loss of the real and personal property and industry in the fifty counties now forming West Virginia had accounted for a percentage of this decline, but only for a part. In comparison with many northern states, which, despite the war, had continued to grow in wealth and productivity, Virginia's predicament stands out clearly. It did, however, fare better than some of the other Confederate states.[14]

Nonetheless, the bar was beginning to rebuild by 1870 and return to its former position of economic and professional ascendency. The United States Census for that year listed 1,075 resident attorneys in Virginia, down substantially from the number listed in 1860, but still a respectable figure.[15] Farmers, physicians, merchants, teachers, and even clergymen outranked attorneys in number, but not in either earning potential or community standing.

As Virginia gradually recovered from the effects of the Civil War, the Commonwealth began to grow and prosper. Virginia's overall population increased at ten-year increments of approximately 15 percent, from 1,225,163 in 1870 to 1,854,184 in 1900. During the same thirty years, capital available for investment and production rose by a respectable 244.8 percent (to nearly $104 million), and the dollar value of industrial products grew by 155.2 percent (to over $132 million). The number of acres of improved farmland in the Commonwealth multiplied, as did the average dollar value per acre of farmland, which climbed from $13.56 in 1870 to $16.25 by 1900. Virginia's economy remained, in comparison with that of many other states, primarily agricultural.[16]

By 1880, 1,355 lawyers resided in Virginia, the vast majority of whom were native-born and below the age of sixty. At that time, they represented 2.1 percent of the total number of practicing attorneys listed for the states and territories in the federal census.[17] The 1890 census listed 1,649 males as resident attorneys, 38 of whom were nonwhite.[18] By 1900, the profession in Virginia had grown to 2,032.[19] Not surprisingly, the greatest number of attorneys were concentrated in the Commonwealth's urban centers: Richmond, Norfolk, Petersburg, and Lynchburg.[20]

Virginia's first black attorney probably was Robert Peel Brooks, who was admitted to practice in Henrico County and Richmond in January 1876.[21] He was joined the next year by Henry B. Fry and William C. Roane. Roane, a well-educated former schoolteacher, remained in practice for some years. In 1880, E. A. Randolph received his LL.B. from Yale Law School and commenced practice in Richmond.[22] Other prominent black members of the Virginia bar in the nineteenth century were Giles B. Jackson, James H. Hayes, and Charles F. Whittle. By the last decade of the century, a number of blacks were successfully practicing in the Commonwealth; most were situated in the state's major urban centers.[23]

Before 1920, there were no women licensed to practice in the state. Although the statutes regulating admission to the bar before 1895 stated that "any person" could be licensed,[24] public sentiment in Virginia at that time opposed the idea of female lawyers.[25] In the early 1890s, Belva Lockwood, the nationally known feminist, attempted to join the Virginia bar, but her application was refused because she was a woman. The United States Supreme Court in 1894 upheld the Virginia court's ruling that construed the statute to exclude women, and the federal court declared that the right to practice law is not a privilege or immunity of a citizen of the United States.[26] The next year, the Virginia statute was amended to permit "any male citizen" to be licensed to practice law.[27]

In 1920, the statute was changed to allow women to practice at the bar.[28] That same year, three women were admitted to the University of Virginia School of Law; two of them, Rosemary Davis of Norfolk and Elizabeth H. Tompkins of Richmond, passed the bar examination and were licensed in 1922.[29]

The nature of legal practice began to change in the last third of the nineteenth century, and the divergence between "country lawyers" and those who practiced in Virginia's urban centers became more pronounced. In the immediate postwar years, most attorneys practicing in the county and circuit courts of the Old Dominion found, because of the economics of the times, that they had to supplement the income they derived from their law practices. A prominent King William County attorney spent nearly as much of his time in the fields as he did in the courtroom, and a Caroline County practitioner taught school until his financial picture brightened.[30] Likewise, lawyers found a need to accept all kinds of cases; specialization was not possible. "In those days," wrote John S. Wise, "the lawyer took whatever grist came to his mill." Equity or common law, civil litigation or criminal defense, debt collection or probate, the practitioner of necessity had "to enter upon the whole of his miscellaneous practice."[31] Partnerships, too, offered aid. Based not on specialization but on the sharing of business, these arrangements provided an access to the law to hungry young attorneys. In one partnership in rural Pittsylvania County for which information survives, the senior member of the firm attended the circuit (superior) courts in his home and surrounding counties, and the Court of Appeals in Richmond, and the junior member practiced in the county (inferior) courts and staffed the office to accept and advise clients.[32]

Of great assistance to Virginia attorneys were the opportunities offered to them by business and industry. A country lawyer would count himself fortunate, as did William R. Aylett of King William County, to receive retainers from the Southern Mutual Insurance Company or the Richmond banking and investment firm of Thomas Branch and Company.[33] But the most beneficial connection of all was that with one of the numerous companies involved in the burgeoning railroad development of the Upper South. With such patronage, a practitioner could quickly move up the economic ladder and secure his fortune.[34] For urban practitioners, the offers of positions as agents for or counsel to large corporations doing business in Virginia became more abundant as the century drew to a close. Along with the greater availability of lawyers in the cities, this allowed, in fact encouraged, specialization among the urban bar, who, like their brothers in the country, had traditionally accepted a caseload of a wide variety of civil and criminal litigation.

In the period 1870 to 1900, most Virginia lawyers, both city and country attorneys, followed their calling as sole practitioners. Before 1870, and after, there were a few partnerships of two lawyers working together; more often than not, they would have resulted from a close family relationship. As the century drew to a close, however, the professional advantages of partnerships became more obvious; they afforded the opportunity to specialize, to acquire an expertise in some one branch of the law. In 1900, there were many two-man law firms, and there was one three-man firm in Richmond. The dawn of the present era broke in 1901 with the formation of the firm of Munford, Hunton, Williams, and Anderson (today known as Hunton and Williams). The four gentlemen were among the leading practitioners of the state, and they combined their efforts to form an organization that could offer expert legal services in all fields of the law along the lines of the large New York City law firms.[35]

The bar of Virginia during the last third of the nineteenth century attracted many talented men, and several of them earned national reputations as legal advocates and scholars. Having discussed the Virginia bar as a group, we now pause to consider some of its more outstanding individual members.

The leader of the Virginia bar during the first ten years of the period under discussion, 1870 to 1880, was William Green. Green was an excellent practitioner and a deeply learned legal scholar. He was one of the three original law professors of the University of Richmond in 1870 and gave the opening address of the law school. He was prevailed upon to supply the lead article which initiated the *Virginia Law Journal* in 1877. In addition to serving as chairman of the executive committee of the Virginia Historical Society, William Green supplied much of the scholarship behind J. W. Wallace's *Reporters*, which was appropriately dedicated to Green. Green, who had established his reputation as a lawyer before the War Between the States, lived on until 1880 to inspire a younger generation with a love of legal scholarship.[36]

Conway Robinson, who died in 1884, was of equal stature. He was admitted to the bar in Richmond in 1827 and rapidly rose in prominence as an advocate. In the 1830s he published a three-volume practice manual for Virginia lawyers; it was an excellent and much-needed work and assured his reputation. In this decade, he served as president and general counsel of the Richmond, Fredericksburg, and Potomac Railroad and was one of the founders of the Virginia Historical Society. His law practice and writing increased to the point that he moved in 1858 to Washington, D.C., in order to be closer to the United States Supreme Court and the Library of Congress. He maintained an office in Richmond, however, since he continued to appear before the Virginia Court of Appeals. His major work was his seven-volume *Practice in the Courts of Justice in England and the United States, 1854–1874*; this work was well received and used on both sides of the Atlantic Ocean.[37]

John Randolph Tucker (1823–1897) achieved as much prominence in his lifetime as his father, Henry St. George Tucker (1780–1848), and his grandfather, St. George Tucker (1752–1827), had in theirs. Ran Tucker made his mark as a practicing attorney, attorney general of Virginia from 1857 to 1865, law professor and then dean at Washington and Lee University, member of Congress from 1875 to 1886, and a legal scholar. He was president of the American Bar Association in 1892.[38] He had a delightful sense of humor that, coupled with his legal erudition, made him a popular speaker at bar association meetings throughout the nation.[39]

The most famous of all Virginia law professors was John B. Minor, who taught at the University of Virginia for fifty years before his death in 1895. Old John B., as he was affectionately referred to by his students, was single-minded in his devotion to legal education and scholarship. By the end of his career, his lecture notes had grown into a six volume encyclopedia of Virginia law, *Institutes of Common and Statute Law*.[40]

One of Minor's most famous students was John W. Daniel (1842–1910), "the Lame Lion of Lynchburg." Daniel had received a crippling wound during the battle of the Wilderness. After the war he studied law at the University of Virginia and then commenced practice in his native Lynchburg. He was a hard worker and a brilliant orator, and he rapidly achieved recognition at the bar. In 1869 he wrote a book on attachments, and in 1876 he published his nationally known book on negotiable instruments. He was perhaps best known as an orator and as United States senator from Virginia from 1887 until his death in 1910.[41]

Thomas Nelson Page, though better known as a novelist, began as a lawyer. From 1874 until 1893 Page was a successful practitioner and one of the leaders of the Richmond bar. While pursuing his profession as a lawyer, he began writing short stories about Virginia and Virginians as they were before the war. The charm of his literary style captivated the nation, and, when his second marriage in 1893 brought financial independence, he gave up the practice of law and spent all of his time writing novels and stories. Page was also active in politics, and he served as Ambassador to Italy for six years during the First World War.[42]

In 1870, the Virginia bar was an unorganized profession. There was a definite professional consciousness,[43] and generalizations were being made about the level of the competency and integrity of the bar. The only organized activities of the bar, however, were occasional meetings to commemorate deceased members.[44]

It was not long before the advantages of an organized association of lawyers began to be apparent. In 1878, the editors of the *Virginia Law Journal* called for a bar association in Virginia.[45] The Bar Association of the City of Richmond was organized in 1885. The call for organization was issued in September 1885, signed by 107 attorneys, and the constitution and by-laws were adopted on October 29, 1885. The stated objects of the Richmond bar association were "to aid in maintaining the honor and dignity of the profession of the law; to promote legal science and the administration of justice; and to cultivate social intercourse among its members.'' A grievance procedure was established,[46] and a law library was created. Although an earlier effort had failed, the Richmond bar association flourished from its beginning. In 1894 there were 118 members, and the law library had forty titles in it. In 1898 there were 129 members, and a code of ethics for lawyers was published. In the following year, a minimum fee schedule was adopted in order to prevent the ''unseemly and unprofessional practice of cutting rates''; by 1899 the law library of the Richmond bar had grown to eighty titles.[47]

It was hoped when the Richmond bar association was founded in 1885 that it would grow into a statewide organization.[48] Accordingly, in 1888, the Bar Association of the City of Richmond issued a call for the formation of a statewide bar association, and the Virginia State Bar Association was established in that year by 128 of the most prominent lawyers from every section of the state.[49] The organization was an instant success, and within five years there were more than 400 members. In 1895, the Virginia State Bar Association with 457 members was second in size only to the New York State Bar Association,[50] and two years later only the bar associations in the populous states of New York, Pennsylvania, and Michigan had more members.[51]

The original standing committees of the Virginia State Bar Association show the purposes and future activities of the association. These committees were admissions, legislation and law reform, judiciary, grievances, legal education and admission to the bar, library and legal literature, and the executive committee.

We have already commented upon the activities of the committees on admissions and on legal education and admission to the bar. The Committee on Grievances was to receive and investigate complaints against lawyers and anything ''affecting the interests of the legal profession, the practice of law, and the administration of justice.''[52] This committee did very little in the first twelve years of its existence, before 1900.[53] A special committee, however, presented a code of professional ethics at the first meeting of the association that was adopted at the second meeting.[54]

The Judiciary Committee was not very active, but it served a useful role in bringing together several strands of ideas. The General Assembly was pressed to give higher judicial salaries; Virginia had been characteristically stingy in this regard.[55] There were numerous and various private proposals to restructure the system of courts,[56] and in 1902 the county courts were severely reorganized.[57] In 1898, in an effort to increase the general respect for the courts, the bar association voted to recommend that the judges of the Supreme Court of Appeals wear judicial robes.[58]

We have deliberately saved till last our discussion of the activities of the Committee on Legislation and Law Reform. These gentlemen in their first annual report, which was given to the second meeting of the Virginia State Bar Association, threw the fat into the fire.

The Virginia State Bar Association threw itself into the middle of the codification question. The first Presidential Address was delivered by William J.

Robertson on the subject of codification, which was then at the forefront of American legal thinking. Robertson had been a judge of the Virginia Supreme Court of Appeals and had served there with distinction during the war and until he was removed by the Reconstruction government for political reasons. He then practiced law with great success in Charlottesville and was honored by being elected the first president of the bar association.[59] In his address, Robertson advocated the adoption in Virginia of a code of pleading and practice similar to the Field Code of New York. Robertson specifically urged the abolition of the forms of action and the merger of law and equity procedure.[60]

This address was clearly part of an organized discussion of the codification movement. The Annual Address at the same meeting was delivered by James C. Carter of New York, a nationally known scholar who opposed the idea of general codification. Carter argued against the general codification of private law and, in passing, criticized the New York Code of Civil Procedure.[61] At the same meeting, the members of the Virginia State Bar Association debated the question whether Virginia should adopt the Field Code of New York.[62]

This was the beginning of a lively debate throughout the state on the subject of law reform.[63] The idea of a wholesale adoption of the Field Code was quickly dropped, and the discussion centered on two related proposals: the abolition of the forms of action and the merger of law and equity procedure. In 1891, a special committee of the Virginia bar association recommended that both of these steps be taken.[64] In 1892, the bar association approved the recommendations of the committee.[65] When the committee presented its proposed draft bills to the bar association the next year, however, the general code of pleading, which included the abolition of the forms of action and the separation of common law and equity procedure, and several miscellaneous proposals were defeated.[66] The bar association did approve a draft bill which would have simplified the pleading of actions based on contracts and also a draft bill to allow equitable principles to be used at common law and common law injuries to be used in equity.[67] The draft bills were thereupon presented to the General Assembly, but none were enacted.[68]

It should not be concluded that these efforts at law reform were useless failures. The seed was planted then that bore fruit later. In 1919, motion pleading was allowed generally in all civil actions,[69] and, although the ancient forms of action were not abolished, they quickly fell into disuse and were forgotten. Other less extensive improvements in pleading and practice have been made from time to time.[70]

The merger of common law and equity procedures is a step that has not been taken in Virginia. In federal practice, this measure, which was promulgated in 1938, has created as many problems as it solved. As long as the civil jury remains in use at common law, the merger of law and equity cannot be complete. In England, civil juries have been generally abolished, and lawyers do not have to consider whether their lawsuits would have been at common law or in equity but for the merger of the courts and procedures.

In 1899, the Virginia State Bar Association turned its attentions to, among other things, the Torrens system of land registry. Land registration is quite different from the recordation of land title deeds, the system used in Virginia since colonial times to protect rights in real property. The purpose of both systems is the same. The enthusiastic proponent of the Torrens System in Virginia was Eugene C. Massie. On his motion, the association voted to study the matter.[71] Massie then proceeded to educate the Virginia bar on the subject and to lobby for its statutory approval.[72] The Torrens System was editorially supported.[73] Finally, in 1916, a comprehensive bill was enacted;[74] however, the Torrens System, though legal now, has never been put into operation.[75]

We come now to the topic of the relationship between the Virginia bar and the corporate world. During the period 1870 to 1900, northern and European industrialists invested large amounts of money in Virginia, and this investment, which was much needed for the economic growth of the state, was encouraged by Virginians in every way they could. The other side of the coin was, of course, outside the control of Virginia commerce and industry, most notably the railroads. The major issue in Virginia politics during this period was the readjustment of the state debt. This was a part of the issue of industrialization and financial credit; even though lawyers were fighting on both sides, this issue was a political rather than a legal one and will not be discussed here.[76]

However, the bar did become involved with the problems of the state control of corporations (many persons in the 1880s feared that the corporations controlled the state government) and the fellow-servant doctrine, which limited the liability of corporations to their employees. Although individual lawyers were very pleased to have railroads and other corporations for clients and represented them very well, nevertheless the bar as a whole took a healthy, independent stance; the Virginia bar as a whole was not in the pockets of the railroads.

In 1890, the subject of the Presidential Address of the Virginia State Bar Association was the economic and political abuses being perpetrated by huge corporations. The laxness of the General Assembly in failing to protect the general public was also noted.[77] Three years later, the bar association heard further criticisms of the corporations. J. Allen Watts pointed out the ease of obtaining corporate charters for undercapitalized companies and the lack of public control over corporations.[78] In order to remedy these problems, the duties of supervising corporations was taken from the General Assembly and given to a new body in 1902 by the new Constitution of Virginia. The newly created State Corporation Commission was erected as a fourth branch of the state government with legislative, executive, and judicial powers.[79] It has been very effective in regulating companies doing business in the Commonwealth.

The fellow-servant doctrine, simply stated, is that "there can be no recovery for an accident caused by the negligence of a fellow servant." The value of this rule is particularly great to corporations who must necessarily perform all their functions and acts by agents or servants. If the fellow-servant doctrine were liberally construed, corporations (and their shareholders) would be totally immune from tort liability; such a result would be monstrous, and the trend since the nineteenth century has been to limit in various ways the operation of this doctrine.[80] In 1885, the editor of the *Virginia Law Journal* condemned the rule in general.[81] Robert L. Parrish, however, expressed his approval of the general rule in an address to the Virginia State Bar Association in 1892.[82] By 1902, public opinion had been marshalled against the railroads, and the new constitution of Virginia abolished the fellow-servant doctrine as a defense available to railway companies. This limitation of the doctrine remains in force today.[83]

In conclusion, we can see that during the period 1870 to 1900 there was steady and continuous progress among the Virginia bar. The fifteen years, 1870 to 1885, was a time of economic and professional recovery from the devastations of the Civil War and Reconstruction. The leaders of the bar were older gentlemen of the ante-bellum era, and they constantly insisted on maintaining the high professional standards of the bar. In general, it was fifteen years of rebuilding, a time of conservatism rather than innovation.

The first bar association in the state was formed in 1885, and the most significant feature of the period 1885 to 1900 was the organized activities of the bar. Before about 1895, the Virginia State Bar Association was not very successful in having its proposals enacted by the General Assembly. After that date, however, the bar association's lobbying techniques were improved to the point that success was frequent. From its inception in 1888, the Virginia State Bar Association was a leader in the area of legal reform—the primary forum for public debate on these issues.

As already noted, the bar association movement was a great success in Virginia. There are several reasons for the instant popularity of the Virginia State Bar Association. To begin with, lawyers are a gregarious and convivial crew, and the meetings of the bar association were always held at popular and fashionable resorts during the summer. The second reason was the desire to improve the legal profession.

Nothing frustrates an attorney more than to argue a case against an incompetent lawyer, because the true issues become obscured by the irrelevant and ignorant points made by the uneducated or obtuse opposing counsel. Justice is served only by the debate of the true issues of the case. A good lawyer can deal with an ignorant one well enough if the judge is reasonably competent, but it offends his professional pride to have to argue against poor workmanship. To improve the level of practice in Virginia, the organized bar sought to increase the educational requirements for admission to practice law. Also, the organized bar began a program of continuing legal education for members of the bar by having lectures on legal subjects during their annual meetings; these papers were then printed and circulated to all members of the bar association.

Furthermore, the conscientious lawyer is deeply offended by dishonesty and laziness on the part of other members of the bar. Most lawyers are proud of their calling and very much resent it when the reputation of the legal profession is besmirched by unethical conduct of other attorneys. Justice was seen to be one of the four cardinal virtues, and the bar had a vital role in the administration of justice. Immoral and dishonest conduct on the part of a lawyer very much offended most members of the Virginia bar, and one of the purposes of the bar association was to eliminate it by having the offender disbarred. Although the association did not have much success along these lines before 1900, the policy was forcefully stated, and in the twentieth century it was implemented.

In general, the history of the Virginia bar from 1870 to 1900 was not a matter of dramatic revolution, but rather, one of slow but steady and constant professional growth.

## NOTES

1. *Virginia Code*, chap. 160, §§1, 3 (1873); *Virginia Code*, §§ 3191, 3193 (1887).

2. "Remarks of J. W. G. Blackstone," *Reports of the Virginia State Bar Association* 7 (1894):21 (hereafter cited as *VBA*); J. L. Anderson and W. M. Lile, "Report of the Committee on Legal Education and Admission to the Bar," *VBA* 7 (1894):49, 50; "Examination for Admission to the Bar in Virginia—The Past—The Future," *Virginia Law Regulations* 2 (1896):310, 312 (hereafter cited as *Va. Law Reg.*).

3. B. B. Munford, *Random Recollections* (New York, 1905), 74.

4. H. R. Pollard, *Memoirs and Sketches of the Life of Henry Robinson Pollard* (Richmond, 1923), 155.

5. *VBA* 1 (1888):6, 7, 12, 15 (remarks of Charles M. Blackford and Holmes Conrad); note also "Legal Education and Admission to the Bar," *Virginia Law Journal* 13 (1889):531 (hereafter cited as *Va. Law Jour.*).

6. "An Act to Regulate the Licensing of Persons to Practice Law in This State," *VBA* 2 (1889):52–54; "Remarks of J. Allen Watts," ibid., 3 (1890):22–23. The bill was resubmitted to the General Assembly in 1894 and was again defeated; ibid., 6 (1893):44–46, 273–75; ibid., 7 (1894):16–22, 49.

7. J. L. Anderson, "Report of the Committee on Legal Education and Admission to the Bar," ibid., 8 (1895):62–68 (see also 26–40).

8. *Virginia Acts of Assembly, 1895–1896*, chap. 41, 49.

9. 93 *Virginia* 5 (1897); "Rules and Regulations Prescribed by the Supreme Court of Appeals of Virginia for Licensing Persons to Practice Law," *Va. Law Reg.* 2 (1896):219–20; ibid. 2 (1897):910–11. They were applauded in "Examination for Admission to the Bar in Virginia—The Past—The Future," ibid., 2 (1896):310–312; J. L. Anderson and C. R. Sands, "Report of Committee on Legal Education and Admission to the Bar," *VBA* 9 (1896):39–43; J. H. Corbitt, "Admission to the Bar in Virginia," ibid., 40 (1928): 286–318.

10. The examination was published: "Questions Propounded by the Court of Appeals to Applicants for License to Practice Law, January 8, 1897," *Va. Law Reg.* 2 (1897):774–77. Later bar exams were published in ibid., 3 (1897–1898):315–17, 465–68; ibid., 4 (1898–1899):270–76, 405–7, 707–9; ibid., 5 (1899–1900):273–77, 422–24, 723–27.

11. *Virginia Acts of Assembly, 1910*, chap. 152, 238.

12. R. Page, *Thomas Nelson Page* (New York, 1923), 67.

13. *Response of Francis Rives Lassiter of Petersburg to a Toast Offered at the Virginia Bar Assn. Meeting. . .Aug. 8, 1895* (Richmond, 1895), 3. As late at 1887, former Con-

federates were being denounced as "traitors"; see "The Appointment of Mr. Lamar," *Va. Law Jour.* 12 (1888):62–63 referring to an editorial in the *Albany Law Journal*.

14. *Ninth Census—Vol. 3: The Statistics of the Wealth and Industry of the United States* (Washington, D.C., 1872), 10, 81, 86, 90, 392–93.

15. *Ninth Census—Vol. 1: The Statistics of the Population* (Washington, D.C., 1872), 674–75. For a comparison with 1860 figures, see J. C. Kennedy, comp., *Population of the United States in 1860* (Washington, D.C., 1864), 524–25, which lists 1,341 resident attorneys in Virginia. The decline in the number of practitioners may be attributed not only to the loss of life during the war, but also to the loss of the fifty counties that formed West Virginia. In 1870, West Virginia boasted 400 resident attorneys.

16. *Census Reports, Vol. 8: Twelfth Census of the United States Taken in the Year 1900; Manufacturers, Part 2: States and Territories* (Washington, D.C., 1902), 904; ibid., *Vol. 5: Agriculture, Part 1: Farms, Live Stock, and Animal Products* (Washington, D.C., 1902), 688–89, 692–93, 695.

17. *Statistics of the Population of the United States at the Tenth Census* (Washington, D.C., 1883), 715–16. This compilation lists one female as a resident attorney, though it is unlikely she ever practiced due to legislative restrictions on entry to the bar. She may have been admitted and practiced in another jurisdiction and resided in Virginia.

18. *Report on the Population of the United States at the Eleventh Census: 1890, Part 2* (Washington, D.C., 1897), 618.

19. *Twelfth Census of the United States—Vol. 2: Population, Part 2* (Washington, D.C., 1902), 541.

20. Andrew Boyd & Co., *Virginia State Business Directory, 1871–1872* (Richmond, 1871); *Chataigne's Virginia Gazetteer and Classified Business Directory, 1890–1891* (Richmond, 1890), 286, 372, 517–20, 773.

21. *Richmond Daily Dispatch*, January 13, 1876, 1; January 14, 1876, 1.

22. E. R. Williams, "Edwin Archer Randolph, LL.B., Rediscovered," *Richmond Quarterly* 3 (1981):46–48; note also the autobiography of a black lawyer in Gloucester County, T. C. Walker, *The Honey-pod Tree* (New York, 1958).

23. *Sheriff's Richmond City Directory, 1877* (Richmond, 1877), 41, 84, 173, 247–49; *Chataigne's Virginia Gazetteer*, 372, 519–20, 773; *Hill Directory of Richmond and Manchester, Va., 1900* (Richmond, 1900), 1004–7. Unfortunately, very little is known about these early black attorneys; however, several are noted in L. J. Jackson, *Negro Office-Holders in Virginia 1865–1895* (Norfolk, 1945).

24. *Virginia Code* § 3191 (1887).

25. "Women as Lawyers," *Va. Law Jour.* 1 (1877):58.

26. Ex parte Lockwood, 154 U.S. 116 (1894); "Mrs. Belva A. Lockwood, Attorney at Law," *Va. Law Reg.* 1 (1895):151.

27. *Virginia Acts of Assembly, 1895–1896*, chap. 41, 49; *Virginia Code* § 3408 (1919) read "all male persons."

28. *Virginia Acts of Assembly, 1920*, chap. 77, 66.

29. J. Ritchie, *The First Hundred Years* (Charlottesville, 1978), 96–99.

30. Diary, 1867–1869, and account book, 1866–1872, of William R. Aylett, Aylett Family Papers, Virginia Historical Society; "Reminiscences of A. B. Chandler," in M. Wingfield, *History of Caroline County, Va.* (Richmond, 1924), 407.

31. J. S. Wise, *The Lion's Skin* (New York, 1905), 174; J. L. Peyton, *Memoir of John Howe Peyton* (Staunton, 1894), 161; F. N. Boney, *John Letcher* (University, Ala., 1966), 227, 230, 237.

32. Chiswell Dabney to Mrs. E. L. Dabney, February 24 and March 13, 1870, Saunders Papers, Virginia Historical Society. On partnerships, see also Pollard, *Memoirs and Sketches*, 152–53.

33. Account book, 1871–1887, of William R. Aylett, Aylett Family Papers, Virginia Historical Society, 16, 18, 22, 52. See also W. Larsen, *Montague of Virginia: The Making of a Southern Progressive* (Baton Rouge, 1965), 21.

34. J. P. Maddex, Jr., *The Virginia Conservatives, 1867–1879: A Study in Reconstruction Politics* (Chapel Hill, N.C., 1970), 61–62; Munford, *Random Collections*, 88; Larsen, *Montague of Virginia*, 22.

35. T. B. Gay, *The Hunton Williams Firm* (Richmond, 1971), 51–54; J. A. Cutchins, *Memories of Old Richmond* (Verona, Va., 1973), 136.

36. P. Slaughter, *Brief Sketch. . . of William Green* (Richmond, 1883); A. C. Gordon, "William Green," in W. D. Lewis, ed., *Great American Lawyers*, 8 vols. (Philadelphia, 1907–1909), 5:255–89; R. A. Brock, *Catalogue. . . of the Library of the Late Hon. William Green, LL.D.* (Richmond, 1880); *American Law Review* 14 (1880): 669.

37. R. A. Claybrook, "Conway Robinson," in W. H. Bryson, ed., *Virginia Law Reporters Before 1880* (Charlottesville, 1977), 57–64; E. B. Merrill, "Conway Robinson," *Albany Law Journal* 29 (1884):165–66; "A Virginian Author," *Va. Law Jour.* 1 (1877):60–61.

38. J. G. Rogers, *American Bar Leaders* (Chicago, 1932), 71–76. James Overton Broadhead and John White Stevenson were also presidents of the ABA during the period covered by this essay. Both were born and educated in Virginia, but Broadhead resided in Missouri and Stevenson lived in Kentucky when elected to that honor; ibid., 1–8, 33–36. Ran Tucker's son, Harry Tucker (1853–1932), was president of the ABA in 1904; ibid., 131–35.

39. J. W. Davis, "John Randolph Tucker," *Washington and Lee Law Review* 6 (1949):139–62; W. R. Vance, "John Randolph Tucker," in W. D. Lewis, ed., *Great American Lawyers*, 8 vols. (Philadelphia, 1907–1909), 7:323–54; R. T. Barton, "John Randolph Tucker," *Va. Law Reg.* 3 (1897):1–17.

40. "Minor, John Barbee," *Dictionary of American Biography* (New York, 1962), 7:26; J. C. Lamb, "John B. Minor," *Va. Law Reg.* 1 (1895): 473–84; W. H. Bryson "The History of Legal Education in Virginia," *University of Richmond Law Review* 14 (1979):155, 186–87, 189.

41. "Daniel, John Warwick," *Dictionary of American Biography* (New York, 1952), 3:68; G. L. Christian, "John Warwick Daniel," *VBA* 23 (1910):73–80.

42. R. Page, *Thomas Nelson Page* (New York, 1923); "Page, Thomas Nelson," *Dictionary of American Biography* (New York, 1962), 7:141; "Thomas Nelson Page," *VBA* 35 (1923):95–97.

43. E. L. Shepard, "Lawyers Look at Themselves: Professional Consciousness and the Virginia Bar 1770–1850," *American Journal of Legal History* 25 (1981):1–23.

44. For example: "The Late Peachy R. Grattan, Esq." 75 *Virginia Reports* (1881) v-viii; "Proceedings of the Staunton Bar upon the Death of A. H. H. Stuart," *Va. Law Jour.* 15 (1891):157–60; the members of the Richmond bar walked as a group in George Wythe's funeral procession in 1806; *Wythe's Reports* (2d ed., 1852), x1. The author wishes to thank Mr. Hunter Martin, secretary, the Richmond Bar Association, for his kind assistance.

45. "Acknowledgment—Bar Association," *Va. Law Jour.* 2 (1878): 704.

46. The grievance committee prosecuted nonmembers as well as members; for an

anecdote in connection with a prosecution for running and capping, see R. Page, *Thomas Nelson Page* (New York, 1923), 80.

47. Bar Association of the City of Richmond, *Annual Reports*, for the years 1886, 1894, 1898, and 1899; "The Richmond Bar Association," *Va. Law Jour.* 9 (1885):754–56; "Code of Ethics," *Va. Law Jour.* 13 (1889):327–32; "Scale of Fees Adopted by Richmond Bar Association," *Va. Law Reg.* 4 (1899):783–84.

48. "The Richmond Bar Association," *Va. Law Jour.* 9 (1885):754–56.

49. "A State Bar Association," *Va. Law Jour.* 12 (1888):422–23; "The Virginia State Bar Association," ibid., 12 (1888):550–51; "The State Bar Association Committees," ibid., 12 (1888):742–43; *VBA* 1 (1888).

50. "The Virginia State Bar Association," *Va. Law Reg.* 1 (1895):73–74.

51. "Report of Secretary," *VBA* 10 (1897):11.

52. "By-Laws," *VBA* 1 (1888):40.

53. Ibid., 12 (1899):18–29, 36–45.

54. Ibid., 1 (1888):14, 25, 61–68; ibid., 2 (1889):25, 179–86.

55. "The Pay of the Circuit Judges," *Va. Law Jour.* 11 (1887):319; "The Judicial System, Again," ibid., 11 (1887):384; *VBA* 2 (1889):50, 149–53; J. P. Harrison, "Suggested Changes in Our Judicial System," *VBA* 12 (1899):233, 242–43.

56. "Report of J. C. Parker of the Special Committee on the Judiciary System of the State," *VBA* 10 (1897):113–126 (note also 24–47); Harrison, "Changes in Judicial System," 233, 244–46; "The Judicial System," *Va. Law Jour.* 10 (1886):61–62; "Jurisdiction of the County Courts," ibid, 10 (1886):124–25; "The Judicial System, Again," ibid., 11 (1887):384; "The Virginia Judicial System," ibid., 12 (1888):65–69.

57. The history of the court was chronicled, and its demise was lamented in H. Conrad, "The Old County Court System in Virginia: Its Place in History," *VBA* 21 (1908):323–50.

58. *VBA* 11 (1898):21–24; for similar proposals, see "Judicial Gowns," *Va. Law Reg.* 3 (1898):660–81; "Judicial Robes," ibid., 4 (1898): 477–79; ibid., 4 (1899):704–705; Harrison, "Changes in Judicial System," 233, 237 argued that "all judges should be required to wear the gown."

59. A. C. Gordon, "Judge William Joseph Robertson," in W. D. Lewis, ed., *Great American Lawyers*, 8 vols. (Philadelphia, 1907–1909), 7:129–59.

60. W. J. Robertson, "Presidential Address," *VBA* 2 (1889):85, 90.

61. J. C. Carter, "The Provinces of the Written and Unwritten Law," ibid., 2 (1889):95–137 (esp. 128, 132).

62. Ibid., 2 (1889):32–39. The abolition of the forms of action had been advocated two years earlier in "Suggested Changes in Civil Procedure in Virginia," *Va. Law Jour.* 11 (1887):69–70, and in "The Code Revision and Law Reform," ibid., 11 (1887):124–25.

63. See S. S. P. Patteson, "Law Reform," *Va. Law Jour.* 13 (1889):461–70, 677–87; "Law Reform," 475; S. C. Graham, "Sacking the Temple," ibid. 13 (1889):809–14; F. H. McGuire, "Remarks on Pleadings in Virginia," ibid., 14 (1890):21–25; S. S. P. Patteson, "Law Reform—A Rejoinder," ibid., 14 (1890):65–70; "Remarks of S. S. P. Patteson," *VBA* 4 (1891):26–35; W. B. Pettit, "Law Reform—A Rejoinder," *Va. Law Jour.* 15 (1891):681–87; S. S. P. Patteson, "Law Reform—A Sur-Rejoinder," ibid., 15 (1891):745–50; W. B. Pettit, "Law Reform—Reply to Sur-Rejoinder," ibid., 16 (1892):1–8; J. R. Tucker, "Address," *VBA* 5 (1892):85–107.

64. *VBA* 4 (1891):26–36, 44–69. It is interesting to note that one of the members of

this committee, all of whom supported these far-reaching changes, was Thomas S. Martin, a man later considered to be an archconservative.

65. *VBA* 5 (1892):22–36.

66. Ibid., 6 (1893):14–62, 72–104.

67. Ibid., 6 (1893):99–100, 102–103.

68. Ibid., 7 (1894):53–68.

69. *Virginia Code* § 6046 (1919).

70. For example: *VBA* 13 (1900):61–62.

71. Ibid., 12 (1899):16. There was a discussion of some of the problems of it during the next meeting of the bar association; ibid., 13 (1900):29–46.

72. E. C. Massie, "The Torrens System of Land Registration," ibid., 13 (1900):299–336; E. C. Massie, "Virginia and the Torrens System," ibid., 14 (1901):283–314; "The Torrens System," *Va. Law Reg.* 5 (1901):797–98; *VBA* 15 (1902):13–34; ibid., 16 (1903):18–40, 351–80; E. C. Massie, "Reform of our Land Laws," ibid., 18 (1905):213–30.

73. *Va. Law Reg.* 5 (1899):123-24, 319; ibid., 9 (1903):58–60; ibid., 10 (1904):918–19, 1001; ibid., 11 (1905):420, 433–48; "The Torrens System: An Open Symposium," ibid., 11 (1905):570–608, 649–63; ibid., 12 (1906):707–43.

74. *Virginia Acts of Assembly, 1916*, chap. 62, 70–88; *Virginia Code* § 5225 (1919); *Virginia Code Annual* § 55–112 (Repl. Vol., 1981); E. C. Massie, *The Torrens System: A Manual* (Richmond, 1916); R. C. Walker, "The Torrens System," *Va. Law Reg.*, n.s. 2 (1916):1–6; E. C. Massie, "Perfection of the Torrens System," ibid., n.s. 2 (1917):750–71.

75. J. V. Buonassissi, "Yes Virginia—There is a Torrens Act," *University of Richmond Law Review* 9 (1975):301–21; J. G. Cosby, "Closing the Closing Gap," ibid., 12 (1978):607–25.

76. The subject is ably dealt with in C. C. Pearson, *The Readjuster Movement in Virginia* (New Haven, Conn., 1917); A. W. Moger, *Virginia: Bourbonism to Byrd, 1870–1925* (Charlottesville, 1968).

77. R. G. H. Kean, "The Tendency to Abuse of Corporate Franchises," *VBA* 3 (1890):79–91.

78. J. A. Watts, "Duty of the Legal Profession in Regard to Needed Changes in Legislation," ibid., 6 (1893):215–45.

79. A. E. D. Howard, *Commentaries on the Constitution of Virginia* (Charlottesville, 1974), 2:967–70.

80. See generally *Michie's Jurisprudence*, vol. 12B (1978), "Master and Servant," §§ 65–78.

81. "Fellow-Servants," *Va. Law Jour.* 9 (1885):60.

82. R. L. Parrish, "Master and Servant," *VBA* 5 (1892):127–50.

83. Virginia Constitution of 1902 § 162; *Virginia Acts of Assembly 1901–1902*, chap. 322, 335; *Virginia Code Annual* § 8.01–57 (Repl. Vol., 1977).

*MICHAEL DE L. LANDON*

# *Another False Start: Mississippi's Second State Bar Association, 1886–1892*

The first formally organized state bar association ever to exist in the United States operated from 1821 to 1825 in Mississippi. Organized in Natchez in May of the former year, it represented an attempt by the leaders of the legal profession in what was then a four-year-old, southwestern frontier state to establish some sort of standards for both admission to the bar and the ethical practice of the law. But with hundreds of new settlers coming in every month from a wide variety of backgrounds, and not a few of them claiming to be qualified lawyers, the imposition of any such standards proved to be impossible. And so, because its main reason for being was frustrated, the organization, though never formally dissolved, after four years of life simply ceased to function.[1] Mississippi's present state bar organization can trace its institutional history back to 1906.[2] Twenty years before that, in 1886, the state's second bar association was founded, but was destined to continue for only a year or two longer than its predecessor had earlier in the same century. The founding, functioning, and final foundering of that second association form the subject matter of this essay.

By the 1890s, as most of America moved into the modern industrial age, bar associations represented an idea whose time had come. A New York State Bar Association had been founded in 1876, and one had been founded in Illinois in 1877. The impetus for creating both of them undoubtedly came from, respectively, New York City and Chicago—the two great metropolitan centers of what had by then become a continental commercial system. The newly built nationwide network of railroads provided that system with its principal arteries. At the same time, those railroads at last made it possible for lawyers to convene quickly and easily, at least once a year, with their professional colleagues from every town and county of a large state at some central location. Railroads even made it possible for lawyers from all over the United States to meet together in one place, if they so desired. In the summer of 1878, out of the 607 lawyers who had been invited by the organizers to attend, some seventy-five lawyers from twenty-one states assembled at Saratoga Springs in upstate New York and established the American Bar Association.[3]

The lawyers who attended that organizational meeting, it has been noted, were a select group drawn from among the recognized leaders of the legal profession in their respective states. Most were business lawyers of the sort that represented very wealthy individual clients or large corporations. Not surprisingly, many of them were railroad lawyers. For the railroads, as Bernard Schwartz has observed, were America's "first big business" and, until the end of the nineteenth century, were unrivalled in size and wealth by any other type of corporation.[4]

Yet another peculiarity has been noted about the group that attended that first meeting in Saratoga Springs. Although it was held in the heart of the northeastern United States, there were present a very large number of lawyers from the former Confederate states. Carleton Hunt of the Louisiana bar had been one of the leading organizers of the meeting. And James O. Broadhead of Virginia was elected the first president of the new association.[5] Apparently, national unity was perceived to be essential to national prosperity. Northern lawyers evidenced a desire for reconciliation, and their southern counterparts displayed an eagerness to be reaccepted into the American mainstream.[6]

Seventeen founder-members of the ABA were from Mississippi—not nearly so many as from Louisiana, which had thirty-six, but more than from any other southern state.[7] Five of the seventeen were from Columbus, a flourishing port town on the Tombigbee River and the site of a railway junction; three were from Aberdeen, only twenty-five miles from Columbus by river or rail; another three were from the Mississippi riverport city of Vicksburg; two came from Jackson, the state capital; and another two from Canton, twenty-five miles north of Jackson on the Illinois Central Railroad.[8] At the 1880 annual meeting, four new Mississippi lawyers were approved for membership; three were from Columbus. The fourth, C. B. Howry, was from Oxford, home of both the University of Mississippi, with its law school, and the federal district court for the northern part of the state. That same year, Howry was appointed the United States attorney for the district.[9]

By then, however, some of the initial enthusiasm for the ABA among Mississippi lawyers seems to have abated. Eleven of the original seventeen had let their memberships lapse. Of the ten that remained, all but Howry were either from Columbus or Aberdeen. Five years later, in 1885, the number of members had dropped to seven. Besides Howry from Oxford, there were three from Columbus, two from Aberdeen, and a new recruit, John Gilland, from Vicksburg.[10]

During the first few years of the ABA's history, as far as Mississippi was concerned, continuous and active membership in the organization was limited to a tiny handful of lawyers. Almost all of them were from the Columbus–Aberdeen area in the central-eastern part of the state through which interstate trade passed daily by both rail and river to and from Alabama, Tennessee, and beyond. As for the exceptions, Gilland had his practice in Vicksburg situated on the Mississippi River midway between Memphis and New Orleans, across from northern Louisiana; and Howry was an extremely well-educated lawyer with wide interests. The latter worked for the federal government and was destined to end his professional career in Washington, D.C., as a judge on the United States Court of Claims.[11]

No doubt all of them considered the opportunity to escape for a while each summer from the humid heat of Mississippi to the cooler climate of Saratoga Springs and the opportunities that the annual meetings provided to meet and socialize with fellow lawyers from other states reason enough for belonging to the ABA. Besides all of that, they surely must have shared the general enthusiasm of most of the other members of the organization in its early days for legal reforms closely patterned after those which had been enacted during the preceding half-century in England, the homeland of common law, culminating with the two, almost revolutionary, Judicature Acts of 1873 and 1876.[12] More efficient and uniform judicial procedures, together with uniform codes of updated laws applied in every state, would be of great value to lawyers who represented clients engaged in interstate commerce on a large scale.

In order to both stimulate local interest in such reforms and build up support for them among state legislators, another major thrust of the ABA from its very beginning was to encourage the establishment of state and other kinds of local bar associations. Under its original constitution, therefore, one member from each state was chosen every year by his fellow members from that state to serve as one of the vice-presidents of the association. And another member from each state was picked by his colleagues to serve on the general council, which functioned as the nominating committee for the election of the association's president and other officers. The ABA vice-president and the council member, together with two or three other members from their state, made up the ''local council'' of the ABA for each state. Its job was to recruit suitable new members for the association from among the reputable and established members of the state bar while, at the same time, to work for the achievement of the ABA's goals within the state's legal system.[13]

For the year 1885–1886, L. E. Houston of Aberdeen was the vice-president from Mississippi, and R. O. Reynolds from the same city was the general council member; Gilland, Howry, and W. H. Sims from Columbus were the other members of the Mississippi local council.[14] Apparently, it was the five of them, and their two fellow ABA members, J. E. Leigh and J. A. Orr—both from Columbus—who organized the Mississippi State Bar Association that came into being at the beginning of 1886. Reynolds, in Aberdeen, seems to have been the prime mover. On December 30, 1885, the *Weekly Clarion*, published in Jackson, the state capital, reported that plans for the proposed new body had been formulated at preliminary meetings held in Aberdeen, Jackson, and, finally, Oxford.[15] On January 4, 1886, a formal organizational meeting was to be held in the United States courtroom in Jackson. Exclusiveness has never been much practiced *within* the white ranks of Mississippi's ''closed society,'' and the paper went on to emphasize that ''all lawyers in the State who can conveniently do so are expected to be present, and such as cannot attend can make application for membership by letter."[16]

A good many Mississippi lawyers could be expected to be in Jackson anyway on Monday, January 4, 1886. The state legislature, a majority of whose members in both the house and the senate were lawyers, was scheduled to begin its regular session at noon on the following day; and the state supreme court would be in session.[17] And, indeed, on January 6, 1886, the *Clarion* was able to report that the newly-established association had attracted a very considerable membership. Many who had not been able to attend the organizational meeting had, nevertheless, sent in their applications with others.[18]

R. O. Reynolds, the paper said, had called the meeting to order.[19] But he and the other members of the small group of ABA activists could not realistically have hoped to fill the top leadership positions in the new organization. They must have known that, if the association was to be an effective force within the state, its highest officers would have to be men who were recognized as leaders of the profession by the power structure. The *Clarion*, in an editorial in its December 30, 1885, issue, had argued that the presidency of the new body should go to no one but Judge A. M. Clayton of Benton County in north Mississippi. Sometimes referred to as the "Nestor of the Mississippi Bar," Clayton, born in 1800, had served as a justice on the state's ante-bellum supreme court from 1842 to 1852, and during the Reconstruction era, he had served a brief term as a circuit judge from 1866 to 1867. "His ripe scholarship, his spotless character, and his enviable career as a lawyer and judge," in the paper's opinion, made him the obvious man for the position.[20] After a draft constitution and set of by-laws, prepared in advance by the organizers and closely modeled on those of the ABA, had been adopted at the organizational meeting on January 4, 1886, Clayton was elected to the presidency without opposition.[21]

In addition to electing a president, the members, in accordance with their new constitution, also elected three vice-presidents, a secretary, a treasurer, and an executive committee of six from among their ranks. Three years later, in 1889, they would begin paying the secretary a salary of $100 per year and, at the same time, would lay upon him the additional duty of maintaining a correspondence in the future with the secretaries of the ABA and other state bar associations whose various publications he was to receive and keep on file. At the same meeting, the treasurer would be voted $50 as compensation for his time.[22] But then, just two years later, in 1891, no doubt because of declining membership and, therefore, income from the annual membership fees of $5, they would vote to make the secretaryship and the treasurership honorary positions once again.[23] Meanwhile, the annual meetings would tend to last a little longer each year. The final meeting in 1892 would consist of sessions held every evening from Monday to Thursday.[24]

The one-day organizational meeting in 1886 concluded with an evening session at which the featured event was a speech delivered by another leading luminary of the legal profession in Mississippi at that time. Edward Mayes, then forty years of age, was son-in-law to probably the best-known public figure of the day in the state—Lucius Quintus Cincinnatus Lamar, who was then serving President Grover Cleveland as his Secretary of the Interior.[25] In 1877, Mayes had succeeded his famous father-in-law as professor of law at the University of Mississippi at Oxford when Lamar had departed for Washington to begin an eight-year career as a United States senator. In 1888, Lamar would be appointed a justice of the United States Supreme Court, while Mayes, in 1889, was to become chancellor of his university.[26] Unfortunately, no record apparently was kept of either the title or the topic of Mayes's address to the newly founded bar association. It was probably on some aspect of his area of specialization, which was property law. The previous week's *Clarion* had announced that the talk would be of special interest to lawyers, though the general public were certainly invited to attend, as well. "That it will be chaste and scholarly we may confidently predict," the paper had told its readers.[27]

Very likely, it had been Howry, also from Oxford, who had arranged for Mayes to be the featured speaker. He himself was elected at the meeting to a seat on the new association's executive council. L. E. Houston, presumably because he was that year's ABA vice-president for Mississippi, was the ABA member elected to the highest office in the Mississippi association, that of third vice-president. R. O. Reynolds was elected chairman of the executive committee.[28] At the 1887 meeting, Reynolds was reelected to that position for a second year, but before the meeting had ended, his death was reported to the membership.[29] It may well have been the most demanding and most time-consuming position, if not the most prestigious, in the whole hierarchy of the state bar association. The fact that he was twice chosen to fill it, combined with the fact that he had convened the organizational meeting, strengthens the impression that he was the prinicipal mover and shaker of the association at its outset.

In the meantime, at the ABA annual meeting in 1886, Reynolds, by being appointed to the grievance committee, had become the first Mississippian to be tapped for membership on a standing committee of the national organization.[30] Six months later, at its second annual meeting in Jackson, the Mississippi association itself adopted a system of standing committees which, like its constitution and by-laws, was modeled on that of the ABA. As in the national organization, a committee was created for "jurisprudence and law reform," one for "judicial administration and remedial procedure," one for "legal education and admission to the bar," and one for "grievance."[31] The ABA also had committees on "commercial law," "international law," "publications," and "obituaries," but the first two were probably considered to be unnecessary in a predominantly rural and agricultural state; the functions of the last two were presumably handled by the executive committee of the Mississippi association. Beginning in 1888, and for as long as it continued to function, the minutes and press reports indicate that memorial resolutions honoring deceased members were an important part of the agenda at every annual meeting.

The association's first president, A. M. Clayton, had been too ill to attend and preside over the 1887 meeting, and he was among those memorialized at the 1890 meeting.[32] His successor as president, for 1887–1888, was W. I. Nugent of the Jackson law firm of Nugent and McWillie that served as the general attorneys for the Alabama and Vicksburg railroad.[33] The other men who served as presidents of the short-lived association after Nugent were J. B. Chrisman (1888–1889), R. A. Hill (1889–1890), R. H. Thompson (1890–1891), L. Brame (1891–1892), and Nugent's partner, T. A. McWillie (1892–1893).[34] It is interesting to note that not only were two of the seven men who served as president partners with one another at the time, but also Thompson, at the outset of his professional career in Brookhaven, Mississippi, from 1871 to 1878, had been in partnership with a fourth, Chrisman. Furthermore, after Nugent's death in 1897, it would be Thompson—who was destined to serve a term as president of the state's third state bar association in 1923–1924 and was to climax his career by the general attorney in Mississippi for the Illinois Central Railroad system in 1926—who would take Nugent's place as McWillie's partner.[35]

Obviously, the leadership of the Mississippi bar in the late nineteenth century was made up of a small, close-knit group whose members were even more likely than the early ABA enthusiasts from Columbus and Aberdeen to be identified with railroad interests. Very little is known about Brame, however, beyond the fact that he was a Jackson lawyer who had belonged, briefly, to the ABA from 1881 to 1883 and served as a circuit judge from 1886 to 1890, but he must have been a highly respected member of the bar in the capital city and in the state.[36] R. A. Hill, too, was apparently respected and even liked, in spite of the fact that he had been serving as the lone United States district judge in Mississippi since 1866, and had dutifully affirmed the constitutionality of numerous items of federal reconstruction legislation that most whites in the state found unacceptable.[37]

If the presidents of the bar association were all men of distinction in their profession, there are also indications that the members as a whole comprised a select minority of the state's lawyers. Even though there seems to have been every encouragement given for all lawyers in the state to join, and in spite of the enthusiasm for the association among members of the profession reported by the *Clarion* in 1886, the total membership seems to have settled down to somewhere around 120 out of a state bar that probably numbered approximately 600.[38] The annual subscription fee was $5, and for 1889–1890, the treasurer reported an income from subscriptions plus initiation fees of $617.[39] What the *Clarion–Ledger* described as "a large interesting and most enthusiastic meeting" of the association on January 6, 1891, was attended by exactly fifty members, if the list of "members present" is accurate and complete.[40] At least half of the names are ones that are quite familiar to any student of the history of Mississippi during that period.

The particular interests of this comparatively small, elite group are presumably reflected in the subject matter of the papers that were read at their meetings. Mississippi was primarily an agricultural state, and a majority of the clients of even these lawyers would have been private landowners rather than corporations. Edward Mayes was invited to address his colleagues for the second year in a row in 1887, and on that occasion read a paper entitled "A Glance at the Fountains of Our Land Titles." In 1891, he read another paper, "The Administration of Decedents' Estates." After Mayes, R. H. Thompson was the member most frequently scheduled to speak, and he spoke on a wide variety of topics.[41] Members of any profession, of course, enjoy hearing about their kind of work and about others who practice it. Judge Clayton's presidential address to the 1887 meeting, read for him because of his illness, observed that the practice of the law, "devoted as it is to all that men hold dear—to the protection and preservation of life, liberty, property, and reputation—has always and must always number among its followers the highest types of moral and intellectual capacity." He pointed out that it had recently been argued by some scholars that the great plays usually ascribed to William Shakespeare had probably been written by Francis Bacon, a lawyer.[42] At the 1889 meeting, McWillie delivered a paper on "The Ancient Advocate."[43]

Besides listening to papers read by their own colleagues, the members apparently were eager to have distinguished jurists from other states address them as well. At their 1889 meeting, John Randolph Tucker, professor of constitutional and international law at Washington and Lee University in Virginia, and the one-time defender of Jefferson Davis in his treason trial,[44] gave a talk on "The Constitutional System of the United States" at a session held in the House of Representatives in the state capitol building and attended by "a large intelligent and appreciative audience, by no means confined to the legal profession or to the sterner sex." His states' rights theme and fine oratory, even though he spoke for ninety minutes, provoked "eager attention and prolonged applause."[45] At the 1890 meeting, however, the secretary reported to the members that their executive committee had sounded out "several distinguished lawyers from distant and adjoining states," but all had "declined on the ground that January was an unusually busy month, and that they could not find time from their business to be on hand at that time."[46] At the 1891 meeting, members were told that "Mr. Hill of Georgia" had telegraphed at the last moment to say he could not come because of ill health in his family; his paper, supposed to have been sent by mail, had not yet arrived.[47] Things worked out better, however, for what was destined to be the last annual meeting in 1892. Judge U. M. Rose of Little Rock, Arkansas, a leading scholar and practitioner, and a future president of the ABA (1901–1902), was able to attend and give a speech that the *Clarion–Ledger* described as "a brilliant production, worthy of the orator and of his magnificent audience."[48]

Magnificence, though, was a scarce commodity in late nineteenth-century Mississippi. A majority of the state's inhabitants lived by single-crop farming, at or only a little above subsistence level. There was very little money about and, therefore, very little money to be made. Foreclosures on mortgages, tax sales, and bankruptcies were everyday occurrences in nearly every community in the state. But the lawyers who belonged to the bar association seemingly were of the category most likely to be representing the foreclosers, those who bought up land cheap at tax sales, and those to whom bankrupts owed money. "Just look over this assemblage of lawyers from almost every part of the State," said Judge Hill in his presidential address at the 1890 annual meeting; "where will you find a better dressed and more prosperous looking class of men?"[49] The problems that could arise in connection with titles derived from tax sales, together with suggestions as to how best to handle them, had been the subject matter of a lengthy paper presented by R. H. Thompson at the 1888 annual meeting.[50]

If tax titles involved many complications, so, too, did common law bankruptcy procedures. The 1887 annual meeting approved a motion offered by L. Brame "that the condition and wants of the country are such as to require a national bankruptcy law. . . ." A resolution in favor of such a law was passed unanimously at the ABA annual meeting in 1889, and in 1890, the Mississippi State Bar Association once again voted their support for it.[51] But even though President Benjamin Harrison had also gone on record as favoring such legislation, not until 1898, after several years of a nationwide depression, would the United States Congress pass the "Nelson" federal bankruptcy act.[52] Meanwhile, at the 1890 Mississippi bar meeting, Solomon Saladin Calhoon, an activist lawyer practicing in Canton and Jackson and a founder-member of the ABA, impatiently put forward a proposal for a state bankruptcy statute. Consideration of his proposal was deferred for a year so that it could be further studied, but like much else that was proposed at the 1890 meeting, it was never in fact revived.[53]

Various other reforms of both the state and the federal legal systems were proposed by members of the association during its brief existence. A motion in favor of abolishing the distinction between law and equity proceedings in Mississippi's courts, as the Judicature Act of 1873 had done in the English courts, was offered at the 1888 meeting. But a vote on it was deferred until the following year, when it was voted down by the majority.[54] R. A. Hill referred back to the proposal a year later in his presidential address to the 1890 meeting. The only good argument for it, in his opinion, was that parties sometimes mistakenly sought a remedy in the wrong court, that is, in chancery instead of the circuit court or vice versa. But that problem, he suggested, could be taken care of by a simple statute authorizing transfer of the pleadings from the one court to the other and arresting the operation of the statute of limitations by holding the first (mistaken) proceeding to have been the commencement of the suit. Later, at that same meeting, a resolution was passed calling for the passage of just such legislation.[55]

Other reforms called for, either by individuals or by committees, at the 1890 annual meeting included a general codifying of all laws—"international and interstate"—a general broadening of the jurisdiction of the federal district courts, and legislation to permit defendants in state criminal trials to take evidence by deposition from nonresident witnesses or witnesses temporarily absent from the state. As with Calhoon's state bankruptcy law proposal, a final vote on all of those suggestions was put off for a year so that they could be further studied. But the members who had gathered did vote approval that same year of continuing the system of judicial appointments by the executive branch of government rather than by popular vote. They also approved resolutions calling for legislation to make it easier to remove clouds on real estate titles, to protect family homesteads from seizure in bankruptcy proceedings (with safeguards, of course, against abuse of that protection), and to give the assignees of rent notes or of landlords' liens for supplies the same remedies for collection as the original payees. They voted down a resolution in favor of giving the justices of the state supreme court the power to reduce excessive awards of damages without referring the cases back to the lower courts, and also a resolution that called for circuit court justices to be given greater powers to disregard the wishes of attorneys for either party when instructing juries.[56]

The consideration of so many reform proposals by the 1890 annual meeting, and their approval of a good many of them, marks the highpoint of activism on the part of this second Mississippi State Bar Association. But their proposals for reform, and even their unanimous support of any of them, by no means meant that the reforms would be enacted into law in the foreseeable future. That could only be done by the state legislature, which has always been the most powerful branch of government in Mississippi. A majority of the members of the legislature were lawyers, certainly; however, most of these lawyers were small-town lawyers with a tendency to conservatism in their attitude toward the law and populism in their attitudes toward politics. Suggestions for major reform with regard to the judiciary and the legal system coming from the elite corps of lawyers who made up the membership of the bar association would be received with a great deal of skepticism, if not downright suspicion. Paradoxically, however, it developed that the 1890 session of the legislature finally approved a measure of reform more widespread and basic than anything that had been discussed by the bar association. At the urging of United States Senator J. Z. George, the state legislature passed legislation providing for a state convention to be elected and to meet at Jackson on August 12, 1890, for the purpose of completely rewriting Mississippi's state constitution.

The constitution then in force, the state's third since it entered the Union in 1817, had been drafted at a "black and tan" convention and adopted in 1869 under the Reconstruction regime. Blacks outnumbered whites in the state by 16 percent in 1890, and black voters, most of them illiterate and very poor, were still an important factor in local, state, and federal elections.[57] Even among the members of the bar association concern over that situation evidently was far deeper than any concern they might have had to see particular law reforms enacted. R. H. Thompson, recalling the convention of 1890 in which he represented Lincoln and Jefferson counties, remarked some forty years later that "the principal purpose for which it was called" had been "to overcome by lawful means" what he described as a "large majority of ignorant and unworthy voters," and to "maintain the purity of the ballot box." In order to achieve that desirable objective, a "formidable obstacle" had to be overcome, he recollected—nothing less than the Fifteenth Amendment to the United States Constitution with its forthright statement that "the rights of citizens . . . to vote shall not be denied or abridged . . . by any state on account of race, color, or previous condition of servitude."[58]

Thompson was one of several members of the leadership elite of the bar association who also played a prominent role in the constitutional convention. At its opening session on August 12, 1890, at the nomination of Edward Mayes, Solomon Saladin Calhoon was elected to serve as its presiding officer.[59] In his speech of acceptance, although he had been active in the bar association and had been a major advocate of reforms at many of its sessions, Calhoon made no mention of any of them. The nearest he came to it was a suggestion of the need to "examine the organic laws of other countries and States with ours in order to apply points of each." He felt, perhaps, that to call for radical legal reforms would simply promote dissension and disunity and so hinder the search for a solution to what, he reminded them, was "the great problem for which we are called together." It was a problem that arose, he said, from the "colossal fact that cannot be obscured by . . . clouds of maudlin sentiments or pseudo philanthropy . . . that there exist here in this state two distinct and opposite types of mankind." Whenever any two or more of the major races of mankind lived together under the same government, each race inevitably, "from the instinct implanted in its nature . . . desire[d] to be in the ascendancy." Of the two major races represented in Mississippi, he observed, "the rule of one has always meant economic and moral ruin. While the rule of the other has always meant prosperity and happiness, and prosperity and happiness to all races."[60] Obviously, the main purpose of Mississippi's 1890 constitution was to be the firm establishment of white supremacy in the state.

"Anglo–Saxon ingenuity," Thompson later recalled with pride, was up to the challenge. The new constitution under one of its own provisions (section 185) went into effect immediately, on November 1, 1890, without ever being referred to the voters of the state for their approval. Section 256 "by a gerrymander of the state made it practically certain that a large majority of the legislative house of representatives would be elected favorable to the best interest of the state." Sections 140 and 143, by providing that the governor and the other executive officials should be elected on the basis of the number of members of the house of representatives from the counties in which they received majorities, made it certain that white voters would also have most of the say in electing them.[61]

At the 1891 annual meeting of the state bar association, Thompson reviewed the new constitution for the members. Pointing out some of the features that made it superior to its predecessor, he noted that the 1869 ban on property and educational qualifications for voters had been "happily omitted" from the Bill of Rights sections; and that the provision guaranteeing the right of all citizens to travel on public conveyances "now lives only in history." A requirement of separate schools for the races and a ban on interracial marriages were other important new features celebrated by Thompson in his speech. But, in spite of all the reforms proposed at the previous year's bar association meeting, concerning the "Judiciary" sections of the new constitution, Thompson had to admit that "fewer changes were made in this department than in any other."[62]

Section 159, he noted, had defined with greater clarity the respective jurisdictions of the state's circuit and chancery courts, and other sections simplified the procedures involved in transfering suits wrongly begun in the one court to the other. So, something had been accomplished in that regard at least. He welcomed the new requirement that one had to have practiced law in the state for at least five years before one became eligible for appointment to a judgeship. The previous constitution had required only two years of residence and said nothing about experience in the practice of law.[63] Although he made no reference to the matter in his speech, he and the other members of the bar association were probably also pleased that judges were still to be appointed by the governor, with the approval of the senate, rather than being elected. No doubt they also approved of the requirement that the circuit and chancery courts were to hold terms at least once every six months in every county.[64] If not very much, at least some of what the association had called for during the previous few years had been realized.

Section 278 of the new constitution authorized the governor to appoint three commissioners whose task it would be to compile a new code of the state's laws that was in line with its new constitution. The task was entrusted to Thompson and two colleagues. And, during the first week of January 1892, even as the bar association was conducting the four sessions of what was to be its last annual meeting, the three were getting ready to present the results of their labors to the legislature for approval. They had nothing to worry about. The new 1892 Code was quickly approved "with very few amendments," as Thompson proudly recalled decades later.[65]

A number of factors no doubt helped to cause Mississippi's second state bar association to cease operating after 1892.[66] The new code sufficiently altered the schedule of sessions for the state supreme court; it no longer sat in Jackson in the first week of each January.[67] Lawyers who were not members of the legislature were left with very little motivation to travel to the state capital at what was often a time of very unpleasant weather. At the same time, the difficulty of attracting interesting outside speakers was probably another cause for discouragement. The financial hard times that affected all of America in the mid–1890s must have made many rank-and-file Mississippi lawyers reluctant to pay the $5 annual membership fee and, even more, to pay the cost of traveling to Jackson and staying there for what had become a matter of several days by 1892. The fact that the secretary and the treasurer ceased to be remunerated for their efforts must have made it hard to find men willing to accept election to either position.

But there can be no doubt that the new constitution of 1890 and the new code of 1892, in combination, were the main cause of the association's collapse. Its most active members presumably had joined it primarily because they hoped it would be an effective lobby for changes they hoped to make with regard to the legal system, the judicial system, and the system of legal education in the state. A felt crisis over race relations suddenly gave rise to a brand-new constitution and a related brand-new code. And, although those documents gave the legal reformers very little of what they had wanted, it must have seemed to them superfluous—perhaps even presumptuous—to suggest any additional, ad hoc changes in the state's legal system until after at least a few years had elapsed.

Meanwhile, although a few of the brightest and best of its lawyers might have wanted it to, Mississippi was not yet ready to join modern industrial America. It is true that the new constitution did include, for the first time in history of the state's fundamental laws, a segment on "corporations" (article VII). Of the article's twenty-three sections, seven dealt specifically with railroads, the only kind of major corporation operating in Mississippi at the time. Some of the seven were populist in spirit; for example, one required a railroad to run its tracks through any county seat that it came within three miles of anyway. But the remainder probably achieved as much as railroad lawyers such as Thompson and McWillie could realistically hope to see accomplished at that time.

Thirty years after what some of them still called "the war of northern aggression" had ended at Appomattox, the great majority of Mississippi lawyers were still concerned only with the everyday problems of petty crimes, family estates, and small-scale farming and retailing that they encountered in their rural small-town practices. For virtually all of them—including the leaders of the bar association, though their horizons were broader—race relations and the problem of keeping the black man in his place were the overriding concern. And conservatism in that regard would tend to encourage resistance to reform in regard to everything else, including the law, for almost another century in the Magnolia State.

## NOTES

1. The minutes of the first state bar association were published in Mississippi Bar Foundation, *Early Mississippi Bar Associations* (Jackson, 1966), 5–20.

2. See Michael de L. Landon, *The Honor and Dignity of the Profession—A History of the Mississippi State Bar, 1906–1976* (Jackson, 1979).

3. Gerald Carson, *A Good Day at Saratoga* (Chicago, 1978), 3–4.

4. *The Law in America* (New York, 1974), 130; Erwin N. Griswold, *Law and Lawyers in the United States* (London, 1964), 73.

5. Carson, *Good Day*, 21.

6. Ibid., 12.

7. American Bar Association, *Report of the Annual Meeting* (1879), 40 and passim (hereafter cited as *ABA Rep*).

8. Ibid., 40. The seventeenth member came from the small community of Oakwood.

The Mobile and Ohio and the Georgia Pacific Railroads intersected at Columbus at that time; the Illinois Central and the Mobile and Ohio intersected at Aberdeen.

9. *ABA Rep* (1880), 8; *Who Was Who* (1897–1942), s.v. "Howry, Charles Bowen."

10. *ABA Rep* (1885), 35.

11. *Who Was Who* (1897–1942).

12. 36, 37 Victoria, c. 66. 39–40 Victoria, c. 59.

13. Carson, *Good Day*, 14.

14. *ABA Rep* (1885), 104, 106, 135.

15. *Weekly Clarion*, December 30, 1885, 2.

16. Ibid.

17. *Weekly Clarion*, December 30, 1885, 2; January 6, 1886, 2. The annual sessions of the legislature always commenced on the first Tuesday after the first Monday in January.

18. *Weekly Clarion*, January 6, 1886, 2.

19. It proved impossible to locate complete sets of minutes for every meeting of the Mississippi State Bar Association from 1886 to 1892. However, all of them are summarized in Dunbar Rowland, *Courts, Judges, and Lawyers of Mississippi, 1798–1935* (Jackson, 1935), 358–60 (hereafter cited as *Minutes, Rowland*). For the organizational meeting, see ibid., 358.

20. *Weekly Clarion*, December 30, 1885, 2; Rowland, *Courts*, 79, 259; Mississippi State Bar Association, *Minutes of the Annual Meeting* (1890), 8 (hereafter cited as Minutes, Annual Mtg.).

21. *Weekly Clarion*, January 6, 1886, 2; *Minutes, Rowland*, 358.

22. *Minutes, Rowland*, 358; *Clarion–Ledger*, January 10, 1889, 1.

23. *Clarion–Ledger*, January 4, 1891, 4.

24. *Daily Clarion*, January 5, 1892, 4.

25. *Who Was Who* (1897–1942), s.v. "Mayes, Edward"; ibid. (1607–1896), s.v. "Lamar, Lucius Quintus Cincinnatus."

26. Ibid.

27. *Weekly Clarion*, December 30, 1885, 2.

28. *Minutes, Rowland*, 358.

29. Ibid., 358–59; *Weekly Clarion*, January 4, 1887, 2.

30. *ABA Rep* (1886), 111.

31. Carson, *Good Day*, 14; *Minutes, Rowland*, 358–59.

32. *Minutes, Annual Mtg*. (1887), 1; *Minutes, Rowland*, 359.

33. *Minutes, Rowland*, 358; Rowland, *Courts*, 240. Nugent's letters home to his wife, written during his service as a Confederate officer, have been published by the University Press of Mississippi, *My Dear Nellie*, Cash and Howarth, eds. (Jackson, 1977).

34. *Minutes, Rowland*, 358–59.

35. Rowland, *Courts*, 222–23, 240–41; Landon, *Honor and Dignity*, 48.

36. Rowland, *Courts*, 350; *ABA Rep* (1881), 89; ibid. (1882), 108.

37. *Who Was Who* (1607–1896), s.v. "Hill, Robert Andrew."

38. The earliest bar list obtainable was published as an appendix to the proceedings of the Mississippi State Bar Association in 1908, and listed 1,026 lawyers in the state. In 1890, the population of the state was about 40 percent lower than in 1910; United States, Bureau of the Census, *Historical Abstracts* (Washington, D.C., 1976), pt. 1, 30. Presumably, the proportion of lawyers in the population remained approximately the same during the two decades.

39. *Minutes, Annual Mtg*. (1890), 18.

40. *Clarion–Ledger*, January 6, 1891, 4.
41. *Minutes, Rowland*, 358–60.
42. *Clarion*, January 5, 1887, 2.
43. *Minutes, Rowland*, 359.
44. *Who Was Who* (1607–1896), s.v. "Tucker, John Randolph."
45. *Clarion–Ledger*, January 10, 1889, 4.
46. *Minutes, Annual Mtg.* (1890), 16.
47. *Clarion–Ledger*, January 6, 1891, 4. This was perhaps Jackson Hill, U.S. Senator from Georgia (1871–1873), who died just three months later, March 6, 1891; *Who Was Who* (1607–1896), s.v. "Hill, Jackson."
48. *Who Was Who* (1897–1942), s.v. "Rose, U. M."; *Clarion–Ledger*, January 5, 1892, 4.
49. *Minutes, Annual Mtg.* (1890), 15.
50. *Minutes, Rowland*, 359.
51. *Minutes, Annual Mtg.* (1887), 1; ibid., (1890), 1, 9, 20.
52. *Minutes, Annual Mtg.* (1890), 20; Ch. 541, 30 stat., 544.
53. *ABA Rep* (1879), 40; *Minutes, Annual Mtg.* (1890), 6.
54. *Minutes, Rowland*, 359; *Clarion–Ledger*, January 10, 1889, 1. Sections 24 and 25 of 36, 37 Victoria, c. 66, had stated that in the proceedings of the newly established Supreme Court of Judicature, whenever the rules of law and of equity came in to conflict, the latter should prevail.
55. *Minutes, Annual Mtg.* (1890), 11, 19.
56. *Minutes, Annual Mtg.* (1890), passim.
57. United States, Bureau of the Census, *A Century of Population Growth* (Washington, D.C., 1909), 82. The size of the black majority over whites in the state increased steadily between 1880 and 1900; ibid.
58. Rowland, *Courts*, 235–36.
59. State of Mississippi, *Journal of Constitutional Convention* (1890), 8–9.
60. Ibid., 10–11.
61. Rowland, *Courts*, 237–38; the section was repealed in 1963.
62. *Clarion–Ledger*, January 7, 1891, 1.
63. Ibid.
64. State Constitution, Sections 158, 164, 171.
65. Rowland, *Courts*, 238–39.
66. According to one report, bar meetings were held in 1893 and 1894, the latter of which was "poorly attended"; Carol C. Morland, "Check List of State Bar Association Proceedings," *Law Library Journal* 63 (1969), 142. Perhaps so, but certainly no new officers were elected and no minutes were kept. I could find no mention of them in the Jackson newspaper.
67. *Mississippi Code* (1880), secs. 1398–99; ibid. (1892), sec. 4338.

*GERARD W. GAWALT*

# *Bibliographic Essay*

The study of the legal profession has attracted increasing attention from legal historians during the past two decades, even though doctrinal studies, concentrating on substantive, constitutional, and procedural law, have remained of paramount concern. Even in these fields, scholars realize that a clear understanding of the profession, both as aggregates and as individuals, could be critical to changes in and interpretations of substantive law.

The scholarly ancestors of today's studies of the legal profession are Charles Warren, Roscoe Pound, W. Raymond Blackard, and Alfred Z. Reed. Their major writings established the twin themes of the conservative nature of lawyers and the decline of the profession during the nineteenth century. Although dated, they are still useful, and the general studies of Warren and Reed have not been superseded. Charles Warren, *A History of the American Bar*, Boston, 1911; Alfred Z. Reed, *Training for the Public Profession of the Law*, New York, 1921; Roscoe Pound, *The Formative Era of American Law*, Boston, 1938; idem, *Interpretations of Legal History*, Cambridge, 1923; idem, *The Lawyer from Antiquity to Modern Times, with Particular Reference to the Development of Bar Associations in the United States*, St. Paul, 1953; W. Raymond Blackard, "The Demoralization of the Legal Profession in Nineteenth Century America," *Tennessee Law Review* 15 (April 1940):314–23.

Their themes and their general concern with the role of bar associations as vehicles for self-regulation and mutual support were refined and their findings expanded by the following members of this traditional school of legal scholars: Anton-Hermann Chroust, *The Rise of the Legal Profession in America*, 2 vols., Norman, 1965; James Willard Hurst, *The Growth of American Law: The Law Makers*, Boston, 1950; Erwin N. Griswold, *Law and Lawyers in the United States*, Cambridge, 1965; William F. English, *The Pioneer Lawyer and Jurist in Missouri*, Columbia, 1947; Clyde Jacobs, *Law Writers and the Courts: The Influence of Thomas M. Cooley, Christopher G. Tiedeman, and John F. Dillon upon American Constitutional Law*, Berkeley, 1954; Arnold M. Paul, *Conservative Crises and the Rule of Law: Attitudes of Bar and Bench, 1887–1895*, Ithaca, 1960; Jerome E. Carlin, *Lawyers on Their Own: A Study of Individual Practitioners in Chicago*, New Brunswick, 1962; and Lawrence M. Friedman, *A History of American Law*, New York, 1973. Although Jerold Auerbach places the legal profession within the same framework, the critical analysis of his book sets it apart: *Unequal Justice; Lawyers and Social Change in Modern America*, New York, 1976.

In recent years, other historians, including several authors of essays in this book, have moved away from the traditional perspective and interpretation of the profession. They argue that in most measurable forms, such as training, recruitment, professionalization of practice, political power, judicial power, and quantitative growth, the profession improved and strengthened itself during the nineteenth century. They conclude, moreover, that the legal profession cannot be categorized as simply conservative and elitist. Seminal work by Daniel Calhoun, Maxwell Bloomfield, and Gerard W. Gawalt has produced a growing list of works that combine a new perspective with varying research techniques and sources of information. See, for example: Daniel Calhoun, *Professional Lifes in America: Structure and Aspiration*, Cambridge, 1965; Gerard W. Gawalt, "Massachusetts Lawyers: A Historical Study of the Process of Professionalization, 1760–1840," Ph.D. diss., Clark University, 1969; idem, *The Promise of Power: The Emergence of the Legal Profession in Massachusetts, 1760-1840*, Westport, 1979; Audra L. Prewitt, "American Lawyers and Social Ferment," Ph.D. diss., Northwestern University, 1973; Maxwell Bloomfield, *American Lawyers in a Changing Society*, Cambridge, 1976; Morton J. Horwitz, *The Transformation of American Law, 1780–1860*, Cambridge, 1977; Wayne K. Hobson, "The American Legal Profession and the Organizational Society, 1890–1930," Ph.D. diss., Stanford University, 1977. The present book of essays expands the work of this school of interpretation.

Biography has always been the backbone of studies of the legal profession. Most writing on the profession during the nineteenth century consisted of books and articles on the bench and bar that can best be described as hagiography. Yet there is much factual data in these works that can prove valuable. Literally hundreds were sponsored and written by admiring lawyers and local bar associations. On a national level, William D. Lewis, ed., *Great American Lawyers*, 8 vols., Philadelphia, 1907–1909, exemplifies this school of writing. Almost every state had at least one work, such as John B. O'Neall, *Biographical Sketches of the Bench and Bar of South Carolina*, 2 vols., Charleston, 1859; or William T. Davis, *The Bench and Bar of the Commonwealth of Massachusetts*, 2 vols., Boston, 1895. This simple group biography has evolved, on the one hand, into more statistics-oriented works of prosopography, such as Gary Nash, "The Philadelphia Bench and Bar, 1800–1860," *Comparative Studies in Society and History* 7 (January 1965):203–20; Kermit Hall, *The Politics of Justice*, Lincoln, 1979; Gawalt, *The Promise of Power*; idem, "Sources of Anti-Lawyer Sentiment in Massachusetts," *American Journal of Legal History* 14 (October 1970):283–307; idem, "National Standardization and Regional Diversity in the Post–Civil War American Legal Profession," AHA Annual Meeting, 1982; and the essays in this volume by Gordon Bakken, Maxwell Bloomfield, Gerard Gawalt, Kermit Hall, and Wayne Hobson. On the other hand, it has produced more sophisticated multibiographical works, such as W. Hamilton Bryson, *The Virginia Law Reporters Before 1880*, Charlottesville, 1977; idem, *Legal Education in Virginia, 1779–1979*, Charlottesville, 1982; and Leon Friedman and Fred L. Israel, eds., *The Justices of the Supreme Court, 1789–1978*, 5 vols., New York, 1969–1978.

Biographical studies of individual lawyers and law firms are too numerous to make a complete listing feasible. A sample of traditional but still valuable biographies and firm studies includes: Robert T. Swaine, *The Cravath Firm*, 3 vols., New York, 1946–1948; Walter K. Earle, *Mr. Shearman and Mr. Sterling and How They Grew*, New Haven, 1963; Otto E. Koegel, *Walter S. Carter, Collector of Young Masters; or, The Progenitor of Many Law Firms*, New York, 1953; Arthur H. Dean, *William Nelson Cromwell, 1854–1948: An American Pioneer in Corporation, Comparative, and International Law*, New York, 1957; Edward S. Martin, *Life of Joseph Hodges Choate*, 2 vols., New York, 1921; Theron G. Strong, *Landmarks of a Lawyer's Lifetime*, New York, 1914; Joseph M. Proskauer, *A Segment of My Times*, Washington, D.C., 1957; Henry W. Taft, *A Century and a Half at the New York Bar*, New York, 1930; William N. Brigance, *Jeremiah Sullivan Black*, London, 1934.

Some of the more recent biographies and firm studies are: William Harbaugh, *Lawyers' Lawyer; The Life of John W. Davis*, New York, 1973; Allan Gal, *Brandeis of Boston*, Cambridge, 1980; William W. Clary, *History of the Law Firm of O'Melveny & Meyers, 1885–1965*, 2 vols., Los Angeles, 1966; David Wigdor, *Roscoe Pound: Philosopher of Law*, Westport, 1974; Erwin O. Smigel, *The Wall Street Lawyers*, New York, 1964; and Charles C. Goetsch, *Essays on Simeon E. Baldwin*, West Hartford, 1981; Mark de Wolfe Howe, *Justice Oliver Wendell Holmes, The Shaping Years, 1841–1870*, Cambridge, 1957; and *Justice Oliver Wendell Holmes, The Proving Years, 1870–1882*, Cambridge, 1963.

Legal education has been examined by many historians, and the following works only illustrate the breadth of available books and articles. The following older but still useful books argue the superiority of law school education over apprenticeship: Charles A. Warren, *A History of Harvard Law School and of Early Legal Conditions in America*, 2 vols., New York, 1908; Joel Parker, *The Law School at Harvard College*, New York, 1871; Frederick C. Hicks, *Yale Law School*, New Haven, 1936; Alfred Z. Reed, *Training for the Public Profession of the Law*, New York, 1921; idem, *Present-Day Law Schools in the United States and Canada*, New York, 1928; Albert J. Harno, *Legal Education in the United States*, San Francisco, 1953.

Representative of more recent books on legal education that assume the superiority of law school training over clinical education, but have a more balanced view of the strengths and weaknesses of law schools are the following: Bryson, *Legal Education in Virginia, 1779–1979*, Charlottesville, 1982; Robert Stevens, *Law School: Legal Education in America from the 1850s to the 1980s*, Chapel Hill, 1983; William R. Johnson, *Schooled Lawyers: A Study in the Clash of Professional Cultures*, New York, 1978; Joel E. Seligman, *The High Citadel: The Influence of Harvard Law School*, Boston, 1978; Jerold S. Auerbach, ''Enmity and Amity: Law Teachers and Practitioners, 1900–1922,'' in *Law in American History*, Donald Fleming and Bernard Bailyn, eds., Boston, 1971, 551–604; Robert Stevens, ''Two Cheers for 1870: The American Law School,'' ibid. 405–548; and Anthony Chase, ''The Birth of the Modern Law School,'' *American Journal of Legal History* 23 (October 1979):329–48; Elizabeth G. Brown, *Legal Education in Michigan, 1859–1959*, Ann Arbor, 1959; and Julius Goebel, ed., *A History of the School of Law, Columbia University*, New York, 1955.

Early students of the legal profession were fascinated by the growth of bar associations. Hollis R. Bailey's, *Attorneys and Their Admission to the Bar in Massachusetts*, Boston, 1907, and Simeon Baldwin's ''The Founding of the American Bar Association,'' *American Bar Association Journal* 3 (October 1917):658–695 are two examples of this early concern with professional institutions of self-regulation and mutual protection. Much of these works also concerned bar associations: Chroust, *The Rise of the Legal Profession in America*, 2 vols., Norman, 1965; and Pound, *The Lawyer from Antiquity to Modern Times, with Particular Reference to the Development of Bar Associations in the United States*, St. Paul, 1953. See also Norbert Brockman, ''The Politics of the American Bar Association,'' Ph.D. diss., Catholic University of America, 1963. Many of these bar association studies have been commissioned by state and local bar associations or the American Bar Association. The following commissioned works are among those quite useful to historians: Gerald Carson, *A Good Day At Saratoga*, Chicago, 1978; James G. Rogers, *American Bar Leaders: Biographies of Presidents of the American Bar Association, 1878–1928*, Chicago, 1932; Edwin R. Sunderland, *The History of the American Bar Association*, New York, 1953; George Martin, *Causes and Conflicts: The Centennial History of the Association of the Bar of the City of New York*, Boston, 1970; and Michael de L. Landon, *The Honor and Dignity of the Profession: A History of the Mississippi State Bar, 1906–1976*, Jackson, 1979.

Little has been written on women in the legal profession, and the literature tends to emphasize the exclusion of women from the profession in the nineteenth century. Nevertheless, the following works offer insights into women in the legal profession: Cynthia Fuchs Epstein, *Women in Law*, New York, 1981; Barbara J. Harris, *Beyond Her Sphere: Women and the Professions in American History*, Westport, 1978; Roberta Frankfort, *Collegiate Women: Domesticity and Career in Turn-of-the Century America*, New York, 1977; D. Kelly Weisberg, ''Barred from the Bar: Women and Legal Education in the United States, 1870–1900,'' *Journal of Legal Education* 28 (1977):485–507; Dorothy Thomas, *Women Lawyers in the United States*, New York, 1957; and Beatrice Doerschuck, *Women in the Law: An Analysis of Training, Practice, and Salaried Positions*, New York, 1920.

Few blacks were admitted to the legal profession in the nineteenth century and, consequently, there are few historical studies. In addition to the article Maxwell Bloomfield wrote for this book, he also wrote ''John Mercer Langston and the Rise of Howard Law School,'' *Records of the Columbia Historical Society of Washington, D.C.* 48 (1971–1972):421–38. See also: Walter J. Leonard, *Black Lawyers Training and Results: Then and Now*, Boston, 1977; Kenneth S. Tollett, ''Black Lawyers,

Their Education, and the Black Community,'' *Howard Law Journal* 17 (1972):325–57; Irvin C. Mollison, ''Negro Lawyers in Mississippi,'' *Journal of Negro History* 38 (January 1930):38–71; and Carter G. Woodson, *The Negro Professional Man and Community, With Special Emphasis on the Physician and the Lawyer*, Washington, D.C., 1934.

The judiciary, like constitutional law, has been a favorite subject of legal historians. Most of the work represents solid scholarship and in some instances, the best of legal history. The following list contains but a few of the more analytical books on the judiciary in the nineteenth century: Kermit L. Hall, ''The Children of the Cabins: The Lower Federal Judiciary, Modernization, and the Political Culture, 1789–1899,'' *Northwestern University Law Review* 75 (October 1980):423–65; idem, *Politics of Justice*, Lincoln, 1979; Philip L. Dubois, *From Ballot to Bench: Judicial Elections and the Quest for Accountability*, Austin, 1980; Horwitz, *The Transformation of American Law, 1780–1860*, Cambridge, 1977; Morton Keller, *Affairs of State: Public Life in Late Nineteenth Century America*, Cambridge, 1977; John D. Guice, *The Rocky Mountain Bench*, New Haven, 1972; Stanley I. Kutler, *Judicial Power and Reconstruction Politics*, Chicago, 1968; John P. Reid, *Chief Justice: the Judicial World of Charles Doe*, Cambridge, 1967; James W. Hurst, *The Growth of American Law: The Lawmakers*, Boston, 1950; and Charles Fairman, *Mr. Justice Miller and the Supreme Court, 1862–1890*, Cambridge, 1939.

Scholars seeking a more comprehensive bibliography should turn to Kermit L. Hall, *A Comprehensive Bibliography of American Constitutional and Legal History, 1896–1979*, 3 vols., Millwood, N.Y., 1983.

# *Index*

ABA. *See* American Bar Association
*A. Hubbs v. George Perkins et al.*, 159–60
*Albany Law Journal*, 79, 80, 81
American Bar Association (ABA): antebellum precursors, 77–78; Baldwin's role, 81–82, 84–85, 87–89, 90, 95–96 n.65, 97 n.72; bankruptcy law views, 194; "Congress of Lawyers," 81; conservatism, alleged, 75–76; elitism, 78, 81; founding, 75, 76, 80, 81, 95 nn. 52, 54, 55, 96 nn.60, 65; ideals behind, 56; lawyers involved in, 85–87, 95–96 n.65; members' status, 78–79; Mississippi lawyers' activities in, 176, 188–91; objectives, 89; professional roots, 76, 79; professional standards, 88, 96 n.72; Saratoga clique, 87–88, 95 n.60; social aspects, 89; Southern lawyers' participation, 188–89
American Law Institute (ALI), 72 n.53
*American Law Review*, 56, 78
American Law Schools, Association of, 109
American Social Science Association, 84
Andrews, James D., 4
Anti-Lynching and Protective Association of Texas, 163
Appellate Court Judges (Midwestern): access, 38–42; age, 37; career duration, 36; corruption charges, 31; critics of, 29–31, 38, 42, 43; direct election of, 29–30, 34; education, 31–32, 33, 47 n.19; family connections, 40, 41, 42, 43–46; independence, 34, 36, 37–38; political experience, 35; tenure, 36–37, 38
Arnold, Thurman, 72 n.53
Aronson, Sidney, 43, 45
*Arthur Mack v. Galveston, Houston & Henderson R.R. Co.*, 159
Austin, Henry C., 135–36
Avery, William H., 131
Aylett, William R., 174

Baldwin, Simeon E.: ABA founding, 75, 80, 81, 85, 87–90, 95–96 n.65; background and career, 81–82; legal education changes by, 83–84; reform efforts, 82–83; work habits, 93 n.44
*Baldwin's Connecticut Digest*, 83
Baltzell, E. Digby, 15
Bancroft-Whitney Company, 134
Bankruptcy, 194
Bar Associations, 77–79. *See also* American Bar Association (ABA); *geographic names of specific bar associations*

Barbour, John H., 165
*Barret v. The Southern Pacific Company*, 139
Beard, John S., 132
Beck, James, 65
Berle, Adolf A., Jr., 63, 66
"The Best Men" (reformers), 82–83
Bicknell, John D.: California law practice, 126, 127, 128, 129, 131; on capitalism, 141; on debt collection, 137; land dealings, 135–36; law library, 133–34; ordinances, 143–44; railroads, 140–42, 143; regulatory law, 140; tort law, 137–40
Biddle & Ward, 15
Biddle, Paul, Dawson & Yocum, 15
Bigelow, Henry, 109
Blacks in legal practice:
—at Harvard Law School, 106
—in Massachusetts, 103, 104
—in Texas: anti-lynching action, 163; bar admission, 155; bar beginnings, 152–53; biographies, 153–54; civil rights actions, 162–65; courts, 158–62; education, 154–55; political affiliation, 164; practice, 156, 165–66; professional misconduct, 156–58; Smith's role, 158–62
—in Virginia, 173
Blaine, James G., 83
Bloomfield, Maxwell, 77
Boston legal practice, 14–16, 17, 99–100. *See also* Massachusetts legal practice
Boston University Law School, 104, 106, 107, 109
Brame, L., 192
Brandeis, Louis D., 16, 21, 63, 66, 100–101
Bressler, Marvin, 44
Bridge, Allen D., 162
Bristow, Benjamin, 85, 86
Broadhead, James O., 12, 86, 89–90, 188
Broadhead, Slayback & Haeussler, 12
Brooks, Robert Peel, 173
Broyles, M. H., 162
Bryan, John D., 131
Bryce, James, 42–43
Bryne, James, 7
Buckalew, Charles R., 85, 86
Bump, Orlando F., 81
Burgess, George O., 155
Butler, William Allan, 87

Cadwalader, Wickersham & Taft, 19
Cairns, John James, 129
Calhoon, Solomon Saladin, 194, 196
California legal practice: advantages, 131; birthplaces, 126–27; and business interests, 141; changes in, 132–33; debt collection, 136–37; delay tactics, 142–43; economic problems, 126; education, 128–29; emigration, 130–31; family background, 129–30; information network, 134; land speculation and titles, 127–28, 135; lawbooks, 133–34; past employment, 131–32; and railroads, 131, 137–40, 145; specialists, 144–45; state Supreme Court, 144; urban practice, 125–26; water law, 141, 145
Cardozo, Albert, 31
Carter, James C., 51–53, 55, 178
Carter, Seth, 161
Carter, Walter S., 17, 19
Carter, Hughes & Dwight, 13
*Carter v. Texas*, 161
Case system, 63, 84, 108
Center, John, 127
Chamberlain, Carter & Hornblower, 17, 19
Chicago, University of, Law School, 72 n.52
Chicago legal practice, 12, 14
Chittenden, L. E., 77
Choate, Joseph H., 16, 52, 65, 100
Chrisman, J. B., 192
Christy, Anna, 104
Cincinnati legal practice, 10, 12–13
Civil code, 52, 55
Civil service, 83, 86
*C. J. Walker v. International & Great Northern Railway Co.*, 163
Clark, John B., 127
Clayton, A. M., 190, 191–92, 193

Cleveland, Grover, 82, 83
Cleveland legal practice, 12, 13
Clifford, John H., 100
Columbia University, 55; Law School, 72 n.52
Committee of One Hundred, 52
Common law, 55, 72 n.53, 178
Connecticut legal practice, 83
Connecticut State Bar Association, 85
Constitutional law, 76
*Constitutional Revolution, Ltd.* (Corwin), 76
Cooley, Thomas M., 85, 86
Corporations: ethics, 61; favors, 60; forms, 58, 59–60, 61; legal ideals, 59; legal limitations, 58, 65; legal services, 8–9, 59–60, 61, 62, 63, 66, 71 n.86; liberalism, 64; Mississippi legal relations, 198; public policy, 64, 65, 66, 67, 68, 70–71 n.39; state regulation, 65; Virginia legal relations, 179–80. *See also* Law firms, large
Corwin, Edward S., 75–76
Court practice, 99. *See also* Appellate Court Judges (Midwestern)
Couts, Cave Johnson, 127
Cravath, Paul D., 9, 19, 20, 65
Crawley, John M., 140
Croly, Herbert, 4
Cromwell, William Nelson, 8
Cuney, Joseph, 154, 158, 159, 162, 164, 165
Currey, John, 132–33
Curtis, Jesse William, 130
Curtis, W. G., 142

Dahrendorf, Ralph, 43
Daniel, John W., 176
Davies, Stone & Auerbach, 17
Davis, Rosemary, 174
Debt collection, 136–37
Dent, Thomas H., 165–66, 168 n.21
Devens, Charles, 85
Dickson, Beitler & McCouch, 15
Dill, James B., 8, 65
Dillon, John F., 4
Divorce law, 159
Drew, Daniel, 79
Dubois, Philip, 34, 36
Dulles, John Foster, 10
Dunbar, William H., 101

Eaton, Dorman, 80, 82
Edmonds, George F., 82, 83
Emott, James, 80
Erie Railroad, 56, 79
Evarts, William M., 76, 80, 85, 86
Evarts, Southmayd & Choate, 16

Fabens, George C., 137–38
Farley, James, 103
Felland, H. F., 127
Fellow-servant doctrine, 179–80
Field, David Dudley, 52, 57, 79, 86
Fires, 138
Fish, Richardson, Herrick & Neave, 17
Fisk, James, 56, 57, 79
Fleischman, Simon, 29–30, 42
Flournoy, George, 129–30
Flower, J. M., 12
Fontaine, Sydney T., 164
Foreign-born in legal practice, 103–4
Foreign Service, 70 n.38
Frankfurter, Felix, 21
Fremont, George W., 152
Freund, Ernst, 72 n.52
Friedman, Lawrence, 31, 38, 42, 106
Fry, Henry B., 173
Fugitive Slave Laws, 85

Gallman, Robert, 45
Galveston, Texas: black community, 153; black legal practice, 153–62; civil rights suits, 162–63; poll tax, 164, 165. *See also* Blacks in legal practice
Galveston, Harrisburg & San Antonio Railway Company, 163
*Galveston Times*, 160–61
George, J. Z., 195
German lawyers, 72 n.50
Gilland, John, 188
Gleason, Henry, 135
Gold market, 56, 57

Goodwin, John D., 127, 130
Goodwin, William N., 130
Gould, Jay, 56, 57, 79
Government and business, 64, 65, 66, 67, 68, 70–71 n.39
Graves, Jackson A., 135, 141
Graves, O'Melveny, and Shankland, 137, 143
Gray, Horace, 161
Green, Alexander, 155, 156–57, 158–59, 162, 164
Green, William, 175
Griffith, J. M., 141
*Griffiths v. Gruner*, 143
Gurney, Ephraim W., 108
Guthrie, William D., 9, 65

Hall, W. Oakley, 101
Halleck, Peachy, Billings, and Park, 126
Hamersley, William, 85
Hammond, Creed, 136–37, 138–39, 143
Hammond, W. G., 79
Hand, Learned, 9
Harmon, Judson, 13
Harmon, Colston, Goldsmith & Hoadly, 13
Harrington, John T., 128
Harrison, Benjamin, 194
Harvard Law School: black student, 104; James Carter and, 52; graduates' marriages, 107; instructional approach, 84, 106, 108; scientific law codes, 55
Haven, Thomas E., 128
Hayes, James H., 173
Haymond, Creed. *See* Hammond, Creed
Henderson, John B., 85, 86
Higby, William, 136
Higginson, Thomas Wentworth, 82
Hill, Arthur Wesley, 128
Hill, R. A., 192, 194
Hill, Walter R., 156, 159, 162, 163, 164
Hilliard, G. S., 104
*History of the American Bar Association*, 75
Hitchcock, George N., 136
Hitchcock, Henry, 85, 86
Hoadly, George, 13, 85, 86
Hoadly, Lauterbach & Johnson, 13
Hofstadler, Richard, 61
Holmes, Oliver Wendell, 108
Hopkins, Mark, 82
Hornblower, William B., 17
Houston, Francis A., 101
Houston, L. E., 189, 191
Howry, C. B., 188, 189, 191
Hubbard, Richard D., 85
*Hubbell's Legal Directory*, 5, 8, 10, 12, 13, 17, 20, 23 n.9
Hughes, Charles Evans, 17, 19
Hunt, Carleton, 84, 85, 86, 188
Hunton and Williams, 175
Hurst, James Willard, 8, 29, 38

Industrialization: California legal practice, 130–31, 138, 144–45; house counsels, 101; Massachusetts legal practice, 97–98, 100; and rise of national law schools, 107, 108; and regulatory law, 140–41; scientific legal approach, 108; tort law, 137–40; water law, 141, 145
*Institutes of Common and Statute Law* (Minor), 176
Irish-American lawyers, 103–4, 106

Jack, David, 142
Jackson, Giles B., 173
Jarboe, Harrison, and Goodfellow, 143, 144
Jenkins, Edward F., 103
Johnson, Edgar M., 13
Johnson, John G., 15
Johnson, William H., 104
Jones, Alice Hanson, 45
Jones, Charles, 89
Jones, W. L., 161
Judges. *See* Appellate Court Judges (Midwestern)

Kansas City legal practice, 12, 13
Kennedy, J. M., 126
Kett, Joseph, 105
King, Rufus, 12
King, Thompson, Richard & Thompson, 12
Koerner, Gustave, 80, 88, 89, 93 n.38

Labor activity, 70 n.31
Laine, T. H., 134
Lamar, Lucius Quintus Cincinnatus, 191
Land: speculation and titles, 127–28, 131, 135; Virginia registry, 179
Langdell, Christopher C., 84, 108, 109
Lathrop, Gardiner, 13
Lathrop, Morrow, Fox & Moore, 13
Latrobe, John H., 187
Law firms, large: autonomy, 100; Brandeis's views, 101; critics, 4, 9; fees, 100; growth, 5–6, 7, 8–9, 16–19, 23 n.9; innovations, 10; legal training, 14; and national law schools, 107–8; New York reform movement, 55; organization, 19–20; personnel, 18–19, 20; regional distribution, 10–14; salaries, 20; standards, 20–22; traditional views, 15–16. *See also* Corporations; *names of specific firms*
Law Library of Los Angeles, 133
Law schools, 64. *See also* Legal training; *names of specific institutions*
Lawton, Alexander R., 85, 86
*Lawyers and the Constitution* (Twiss), 76
Lawyers' status, 78–79
Legal forms, 58, 59–60, 61
Legal realism, 64
Legal reform: *Baldwin's Connecticut Digest*, 83; changing legal practices, 59–62, 71 n.44; disintegration, 58–62; evils perceived, 54; ideal, 51–52, 53–54, 55, 56, 63; institutions, 52–53, 55; lawyers involved, 67–68 n.6; legal realism movement, 64; in politics, 56; public policy, 64, 65, 66, 67, 72 n.52; restatements, 72 n.53; scandals, 56–57; as science, 55–56, 57, 63, 72 n.52; specialization, 66; U.S. Supreme Court view of, 65
Legal training: Baldwin on, 83–84; bar admission standards, 76–77; of California lawyers, 128–29; of Massachusetts lawyers, 105–8; and rise of national law schools, 105–8; and public policy, 72 n.52; quotas, 103; reading law, 128–29; as science, 108–9; standards, 88, 91 n.14, 95 n.61; of Texas black lawyers, 154–55; vocational vs. theoretical, 108–9
Legislation, uniformity of, 88
Leigh, J. E., 189
Lewis, J. Vance, 154, 156, 157–58, 161, 162
Lewis, M. G., 162
Lewis, William Draper, 20
Liability, 138–39
Libel law, 160–61
Lieb, S. F., 143
Lilienthal, Jesse W., 128
Lockwood, Belva, 174
Lodge, Henry Cabot, 82
Lorrobee, Charles H., 142–43
Luce, McDonald, and Torrance, 134

McBeth, Charles D., 156
McCafferty, Matthew J., 103–4
McDowell, T. K., 129, 135
McMurtrie, Richard, 85, 86
McWillie, T. A., 192, 193, 198
Markey, John, 127–28
Mason, L. W., 133
Massachusetts legal practice: blacks in, 104–5; ethnic composition, 103–4; fees, 99–100; marriage patterns, 102; mobility of lawyers, 102; property and wealth, 98–99, 101, 104; urban concentration, 97–98; women, 103, 104, 105. *See also* Boston legal practice
Massie, Eugene C., 179
Matthews, Stanley, 85, 86
Maxwell, Lawrence, 12
Mayes, Edward, 190–91, 193, 196
Milwaukee legal practice, 13
Minor, John B., 176
Mississippi legal practice: ABA members, 188–90; bankruptcy law, 194; bar associations, 187, 189–93, 197–98; conservatism, 198; corporations, 198; reform proposals, 194–95; state constitution, 195–98; tax titles, 193–94; types, 192–93, 199 n.38; voting rights, 196–97
Mississippi State Bar Association, 190–98
Morris, Robert, 104

Munford, B. B., 171
Munford, Hunton, Williams, and Anderson, 175
Municipal regulations, 140–41
*Munn v. Illinois*, 76
Murray, David, 129

NAACP, 165, 166, 170 n.61
Nader, Ralph, 65
Nash, Gary B., 106
National Association for the Advancement of Colored People (NAACP), 165, 166, 170 n.61
*The Negro Professional Man and the Community* (Woodson), 151
New York City, Bar of, 51, 56, 57, 64, 66, 77, 79–80, 187
New York City legal practice, 10, 11, 13, 14, 16. *See also* Legal reform
Nicoll, DeLancey, 65
Nicoll, Henry, 80
Noble, W. H., 161
Norton, Charles Eliot, 82
Nugent, W. I., 192
Nutter, George R., 21

O'Connor Act of 1876, 140
O'Conor, Charles, 56, 85, 86
O'Melveny, Henry O., 141
Orr, J. A., 189

Page, Thomas Nelson, 176
Page, William D., 17
Parker, Alice, 104
Parrish, Robert L., 180
Payne, John Barton, 12
Perkins, Allen G., 154, 156, 159, 162, 163, 164, 165
Phelps, Edward J., 76, 85, 86
Philadelphia legal practice, 10, 11, 14–15
Picher, O. H., 128
*Plessy v. Ferguson*, 151
Poché, Felix P., 84, 94 n.52
Poland, Luke, 86
Pollard, H. R., 171
Poll tax, 164–65
Porter, John K., 85, 86
Pound, Roscoe, 20–21, 72 n.50, 123 n.38
*Practice in the Courts of Justice in England and the United States, 1854–1874* (Robinson), 175
Price, W. A., 152
Prichard, Frank P., 15
Progressive reform, 64–65, 66
Property-holding lawyers, 98–99
Pullman Palace Car Company, 139

Railroads: and ABA founding, 187; in California legal practice, 131, 137–39; civil rights actions, 162–63; as legal clients, 13, 188; and legal reform, 56; Mississippi legal interests, 192, 198; regulatory law, 140; reorganization, 6, 8; in Southern legal practice, 174; and tort cases, 137–39; in Virginia legal practice, 179–80. *See also names of specific railroads*
Randolph, E. A., 173
Rankin, W. T., 139
Rapid Transit Act of 1894, 65
Rawle, Francis, 87
Reed, Lansing P., 8
Reed, Smith, Shaw & Beal, 17
Reform movement. *See* "The Best Men"; Legal reform; Progressive reform
Regulatory law, 140–41
Restatements, 72 n.53
Reynolds, R. O., 189, 190, 191
Richards, J. M., 136
Richardson, J. M., 126
Richmond, Bar Association of the City of, 176–77
Roane, William C., 173
Robertson, William J., 177–78
Robinson, Conway, 175
Roosevelt, Theodore, 82
Root, Elihu, 4, 8, 9, 65, 66, 71 n.43
Ropes, John C., 95 n.65
Rose, U. M., 193
Rosecrans, William S., 135, 137
Ruffin, George, 104
Ruger, William C., 96 n.72
Russel, G. L., 141

Sagi, Philip C., 44
Saratoga clique, 87–88, 95 n.60
Sawtelle, Lelia Robinson, 104
Schneider, Joseph, 43
Schurz, Carl, 82
Scott, S. H., 152
Sedgwick, Arthur G., 108
Semmes, Thomas Jenkins, 87
Seward, Guthrie & Steele, 19
Shearman, John, 57
Shepard, Edward M., 65
Sims, W. H., 189
Slocum, M. F., 81
Smith, Frank B., 101
Smith, Henry, 89
Smith, Milton, 131
Smith, Wilford H., 155, 158–62, 165, 169 n.46
Social mobility, professional, 105
Sohow, Lee, 45
Soule, Augustus L., 101
Southern Pacific Co., 131, 134, 137–39, 142, 143
Squire, Sanders & Dempsey, 13
Stanley, E. W., 96 n.72
Stephen, Mary E., 104
Sterling, John, 57
Stetson, Francis Lyne, 8, 20
Stetson, Jennings, Russell & Davis, 8
Stimson, Henry L., 8
Stone, Harlan Fiske, 20, 22
Storey, Moorfield, 16
Strong, Theron G., 10
Stubbs, James B., 161
Studebaker, John Mohler, 131
Sullivan & Cromwell, 8, 10
Supreme Court, U.S., 65, 76, 95 n.60, 174
Swanston, Henry H., 158, 159
Swasey, George R., 109

Taft, Henry W., 17
Texas. *See* Blacks in legal practice; Galveston, Texas
Thayer, James B., 110
Thayer, John R., 100
Thompson, Isaac Grant, 80
Thompson, R. H., 192, 193, 194, 195, 196, 197
Thompson, Samuel J., 12
Tilden, Samuel J., 82
Tollett, Kenneth S., 151
Tompkins, Elizabeth H., 174
Torrens system of land registry, 179
Torrey, George A., 103
Tort law, 137–40
Towne, A. N., 142
Train, Charles, 85, 86
Treasher, C. W., 126
Trumbull, Lyman, 85, 86
Tucker, John Randolph, 85, 86, 176, 193
Turner, John L., 152
Tushnet, Mark, 30, 40
Tweed Ring, 57, 79, 86
Twiss, Benjamin, 75–76

Ullman, Charles S., 81
United States Law Association, 81
United States Supreme Court, 65, 76, 95 n.60, 174
Untermayer, Samuel, 21, 66

Vanderbilt, Cornelius, 56, 79
*Virginia Law Journal*, 175, 176, 180
Virginia legal practice: bar associations, 176–81, 183 n.38; black membership, 173; business influence, 174–75; Civil War impact on, 172–73; corporate relations, 179–80; court reorganization, 177; land registration, 179; law codification, 177–79; leading lawyers, 175–76; licensing, 171–72; partnerships, 175; women in, 173–74
Virginia State Bar Association, 177–81
Voting rights, 196–97. *See also* Poll tax

Wadhams, Frederick E., 30
Wallis, S. Teakle, 85, 86
Ward, P. H., 126
Wardell, Allen, 20
Warnack, William, 136
Warner, William, 127
Water litigation, 141, 145
Watts, J. Allen, 179
Westoff, Charles, 43–44

Whiskey Ring, 86, 87, 90
White, Horace, 82
Whittle, Charles F., 173
Wickersham, George, 66
Wiley, Joseph E., 152
Williams, Cornelius, Jr., 154, 155, 159, 162–63, 164
Williston, Samuel, 16
Wilson, Benjamin D., 127
Wilson, D. Webster, 154, 162, 163, 165
Wilson, Woodrow, 4, 72 n.52
Winans, Joseph W., 133
Winkler, Flanders, Smith, Bottum & Vilas, 13
Winston, Payne, Strawn & Shaw, 12
Wise, John S., 174
Women in legal practice: in Massachusetts, 103, 104, 105, 106; in Virginia, 173–74
Wood and Torrey, 99
Woodson, Carter G., 151
Wright, George, 86
Wright, Brown, and Quimby, 99

Yale Law School, 72 n.52, 83, 84

# *About the Editor and Contributors*

GORDON MORRIS BAKKEN is Professor of History at California State University, Fullerton. He is completing the first volume of legal history of California and is author of *The Development of Law on the Rocky Mountain Frontier: Civil Law and Society, 1850–1912* (Greenwood Press, 1983).

MAXWELL BLOOMFIELD is Professor of History at the Catholic University of America and Lecturer in Legal History at the Catholic University Law School. He has written extensively on the history of the American bar, with special emphasis on the relationship between legal professionalism and broader societal values. His publications include *American Lawyers in a Changing Society, 1776–1876*, and he is co-author of the recently published *Law and American Literature*.

W. HAMILTON BRYSON is Professor of Law at the University of Richmond. His principal research interests are in the areas of English and Virginia legal history; he has also written a manual of Virginia civil procedure and practice. Recent publications include *Legal Education in Virginia, 1779–1979: A Biographical Approach*, and *Handbook of Virginia Civil Procedure*.

GERARD W. GAWALT is a Historical Specialist in the Manuscript Division, Library of Congress, and associate editor of *Letters of Delegates to Congress, 1774–1789*. He has held appointments at George Mason University, Assumption College, and Clark University. He has written and lectured extensively on the American legal profession and the growth of a professional class in America. His publications include *The Promise of Power: The Emergence of the Legal Profession in Massachusetts, 1760–1840* (Greenwood Press, 1979).

ROBERT W. GORDON is Professor of Law at Stanford University and has also taught at the Buffalo, Wisconsin, and Harvard Law Schools. He has written articles on legal theory, legal historiography, and the history of the legal profession; he has also contributed essays to *Law and Society in American History: Essays in Honor of James Willard Hurst* (which he edited) and to *Professions and Professional Ideologies in America*.

KERMIT L. HALL is Associate Professor of History and Affiliated Associate Professor of Law at the University of Florida, and he previously held appointments at Vanderbilt University and Wayne State University. His principal research interests involve United States constitutional and legal history, especially the development and impact of methods of judicial selection. Professor Hall is the author of *Politics of Justice* and *Judicial Review in United States Constitutional History*, and the editor of *The Constitutional Convention as an Amending Device* and *A Comprehensive Bibliography of United States Constitutional and Legal History* (3 vols.).

WAYNE K. HOBSON is an Associate Professor of American Studies at California State University, Fullerton. His principal research interests are the history of the American legal profession and the history of American ideas about crime and violence. He has published articles on professionalism and progressivism and on crime and American culture.

MICHAEL DE L. LANDON is Professor of History and History Graduate Adviser at the University of Mississippi, where he has been on the faculty for twenty years, and has also been a visiting faculty member at the University of Wisconsin (Madison). His research has been concerned with the role played by lawyers in the social, economic, and political histories of early-modern England and Mississippi. His books include *The Triumph of the Lawyers* and *The Honor and Dignity of the Profession.*

JOHN A. MATZKO has been a member of the History Department at Bob Jones University for eight years. He is currently completing a study of the early years of the American Bar Association.

E. LEE SHEPARD is Librarian of the Department of Archives and Manuscript Acquisitions, Virginia Historical Society, Richmond. He has recently published articles on the early Virginia bar in the *American Journal of Legal History* and the *Journal of Southern History*, and is currently engaged in research for a biography of lawyer Conway Robinson.

www.ingramcontent.com/pod-product-compliance
Ingram Content Group UK Ltd.
Pitfield, Milton Keynes, MK11 3LW, UK
UKHW020811290926
15470UKWH00003B/1099

9 780313 240218